ATLANTA BRAVES

A Curated History of the Braves

MARK BOWMAN

THE FRANCHISE

TRIUMPH
BOOKS

No part of this publication may be reproduced, stored in a retrieval system, or transmitted in any form by any means, electronic, mechanical, photocopying, or otherwise, without the prior written permission of the publisher, Triumph Books LLC, 814 North Franklin Street, Chicago, Illinois 60610.

Library of Congress Cataloging-in-Publication Data available upon request.

This book is available in quantity at special discounts for your group or organization. For further information, contact:

Triumph Books LLC
814 North Franklin Street
Chicago, Illinois 60610
(312) 337-0747
www.triumphbooks.com

Printed in U.S.A.
ISBN: 978-1-63727-568-9
Design by Preston Pisellini
Page production by Nord Compo

CONTENTS

PART 3 The Cities

PART 4 The Champions

PART 5 The Architects

PART 6 The Future

Foreword

THE ATLANTA BRAVES ARE AN ICONIC FRANCHISE. WE ARE one of the best-run franchises from top to bottom. We win. We didn't win for a long time when we first got to Atlanta. But a transition came in 1991, and the torch has been passed from mentor to mentor for the last 30-plus years. We've elevated ourselves and become one of the elite franchises in all of sports. I dare say in the last 30 years nobody has won more division titles than the Atlanta Braves and I don't think it's even close.

It's hard to be that consistent for that long. And quite honestly, I don't see it changing anytime soon. Because the pieces are in place at the highest levels of this organization and with the product on the field.

I don't think it's unfair to say that we will have sustained success for the foreseeable future. That's hard to do in today's professional sports, because it's so hard to keep everybody together like we were able to do in the 1990s and into the early 2000s.

But when you're run well from the top down, and you've got consistency day in and day out at the highest level, you're able to do things like this. It's been a pleasure to be a part of this. I came in at the ground level. I was part of one of the first drafts that helped turn this organization around. I've said it often—I was born into this organization. I grew up in this organization. I got to reap the benefits of all the winning we did at the major league level and I'm still doing it as a coach now at 51 years old.

The message hasn't changed in 30 years. We're going to win our division and give ourselves a chance to play for a world championship every single year. That's what's expected of you. If you are not pulling in the same direction as the other 25 guys, you're not going to be here for long, and that's pretty awesome.

It's great to be part of an organization that has so many iconic figures. I think the fan base identifies with each and every one of us. We're small-town kids who busted our humps to make it to the big leagues. We stayed as loyal as we possibly could to this organization and fan base. I can't speak for everybody, because I'm one of the only guys who played my whole career for the Braves.

But I was a Southern kid playing Major League Baseball in a Southern town. I drive a pickup truck. You know, people from Braves Country can relate. I haven't changed since I got drafted. I'm still that same country kid. I still love my organization. When I walk into that stadium every day and I look up there and see that red No. 10 hanging in the rafters, I still get chill bumps. I wish one more time I could run out on that field to third base and listen to the gratitude given by the Braves faithful.

I know every single guy who has his number up there in those rafters, whether it's Murph or Smoltz, Glav or whoever it may be, they feel the same way I do. They may have played for other teams, but they will always be part of Braves royalty.

This book will give you a better understanding about the decisions and people who have made the Braves the greatest organization in professional sports.

Chipper Jones, *the Braves' first-overall pick in the 1990 MLB Draft, played his entire career in Atlanta, winning the World Series in 1995. In 2018, in his first year of eligibility, he was inducted into the National Baseball Hall of Fame. He currently serves as a Braves assistant hitting consultant.*

PART 1

THE DECISIONS

1

Hiring Schuerholz

HISTORY WAS CREATED IN BOSTON IN 1871, WHEN THE RED Stockings became a charter member of the National Association of Professional Base Ball Players. The team would be become known as the Beaneaters, Doves, Rustlers, Bees and Braves during its long stay in Boston. This tenure marked the start of what remains the longest continuously operated professional baseball organization.

History was extended when the Braves relocated from Boston to Milwaukee before the 1953 season. Warren Spahn and Eddie Mathews made the move and then welcomed another future Hall of Famer in 1954, when Hank Aaron began his iconic career. This trio would lead the Braves to a World Series title in 1957 and a second straight National League pennant the following year.

History was again extended in 1966, when the Braves moved from Milwaukee to Atlanta and became the first professional team in the Deep South. Aaron would break Babe Ruth's home run record in 1974 and Ted Turner would use his cable satellites to begin making the Braves America's Team a short time later.

These were all great moments. But to truly understand the greatest era in Braves history, it seems best to go back to a summer day in 1990, when Major League Baseball Commissioner Fay Vincent came to Atlanta and attended a game with longtime Braves executive Terry McGuirk, who at the time held multiple leadership roles within Ted Turner's empire, including serving as president of Turner Sports.

As they were at Atlanta-Fulton County Stadium, McGuirk mentioned the Braves were searching for a general manager and had chosen Royals GM John Schuerholz as their top target. Vincent's response served as both a reality check and motivator.

"'You think John Schuerholz is going to come to this place? Are you out of your mind?'" McGuirk remembers Vincent responding.

Vincent wouldn't have been the only person who would have responded in this manner. Schuerholz helped build the Royals from the ground up, became MLB's youngest GM in 1981 and constructed Kansas City's first World Series–winning team in 1985.

As for the Braves, they were enduring their 17th losing season during what was their 25th season in Atlanta. This would also be the sixth straight season they would lose at least 89 games.

"We were like the lowest form of baseball," McGuirk said. "Nobody had any respect for the Atlanta Braves at that point. [Vincent] was a little bit of a snob and egalitarian about baseball and business. It really pissed me off. I had been busy doing a lot of other things, but I didn't think we deserved this. So, we doubled my interests and efforts to get John Schuerholz here after he said this."

Vincent was wrong.

When it became clear Bobby Cox was vacating his general manager title to exclusively serve as the Braves' manager midway through the 1990 season, Schuerholz repeatedly quizzed former Braves president Stan Kasten about his plans to fill this void. Kasten initially grew excited thinking his top choice would be willing to fill the position.

Schuerholz made two recruiting trips to Atlanta, where he talked to Kasten and McGuirk within their plush offices at the CNN Center, which were far nicer than the ones at the ballpark.

Kasten kept the mood light, waving a rubber chicken, swinging a baseball bat and doing whatever he could to make Schuerholz comfortable. It worked. Schuerholz returned to Kansas City and told his wife, Karen, about the fun they had. But there was still a pull that would make him hesitant to migrate to Atlanta.

"We had been talking privately and with permission for several weeks, call it a month," Kasten said. "So, when I called to get a deal finalized, [Schuerholz] said, 'Yeah, I just can't do it. I can't leave Kansas City."

Kasten remembers the events of Friday, October 5, 1990, vividly. He was disappointed by what he heard from Schuerholz. But there was work to be done. The team still didn't have a GM and Cox was in the hospital recovering from a surgical procedure to reconstruct both of his knees.

So, it was Kasten who spent that afternoon recruiting Atlanta Falcons All-Pro cornerback Deion Sanders, who would sign with the Braves three months later. Kasten knew Sanders would interest Schuerholz, who had another two-sport superstar in Bo Jackson during his latter years with the Royals.

As all of this was happening, Schuerholz continued to weigh his commitment to Kansas City, a city where he had spent

20-plus years. Karen had spent all but eight months of her life calling the Missouri town her home. Their two children, Gina and Jonathan, had been born and raised there. Plus, there was a sense of loyalty to Royals owner Ewing Kauffman.

"When I finally decided that I was going to stick with my decision to go to the Braves, it was very traumatic for me and Mr. Kauffman," Schuerholz said. "We both cried at the end of the conversation. He was really sad to see me go. But for me and my young family, that was the right thing to do."

Schuerholz left his native Baltimore to help build the expansion Royals in 1968. He became the club's general manager in 1981 and built the franchise's first World Series title team in 1985. He wasn't George Brett or Frank White. But he was a legendary figure within the Kansas City sports world.

Kasten and McGuirk were ready to move on, feeling the ties to Kauffman and Kansas City might be too strong. But everything changed near the end of the same weekend that began with Schuerholz declining Atlanta's offer.

"Sunday morning, I go out to the gym and when I get home, my wife, Helen, says to me, 'John Schuerholz called,'" Kasten said. "As soon as she said that, I knew what was happening. But I said, 'How did the call go?'"

Kasten acted accordingly after his wife told him Schuerholz had asked if the position had been filled.

"I called him and he said, 'Stan, I don't know what to tell you, but I think I made a mistake,'" Kasten said. "And I go, 'Yes, I know that,' because that's me. We talked some more. He was all-in and the franchise has been flying ever since."

Schuerholz's impact was felt immediately as the 1991 Braves finished one win shy of a World Series title and won the first of a record-setting 14 consecutive division titles. An organization that was viewed as the game's laughingstock suddenly became the envy of the professional sports world.

The Braves participated in five of the eight World Series played from 1991 to '99. Critics have often focused on the fact the 1995 club was the only one to win a World Series during the run of 14 straight division crowns. But it's still a streak that is celebrated and attributed to the great partnership formed by Schuerholz and Bobby Cox.

"It was tough to leave [Kansas City], a place where we loved to live and a place where I'd given a lot of my life," Schuerholz said. "But there was something about the draw to Atlanta that made it special. Then, to know Bobby Cox was going to be a part of this and to have a chance to be a part of it with him, I made the right decision."

It didn't take Schuerholz long to make an immediate impact. His acquisitions of Terry Pendleton, Otis Nixon, Rafael Belliard and Sid Bream were aimed toward improving the defense that would support starting pitchers Tom Glavine, John Smoltz and Steve Avery as they attempted to prove themselves.

With a much-improved defense and a revitalized Pendleton marching his way toward the NL MVP Award, the Braves won the NL West in 1991 and won the first of their five NL pennants in the '90s.

Schuerholz added to his success when he signed Greg Maddux after the 1992 season and traded for Fred McGriff ahead of the trade deadline in '93, just before his club surged over the season's final months to win a third straight division title. Maddux and McGriff both played key roles when the Braves won Atlanta's first World Series title in '95.

While Schuerholz can also be lauded for bringing Gary Sheffield to Atlanta for two seasons (2002–03), his critics will point out the long-term effects of trading top prospect Adam

Wainwright for one year of J.D. Drew in '04. The club also needed some time to recover from the decision to use a group of top prospects for what amounted to one calendar year of Mark Teixeira (2007–08).

But there's no denying Schuerholz's long-standing success; during his 17-season reign as GM, the Braves produced an MLB-best .593 winning percentage. Cox served as his manager throughout this entire tenure.

It was a relationship that actually began way back in 1976, long before these Hall of Famers became household names in the baseball world.

Recognizing there was a good possibility the Royals would serve as his team's opposition in the 1976 American League Championship Series, Yankees owner George Steinbrenner sent Cox, who was Triple A Syracuse's manager that year, on a late September scouting mission to Kansas City.

Cox arranged his ticket and parking requests through Schuerholz, who at the time was running the Royals' minor league system. These two men had never previously met, but the time they shared together during that week in Kansas City enabled them to form a bond that significantly influenced their careers and the construction of the greatest era in Braves history.

"I had never met [Cox], but while socializing, shall I say, one night after a game, we got to know each other pretty well and got to know it was an easy friendship and easy relationship," Schuerholz said. "Mutual respect was already there."

McGuirk recognized the connection not long after persuading Schuerholz and Cox to make the moves that created this dynamic partnership.

"There's such a close relationship between the two of them," Braves chairman and CEO Terry McGuirk said. "When others proxied or surrogated for them at one time or another, it just didn't work. It just showed how unique that chemistry was. Both of them were a man's man. They related on that kind of a basis."

Cox's personality and managerial approach mirrored those Royals manager Dick Howser possessed before passing away in 1987 after developing a brain tumor. The similarities between these two close friends aided the transition for Schuerholz, who had teamed with Howser to win the 1985 World Series.

"We never butted heads," Cox said. "We were on the same page all of the time. He could see what we needed, and I could see what we needed. Some of the decisions were tough, but I don't remember ever where there was an argument about something.... John always listened. Everybody was important in the room."

While Schuerholz is a man who appreciates the country-club lifestyle, Cox feels more comfortable in a country-music bar. Though their personalities and backgrounds might have been different, they shared a passion to succeed and, more importantly, proved willing to achieve their goals while showing utmost respect in communicating with each other, their players and the other members of the Braves organization.

"We thought so much alike about the kind of team we wanted and the kind of players we wanted to have to make up that team, and the kind of environment we wanted to create and maintain and sustain," Schuerholz said. "We were like two peas in a pod. We were like Siamese twins in terms of our intellectual property and our thinking of how this organization ought to be built and run and sustained."

2

Bringing Bobby Back

When Bobby Cox won a World Series ring while serving as Yankees manager Billy Martin's first base coach in 1977, his primary responsibilities were to keep Martin out of barroom fights and to make sure Reggie Jackson remained happy during what was his first season in New York.

And of course, to keep owner George Steinbrenner happy, Cox was among the many Yankees tasked with keeping Martin and Jackson from killing each other.

These great challenges introduced him to three of the biggest personalities baseball has ever seen. In a way, those experiences prepared him for life with Ted Turner, whose limited knowledge of baseball didn't prevent him from recognizing Cox was a tremendous leader.

Shortly after the 1977 World Series concluded, Turner gave 36-year-old Cox his first job as a big-league manager. Unfortunately, he didn't give him a big-league-caliber team. The Braves lost 90-plus games during Cox's first two seasons, went 81–80 in 1980 and then sputtered during both halves of the strike-shortened 1981 season.

When he was called into Turner's office on October 7, 1981, Cox knew what was about to happen. But the eccentric owner, who seldom was at a loss for words, was so hesitant to make a change he didn't say anything. After a long silence, Cox asked if he was being fired. Turner just nodded.

"I like Ted," Cox told the *Atlanta Journal-Constitution* hours after the meeting. "I respect him and thanked him for the four years. It went fast for me because we showed improvement. When I came, we had little more than an expansion team and it has come leaps and bounds. I think everybody did a good job and I think the team will be a contender soon if they make the right trades."

Cox again showed great professionalism the following day, when he attended the press conference that featured Turner adding confusion to his decision by saying the optimal replacement would be somebody like Cox.

What Cox did while serving as Atlanta's manager from 1978 to '81 proved fruitful, as the Braves won the National League West the year after he left.

As that 1982 Braves team won its first 13 games, manager Joe Torre credited the historic start to what Cox had built over the previous four seasons.

Cox also built something special while serving as the Blue Jays' manager from 1982 to '85. Still, after guiding Toronto to its first American League East title in 1985, he jumped at the chance to return to Atlanta, where he had maintained a home throughout his Blue Jays tenure.

Though he loved his time in Toronto, Cox and his wife, Pam, were ready to build their life together in her native state of Georgia. It was where they had met and it was where they were raising their youngest daughter, Skyla, who was an infant at the time.

But thoughts of Cox returning seemed to fade when the Braves named Chuck Tanner as their new manager following the 1985 season. Tanner was well liked, and he had won a World Series while skippering the Pirates in 1979.

The one knock against him was that he wasn't Cox, who had befriended countless folks during his first tenure in Atlanta. This included both Bill Acree and John Holland, who both spent at least five decades filling various roles within the clubhouse.

"We had heard that Bobby was going to come back and manage," Holland said. "Bill called me down to his office and said Bobby wasn't going to be the manager. So then, he called me back an hour later, he said, 'Bobby is coming, but he's going to be the general manager.' We were, like, dancing. It was so great. We were so happy Bobby was coming back."

Instead of heading back to the familiar dugout environment, Cox was returned to fill a seat in the Braves' front office. Turner brought him back to replace John Mullen as the team's general manager.

"Basically, Ted doesn't have a lot of time to run the ballclub anymore," Cox told the AJC the day he was named GM. "He wants people working for him that he thinks can do the job. He still wants to be around the club very much. He'll be advised about everything that goes on."

Mullen, Hank Aaron and highly regarded scout Paul Snyder had served as Turner's top lieutenants over the previous few years. The four were linked to numerous questionable decisions, including the ill-fated Brett Butler–for–Len Barker trade and the decision to replace Torre with Eddie Haas as manager during a 96-loss 1985 season.

They also had all voted against keeping Cox as the Braves' manager beyond the 1981 season.

So, it was no surprise that with Cox's return to run the baseball operations side, Mullen, Aaron and Snyder lost power. But most importantly, Turner stayed out of the way. His money was appreciated. His limited knowledge about baseball was hazardous whenever he made himself part of on-field decisions.

"The one thing Ted did realize is when he wasn't successful or when he wasn't good at something," McGuirk said. "You had this cavalcade of not-very-smart general managers who had been there. Now, all of a sudden, Bobby Cox was back, a real baseball guy and a trusted winner. A guy who just had everybody's respect."

That respect quickly grew as Cox overhauled the farm system by placing the focus on acquiring and developing pitchers. Tom Glavine was already in the system. But during Cox's first few years running the baseball operations department, the team would draft Kent Mercker, Steve Avery and Turk Wendell, who was used to acquire catcher Damon Berryhill and Mike Bielecki.

Cox also sent Doyle Alexander to the Tigers for a Double A pitcher named John Smoltz in 1987. He landed Ryan Klesko (1989) and Chipper Jones (1990) during the final two drafts he oversaw as the Braves' GM.

Subscribing to Branch Rickey's philosophy to gain quality from quantity, the Braves added scouts, coaches and minor league affiliates. The franchise's future steadily brightened as the likes of Glavine, Smoltz, Steve Avery, David Justice, Jeff Blauser, Ron Gant and Mark Lemke rose through the system.

With all of these players at the big-league level by 1990, Cox began to get the itch to return to the dugout. He made a significant impact during his tenure as the GM. But the team was in the midst of a seventh straight losing season and it was time for him to reap the fruits of his labor.

"I remember sitting him down, having lunch with him in the summer of 1990," McGuirk said. "I said, 'One of two things is going on here. Either you're a terrible general manager and you've given these managers terrible players. Or you're a really good general manager, you've got great players and you've just hired some bad managers. It has to be one or the other.'"

Kasten and McGuirk knew the timing was right for Cox to move back in their manager's role.

They got their wish on June 22, 1990, when Cox agreed to fire manager Russ Nixon and replace him with himself. The Braves went 40–57 over the remainder of the season. But Cox remained in that role and another 15 seasons would pass before the club experienced another losing season.

"We kept pounding away at him and eventually he stepped in and took the position," McGuirk said. "The antipathy he had for that moment was that he was so loyal to the people who worked underneath him, he couldn't take firing a guy and then taking his job. It was only after failure after failure that he took the job."

Schuerholz was lured to Atlanta approximately four months later. One year after his arrival, he and Cox celebrated the first of the 14 consecutive division titles they would capture while forming one of the greatest manager or head coach/GM combos the professional sports world has ever seen.

"We never butted heads," Cox said. "We were on the same page all of the time. He could see what we needed, and I could see what we needed. Some of the decisions were tough, but I don't remember ever where there was an argument about something.... John always listened. Everybody was important in the room."

Cox was inducted into baseball's Hall of Fame in 2014 and Schuerholz celebrated this same honor in 2017.

"He and I were together, shoulder to shoulder on almost every element we talked about," Schuerholz said. "It was a great place to be a major league executive on a team that was ascending and we were beginning to ascend."

3

Hank Aaron Signs

Henry Louis Aaron was a larger-than-life superstar who drew the utmost respect from both clubhouse attendants and heads of state.

As Aaron celebrated his 75th birthday at the Atlanta Marriott Marquis on February 5, 2009, he was surrounded by many dignitaries, including Bud Selig, President Bill Clinton, former New York Governor Mario Cuomo and former United Nations Ambassador Andrew Young.

Taking his turn to speak, Clinton once thanked Aaron for helping him carry the traditionally Republican state of Georgia in 1992 and gain his first term in the White House.

When Clinton visited Atlanta a week before the election, he spoke to a crowd of approximately 25,000, half of which he believes showed up just because Aaron was also on the stage. Clinton said Aaron has never allowed him to forget that he won

Georgia by 13,000 votes, which would have essentially accounted for that half who showed up to see the baseball legend.

Echoing a sentiment held by countless baseball fans, Clinton concluded this speech by looking at Aaron and saying, "We all have to acknowledge that you have given us more than we could ever give you."

Long before Cox, Schuerholz, Chipper, Maddux, Glavine or Smoltz, Henry Aaron joined the Braves and became one of the most influential, successful and beloved players to ever wear a baseball uniform. His impact extended far beyond his 755 home runs or 3,000-plus hits.

"I've been asked many times over the past few days to describe Henry Aaron in one word," Chipper Jones said during a memorial service held a few days after Aaron's death in 2021. "Without hesitation, that word is 'beautiful.' The swing, the smile and the spirit were all beautiful."

Knowing the impact Aaron had on the Braves over seven decades, it's important to look at how the organization was fortunate enough to land this young player, who left his native Mobile, Alabama, to play for the Negro League Indianapolis Clowns in 1952.

Scout Bunny Downs found Aaron as he played for the semi-pro Mobile Black Bears for $3 per game. His mother limited Aaron to playing just home games. But the experience still propelled him to Indianapolis, where he made $200 per month while helping the Clowns and what was left of the Negro Leagues

When Jackie Robinson integrated baseball five years earlier, he opened the door for Roy Campanella, Larry Doby, Satchel Paige, Monte Irvin, Sam Jethroe, Willie Mays and others to join MLB clubs. But the exodus of star power also led to the demise of the Negro Leagues.

Still, for the 18-year-old Aaron, the Negro League provided the opportunity he needed to introduce himself quickly and authoritatively to the baseball world.

In *I Had a Hammer*, an autobiography Aaron wrote with Lonnie Wheeler, Kansas City Monarchs manager Buck O'Neil was quoted as saying:

> The first time I saw Aaron, we were playing the Clowns down in Alabama or Louisiana during the spring. I noticed this young boy hitting in the fourth spot and I said, "[Clowns manager Buster Haywood], what's this kid doing hitting fourth? He said, "Buck, you just wait and see him swing the bat.' Well, I had some pretty good pitchers who had been around the block a few times and the first time he came up I told the pitcher to throw this kid a good fastball. He threw a good fastball and the kid hit it up against the right field fence. The next time he came up, I had my best left-hander in there and I said to him, now throw this kid a good fastball. He threw his fastball on the first pitch and the kid hit it against the center field fence. I looked over at Buster and Buster was just laughing at me. The last time, I had the star of my staff in there, an old pro named Hilton Smith, and I told Smith to throw this kid some curveballs. The kid hit a curveball over the left field fence. I told Buster then, I said, 'Tell you what. You and I both know by the time you get to Kansas City to play us, this kid won't be with you anymore.' No way a hitter like that was going to stay around the Negro League."

Attempting to sell some of his players, Clowns owner Syd Pollock sent Braves farm director John Mullen a letter. It concluded with, "We got an 18-year-old shortstop batting cleanup for us."

The Braves had scout Dewey Griggs spent a month scouting Aaron and the Clowns, who in Aaron's memory never actually played a game in Indianapolis while he was with the team. They were more like the Harlem Globetrotters in that they really didn't have a home.

Griggs suggested the young second baseman end his days of hitting cross-handed. Aaron responded by homering in the game that followed and then showed his speed by bunting for a hit in his next plate appearance. This prompted Griggs to send Mullen a note that ended with, "This boy could be the answer."

Mullen wasn't going to squander this opportunity. The Braves had pursued Willie Mays during his high school years in Birmingham and missed out on the opportunity to sign him, when the Giants offered $15,000 more.

Two years later, Aaron chose the Braves over the Giants because they offered $100 more per month and correctly spelled his name.

In the autobiography he penned with Wheeler, Aaron wrote that the Braves offered $350 per month. The Giants offered $250 per month and spelled his name "Arron" on their telegram.

A couple weeks later, Aaron endured the first flight of his life, landed in Eau Claire, Wisconsin, and spent the remainder of the 1952 season playing there. Bill Bruton and Roy White had played in this mostly white town two years earlier. But the friendly citizens were still adapting, and Aaron admitted he was too.

"It was strange for those white folks in Eau Claire to be around black people, and it was just as strange for me to be around them," Aaron said in his autobiography. "There was nothing in my experience that prepared me for white people. I wasn't much of a talker anyway, but in Eau Claire, you couldn't pry my mouth open."

Along with having to get used to this environment, Aaron was involved in a couple of unfortunate incidents. While turning a double play, his throw to first base knocked the oncoming baserunner unconscious.

While toying with the idea of switch hitting a few weeks later, he swung from the left side, lost control of the bat and helplessly watched it hit a teammate during batting practice.

All of this just added to the despair and loneliness he was feeling while attempting to find comfort with this new life. But when Aaron called home to say he was returning to Mobile, his brother convinced him to stick with the opportunity he had.

So, Aaron finished the season with Eau Claire and then spent a portion of spring training in 1953 at an Air Force barracks in Waycross, Georgia. Players could go to town on the weekends to get a haircut or shoot pool.

Aaron missed the bus back one night and was nearly shot by armed guards when he made the long walk back and climbed a fence to return to the barracks. Mullen gave him a Bulova watch the next day and told him to never be late again.

Aaron spent the 1953 season integrating the South Atlantic League in Jacksonsville, Florida, where he and two other Black teammates were not permitted to live or eat with white teammates.

Milwaukee's Double A team at the time was located in Atlanta. The club could have sent him there to begin the season. But that may have been only a slightly friendlier environment in the early 1950s. By going to Jacksonville, Aaron certainly prepared for some of the racial inequalities he would continue to experience after he reached the majors the following year.

Syndicated sports columnist Harry Grayson famously wrote, "He led the South Atlantic League in everything except hotel accommodations."

While playing in segregated towns certainly wasn't easy, 1953 wasn't all bad. Aaron was named the MVP of the Sally League and got engaged to his first wife, Barbara Lucas, the sister of Bill Lucas, who would become baseball's first black general manager (though Ted Turner never officially gave him the title).

Needing money for himself and his new bride, Aaron went to Puerto Rico that winter and began to transition from middle infielder to outfielder. This would suit him perfectly when he returned to spring training with the Braves.

Bobby Thomson, the man best known for giving the New York Giants the 1951 NL pennant with a walk-off homer, was slated to be Milwaukee's starting left fielder before he broke his ankle on March 13, 1954. Aaron filled the void and was given a major league contract when he homered the next day.

Aaron went 0-for-5 when he made his MLB debut as Milwaukee's left fielder during a 9–8 Opening Day loss to the Reds at Cincinnati's Crosley Field. This ballpark was also the site of Aaron's 3,000th hit in 1970. Four years later at the Reds' new home, Riverfront Stadium, the Braves slugger tied Babe Ruth by hitting his 714th homer.

Gordon Graham, a sports columnist from Lafayette, Indiana, had a good take after Aaron's debut.

"If somebody gave us our choice of a team which was most likely going to be a winner three years from now, we believe the Milwaukee Braves would be our selection. Their infield is remarkably young even through the six-deep of [Joe] Adcock, O'Connell, [Johnny] Logan, [Eddie] Mathews, Dittmer and Smalley. The catcher [Del] Crandall is still a kid, although recognized as one of the best in the game, and already the team captain. The pitching is youthful as we mentioned and at least two of the rookie outfielders, Queen and Aaron, looked like sureshot power additions in a year or two."

Well, that proved to be a pretty good prediction. The Braves won the World Series three years later with the help of Aaron, who became a sureshot legend over the two decades that followed.

4

Drafting Chipper

A DAY BEFORE CHIPPER JONES BECAME JUST THE SECOND TOP overall selection to be enshrined in baseball's Hall of Fame, legendary scout Paul Snyder sat outside a Cooperstown home and revealed the Braves didn't initially even have Jones on their draft board.

In other words, they didn't even have a scouting report on Jones, a few months before taking a chance on the man who now stands as one of the most influential and revered players in franchise history.

"I think we did the right thing," Snyder said. "It's certainly easy to say that as we sit here right now at the Hall of Fame."

As the Braves prepared for the 1990 draft, with Cox serving as the general manager and Snyder as the scouting director, Todd Van Poppel was widely considered to be the best available prospect.

Jones wasn't on Atlanta's radar until February, when Hep Cronin opted to drive to Jacksonville, Florida, simply because a fellow scout he regarded as wise said he planned to spend the next day watching a young shortstop from The Bolles School.

Cronin's initial report led to a visit from Snyder, who then prompted Cox and many of the organization's top evaluators to come see this switch-hitting shortstop who had previously eluded their attention.

"The Braves were close to the vest," Jones said. "I never had a meeting with the Atlanta Braves. I heard rumblings they were at some games, but I never met Paul Snyder. I never met Bobby Cox. I never saw Jimy Williams. I know he came and saw me play. They even said Hank Aaron came to watch me play. It wasn't until two nights before the draft that I got the famous phone call."

Long before the famous call was the savvy scouting evaluation Snyder made while sitting in a car parked near a field at the Tigers' spring training complex in Lakeland, Florida.

The Braves heard the Tigers had invited Jones for a workout and wanted to take advantage of the chance to see—or in this case, hear—what he could do with a wood bat. So, an undetected Snyder put himself within earshot and was introduced to the melodious sounds produced by the swing of the kid who would become one of the best switch-hitters in baseball history.

"They say if you can't see, you can scout if you can hear," Snyder said. "We sat in the car and listened for the wood bat to ring. There were a lot of things that had to happen quickly that year—because we didn't have a lot of advanced scouting reports on him from his early years."

Jones laughed a little more than 30 years later, when he first heard the story about Snyder's trip to Lakeland.

"I didn't have a good workout in Lakeland, or maybe as good as I would have liked to," Jones said. "So, maybe, I'm glad that he didn't actually see that workout."

After Jones impressed enough to quickly establish himself as a potential top overall pick, he enhanced the difficulty of the Braves' decision when he broke his right hand punching a teammate who was jealous of the extra attention Jones was receiving.

Three days before the 1990 MLB Draft, Cox traveled to Dallas to meet with Van Poppel and his family. The pitcher was graduating from high school the next day and his family continued to make it clear he would stick to his commitment to the University of Texas even if the Braves took him with the overall pick.

So, the Van Poppels refused to talk to Cox, just like they had twice previously done so with Snyder.

With the sports world still assuming Van Poppel was at the top of the Braves' wish list, Cox told team president Stan Kasten he might go another direction.

"Bobby said, 'I've got to tell you, my so-called second choice, I might like him even better [than Van Poppel],'" Kasten said. "I told him I was going to support him either way and that this was his call. He was always super comfortable with Chipper Jones."

Cox's short tenure as the New York Yankees' third baseman allowed him the chance to play with Mickey Mantle, one of the greatest switch hitters to ever play the game. His visits to watch Jones play in high school introduced him to the young version of somebody who would also earn his place among the elite switch hitters.

"I was hitting balls out of the park left-handed and right-handed," Jones said. "The switch-hitting thing is the reason

I was the No. 1 pick in the draft. If I'm not a switch hitter, I don't go No. 1."

Snyder essentially confirmed this as he reminisced about a stretch during Jones' senior year when he was starting to grow hesitant about swinging from the left side. So, Snyder was thrilled to arrive at a game and have Larry Wayne Jones Sr. say his son would be hitting lefty against the right-handed pitcher that night.

"He said, 'You can stay right here tonight, fellows, he's going to hit left-handed,'" Snyder said. "The first swing he took that night, it was a line drive right out onto the street."

When Cox told Snyder to focus on Jones, a call was placed to Jones' father, who had to make approximately five different calls before reaching his son to tell him he needed to immediately leave his senior prom in Jacksonville and make the hour-plus trek home to talk to the Braves.

"There was one [furious] lady," Jones said. "But I dropped everything and left. Up until that point, that was going to be the most important thing that happened to me."

During that conversation, Jones got the feeling he was going to be the No. 1 overall pick. It wasn't until that point he ever thought the Braves were a legit option for him.

Jones received a $275,000 signing bonus after the Braves took him with the first overall selection. He might have been able to get more. But he had no desire to negotiate at the expense of delaying the start of his playing career.

"It's not often that guys get to be as good as you think they have a chance to be," Snyder said. "This was one time that it did."

Van Poppel received a $500,000 signing bonus after the A's took him with the 14th overall selection. It didn't take long to realize which team gained a bargain and which team acquired a bust.

As Jones was constructing his Hall of Fame career, Van Poppel was proving to be nothing more than a below-average starter and an average low-leverage reliever. The big right-handed pitcher made one start for the A's in 1991 and didn't return to the majors until 1993. He bounced around the league as a starter for a few years and finally found some success as a Cubs reliever in 2000 and 2001.

By this time, Jones had won a National League MVP Award and earned five All-Star selections. He helped the Braves reach the World Series three times during this span, including in 1995, when he capped his rookie season by celebrating Atlanta's first World Series title.

Jones became a first-ballot Hall of Famer who stands with Ken Griffey Jr. as the only players to be enshrined in Cooperstown after being taken with the first overall pick in the MLB draft. Van Poppel posted a 5.58 ERA during an 11-season career that included stints with six different clubs.

Van Poppel might have made the decision easier. But there's no doubt the decision to select Jones stands as one of the most influential and fruitful decisions not only in Braves history, but in all of baseball history.

Jones made his major league debut in 1993, returned from the first of two torn left anterior cruciate ligaments to begin his reign as Atlanta's third baseman in '95 and then proudly retired as a Brave at the conclusion of the 2012 season. His final two seasons were the only ones he spent without Cox, the man who teamed with Snyder to make one of the most influential decisions in team history, as his big-league manager.

"Bobby is the man," Jones said. "He's the guy who drafted me. I spent 23 years in this organization trying to make him proud and trying to make him look good. He went out on a limb and drafted me with the first pick over Todd Van Poppel. It might not have been the popular pick at the time. But I spent two decades trying to make him look good."

5

Trading for Smoltz

WHEN JOHN SMOLTZ CALLED HIS FATHER NEAR THE END OF July in 1987, he was a distraught 20-year-old pitcher who felt like he wasn't getting any guidance as he produced an ugly ERA for the Detroit Tigers' underperforming Double A affiliate in Glenn Falls, New York.

Little did he or the baseball world know what was about to happen.

As Smoltz was in the dugout watching a game on August 12 of that same year, he received two notes. One told him to call home immediately. The other said to call the Tigers' front office. Concerned something might have happened to a family member, he called home first and learned that he had been traded to the Atlanta Braves.

"My dad is a jokester, so I thought he was just trying to loosen me up or make me laugh," Smoltz said. "So, I said, 'Dad, that's not funny.' He said, 'No, I just saw it on the news. The local news guy had called to say you had been traded for Doyle Alexander.'

"I remember saying, 'Dad, I'm serious. If you're joking with me, I'm going to come home and we're going to have it out.' Then, I remembered in this other hand, I was holding this note that said to call the Detroit Tigers front office."

Long before he became a Hall of Fame pitcher, Smoltz was a young, struggling minor leaguer who had to say goodbye to his dream of playing in his home state for that same Tigers team he had loved since childhood.

It was a trade that impacted two organizations in far different ways. The Tigers won the American League East with the help of Alexander, who went 9–0 with a 1.53 ERA after being acquired from the Braves.

To fill Alexander's roster spot, Atlanta promoted a young left-hander named Tom Glavine. This marked the first of thousands of times Glavine and Smoltz's names have since been linked.

The Braves got more than two decades of Smoltz, who spent this time establishing himself as a Cy Young Award winner, one of the greatest postseason pitchers of all time and the only player who was part of Atlanta's 40-man roster throughout the team's run of 14 consecutive division titles. The only year he wasn't on the active roster was 2000, when he was recovering from Tommy John surgery.

"I remember when we got him I was with [Pirates general manager] Syd Thrift and I asked him, 'What do you think about the guy we just got?'" Braves president Stan Kasten said. "He said he thought he was a No. 2 [starter], which was damn good."

Bobby Cox remembered his scouts Paul Snyder and John Hagemann being much higher on the lanky right-hander they had just acquired.

"When we made the trade, they both said he's going to be a Cy Young Award winner," Cox said. "It only took him a few years to do it."

It's safe to say Smoltz turned out to be more than a No. 2 starter. But he certainly had doubts he'd even be considered that highly as he made the long drive in a red Z24 Chevy Cavalier from upstate New York to Richmond, Virginia, where he had been assigned to the Braves' Triple A team. MLB rules at that time stipulated that, if traded for a MLB player, a minor leaguer had to go up a level for the remainder of the season.

"The first feeling that comes to mind is that I'm not wanted," Smoltz said. "Then, about four hours into the trip, I realized the Atlanta Braves wanted me. All I knew was that they weren't very good, they were on TBS and they had Dale Murphy."

Bobby Cox, the Braves' general manager who orchestrated the trade, farm director Bobby Dews and scouting director Paul Snyder were among those who went to Virginia to see Smoltz make his first professional start against a talented Tidewater bunch. This start didn't go well. Nor did the other two that were completed before the season concluded.

But Smoltz's life and career trajectory changed when he went to Instructional League in September and worked with pitching guru Leo Mazzone and a minor league manager, Brian Snitker, who in those days had no trouble acting like a drill sergeant.

"I met Leo for the first time," Smoltz said. "I was scared to death of Snit. To know Snit for the next 30 years, he's been more like a gentle giant. But he was a sergeant running this Instructional League in West Palm Beach."

Smoltz spent just two years within the Tigers organization, but that was long enough for him to feel like his mentality and mechanics were destroyed by too much tinkering. So, it was a relief when Mazzone told him to just throw a pitch as athletically as he could. In other words, don't think about anything. Just throw a pitch.

"I threw it and he goes, 'That's perfect,'" Smoltz said. "I was like, 'Really?' Because I had been doubting everything. He said, 'Just throw like that and we'll upgrade your pitches.' So, we worked on the slider he always preached, and it really became my signature pitch."

Smoltz posted a 4.87 ERA over 38 starts during the two minor league seasons he completed before he was introduced to Mazzone. He posted a 2.79 ERA over 20 starts for Richmond in 1988 and suddenly found himself at the major league level.

"If he doesn't stay in Atlanta, something is wrong," Mazzone told the *Atlanta Journal-Constitution* at the time of Smoltz's promotion. "This isn't any shuttle run for him. Now, he can see what it's all about and come out of spring training next year as a front-line starter."

Mazzone served as Richmond's pitching coach that year. As a reward for what he had done, Cox made sure Mazzone was at Shea Stadium on July 23, 1988, when Smoltz made his MLB debut against a Mets team on its way to 100 wins and an NL East title.

Providing a glimpse of what he would do in so many of the big games that would follow, Smoltz limited the Mets to one run and four hits over eight innings. He posted a 5.48 ERA over the 12 starts he made for Atlanta that year and found himself light years away from where he was the previous year, when he felt lost in Glenn Falls.

Smoltz's grandfather was a longtime employee at Tigers Stadium. This was just one of the many variables that made the Tigers seem like a storybook fit. But there were problems from the start.

Smoltz wasn't taken by the Tigers until the 22nd round in the 1986 MLB Draft. His stock skyrocketed that same summer as he pitched the junior Olympic circuit. But he was stuck to his commitment to attend Michigan State until the night before his first class, when his dad convinced the Tigers to give him first-round money.

Tigers general manager Bill Lajoie seemed to hold this against Smoltz. The young pitcher remembers Lajoie yelling at him for seemingly no reason at the start of his first spring training. Some of that bad blood may have influenced what still stands as the best and most impactful trade in Braves history.

"I look back on that trade and that drive and the Braves' coaching philosophy, that was all huge for me," Smoltz said. "That's what I thought I was going to get with Detroit."

Pairing with Mazzone proved to be the right fit for Smoltz, who remembers getting to the big leagues and suddenly having Atlanta's pitching coach instruct him to throw two-seam fastballs and sliders. This didn't sit well with the fiery Mazzone, who was still Richmond's coach when he first saw this change.

"Leo called and said, 'What are you doing?' Smoltz said. "You're a four-seam backspin, throw-and-turn slider guy.' I said, 'I know, Leo, but this is what they want me doing at the big-league level. What am I supposed to do?' He said, 'You're supposed to go for it.' So, I went for it.'"

Mazzone was reunited with Smoltz near the end of the 1990 season and they remained together until the 14th straight division title was won in 2005. It's a streak that may never be matched and one that might never have happened without Cox trading the Tigers a rental in exchange for a Hall of Famer.

"That trade gave Detroit everything they needed [in 1987]," Smoltz said. "But after that, they went a long time without winning. Ironically, I went to a team that went a long time without winning. But then I got to be part of a team that won for a long time."

6

The Dark Days

GIVEN THE IMPACT BOBBY COX HAD ON THE BRAVES organization, maybe it shouldn't have been surprising to see the franchise head toward some of its darkest days not long after he ended his Hall of Fame managerial career with a loss to the Giants in the 2010 National League Division Series.

The Braves collapsed down the stretch in 2011 after two of their top starters, Jair Jurrjens and Tommy Hanson, suffered injuries. They returned to the playoffs the following year and won the 2013 NL East with the help of Justin Upton, who had been acquired from the D-backs the previous winter.

Justin Upton experienced success in Atlanta. His brother B.J. didn't after being given a franchise-record five-year, $75 million contract in November 2012. Nor did Dan Uggla, who signed a five-year, $62 million deal before the 2011 season. Former Braves GM Frank Wren's last bad contract was the three-year, $23.5 million given to Chris Johnson after a lot of good fortune helped the third baseman surprisingly compete for a batting title in 2013.

The Braves entered the 2014 All-Star break leading the NL East, but Wren's future became cloudy just a couple weeks later. As Bobby Cox, Tom Glavine and Greg Maddux were being inducted into Baseball's Hall of Fame in Cooperstown, speculation grew that the team might soon part ways with Wren.

Initially, the Braves thought about parting ways with Wren in August, while the team was in Pittsburgh and Cincinnati. Cox never liked Wren, but he stepped in and said a team shouldn't get rid of a GM while it was still in contention.

But as the team continued to fade, the executives knew something had to be done. They had just broken ground on the land on which they built Truist Park and The Battery. The plan was to move into this new stadium with a winning team.

"This was essentially the same team we had in 2013," Braves chairman Terry McGuirk said. "We were going to make a few adjustments, but we were going to deliver a winning team into the new stadium when we finished it. Then, son of a gun, we had to destroy it, break it down, because this team was dead and was going nowhere."

Wren was dismissed once the Braves fell out of contention in September. A few days later, the Braves introduced John Coppolella as the new GM. Coppolella was a nervous wreck during his press conference. In hindsight, this should have been viewed as a bad omen.

Serving as team president, Schuerholz approved Coppolella's ascension and assigned John Hart to serve as the president of baseball operations. Hart's primary job was to oversee Coppolella and help guide him through a massive rebuild.

Everything seemed to start auspiciously as Hart and Coppolella teamed to gain strong returns for some of the team's top stars. By sending Jason Heyward to the Cardinals, they netted Shelby Miller, who produced the finest season of his career of 2015 and then was used to acquire Dansby Swanson.

By sending Justin Upton to the Padres, the Braves gained Max Fried. Craig Kimbrel was sent to San Diego a few months later, in a deal that included a draft pick Atlanta used to gain Austin Riley.

When the Braves won the 2021 World Series, Fried threw six scoreless innings in the decisive frame and Swanson fielded the game-ending grounder. As for Riley, he finished sixth in National League MVP balloting that year.

The Braves also greatly benefited from the first MLB draft of the Coppolella and Hart era. They gained Kolby Allard, Michael Soroka, Austin Riley and A.J. Minter during the first day of the 2015 MLB Draft. Ian Anderson was taken with the third overall pick in 2016. And Kyle Wright, who was taken with the fifth overall pick in 2017, provided the most influential relief appearance of the 2021 World Series.

Coppolella and Hart's fingerprints were all over that title. But they were long gone by the time they got to reap the fruits of their labor.

To fully understand how the Braves became mired in scandal, it's best to go back to when Coppolella was searching for a job out of college.

As Coppolella neared the end of his senior year at Notre Dame, he had already accepted a $90,000 salary and $10,000 signing bonus to work in the planning and logistics department at Intel. But dating back to his freshman year, when he had sent letters seeking employment to every major league organization and minor league affiliate, he has had an intense desire to work in baseball, an industry he was introduced to during his early childhood. His father moonlighted as an Angels parking lot attendant at Anaheim Stadium.

Thus, when the Yankees informed him that he was a finalist for a baseball operations internship that would pay $18,000 and almost certainly not lead to a full-time job, he suddenly lost interest in the financial security Intel would have provided as he attempted to pay off his enormous student loan debt.

"The whole thing for me in life and the way I see things is, it's not as much about the outcome as it is the process," Coppolella said shortly after the Braves gave him the GM responsibilities. "I was thinking, 'If I don't go for this now, I'm always going to wonder, what if?'"

So in the midst of a family trip from South Bend, Indiana, to New York City during the spring of 2000, Coppolella completed a three-step interview process with the Yankees by stopping at pay phones in Cleveland, Pittsburgh and Philadelphia. Somewhere in the middle of New Jersey, he informed his parents that he had gotten the Yanks job and that they would now need to head south to Tampa to help set him up for the new world that awaited.

"I said, 'I have a chance to run down a dream,'" Coppolella said. "[My parents] weren't happy about it."

When Coppolella began his internship, he shared an apartment with two guys he had never met, and he fulfilled his financial obligations—car payment, car insurance, rent and living expenses—by taking on a second job that made him "the worst employee Chili's has ever had." But during that seven-month stretch working in the restaurant world three to four nights per week, all he cared about was making the most of the opportunity the Yankees had provided.

"If it hadn't worked out with the Yankees and it would have just ended with the internship, I'd have been all right, because

I would have looked back and known I couldn't have worked any harder," Coppolella said. "If it was not meant to be, it was not meant to be. I did everything they asked and more. I went in with zero expectations. It wasn't about what I'm going to get or what they were going to pay me."

Steinbrenner wanted many of his vice presidents and top members of the scouting and player development departments working alongside him in Tampa, so Coppolella was surrounded by some of the Yankees' most influential people.

But instead of being intimidated by the environment he entered five days after graduating from Notre Dame, Coppolella immediately impressed with the work ethic he acquired growing up in a middle-class Southern California household supported by his father, a U.S. Postal Service employee for 35 years, and his mother, an elementary school teacher.

"He was an on-the-job guy," said Billy Connors, who served as the Yanks' vice president of player personnel. "Everything was baseball. He just dedicated himself so much. He wanted to learn and better himself. He wasn't stepping on anybody's heels or anything like that. He was just doing his job and wanting to be respected for what he did."

Along with handling administrative duties aimed toward tracking prospects and preparing for the annual First-Year Player Draft, Coppolella spent his earliest years with the Yankees handling some far less glorious tasks, like picking up players from the airport or occasionally cleaning toilets. He also volunteered to help fulfill Steinbrenner's wish of having one employee answer the phones at the stadium every Sunday morning during the offseason.

"I would read about prospects, read about our own players and try to learn as much as I could while I was there those mornings," Coppolella said. "There was always one call every week [from Steinbrenner] at 11:55. He would say, 'Hello, young sir. Has anyone called today?' I'd say, 'No, you were the only call.' Then he'd say, 'At 12 o'clock and not one minute earlier, you're free to leave.'"

An early exit is not something Steinbrenner had to worry about with Coppolella, who was usually the first to arrive and the last to leave the Tampa office. His determination to succeed meant he was provided entrance by a security guard. The fact that he did not have a key until he was hired full-time in January 2001 had something to do with him staying later than the other employees throughout his internship.

"I would get there at 9 in the morning, just because [Steinbrenner] would keep you there late at night, so you never wanted to come in too early," said Gordon Blakeley, who served as a vice president during a portion of his long tenure with the Yanks. "[Coppolella] would have already been there for two hours working on stuff. Then he would leave after everybody at 8 or 9 o'clock at night. I'm talking seven days a week."

Some of the Yankees employees were annoyed by Coppolella's quirkiness. But he stuck because top international scout Blakeley befriended him and made sure Steinbrenner knew the value the new kid could bring.

This connection to Blakely would prove significant a decade later.

Coppolella's tireless work ethic continued to be on display after Schuerholz hired him to become part of the Braves' baseball operations staff in 2006. But Coppolella never felt respected once Wren became the GM and leaned heavily on his assistant GM, Bruce Manno, whose leadership style irked more than a few folks within the organization.

Once the Braves parted ways with Wren and Manno, Coppolella began building his new staff. One of his first hires was Blakely, the man who had the greatest impact on his earliest days in the baseball profession.

Fast-forward a couple years to when the Braves signed five of the top 25 prospects on the international market. This 2016 crop, headlined by top international prospect Kevin Maitan, was projected to have a monumental impact.

"This is a great day for the Atlanta Braves, our fans, and our future," Coppolella said at the time. "We are excited about the impact these signings will have on our franchise for years to come."

This signing class had a monumental impact, just not the way the Braves envisioned or wanted.

When the Braves were in Denver for a three-game series in August 2017, Coppolella asked highly regarded scout Rick Williams to assess the organization. Williams had seemingly been Coppolella's right-hand man. But the GM's relationship with many acquaintances began to deteriorate during what would be his final season.

Williams offered a couple opinions, including his belief there needed to be just one person leading the farm system. Dave Trembley, Jonathan Schuerholz and Dom Chiti were basically sharing the role at the time. Coppolella got agitated and walked away from the conversation.

A short time later, the Braves announced assistant GM Billy Ryan and Williams had been demoted. Just a few weeks earlier, Ryan had questioned why Max Fried had been brought from Double A to the majors. Starting his service clock at that time during a losing season didn't make sense.

Ryan stood up to Coppolella and grew frustrated during that 2017 season. Unfortunately, his connection to Coppy led to him leaving the baseball world just a few years later.

A little more than a week after these demotions were announced, MLB received an anonymous letter detailing some of the Braves' transgressions on the international market.

The demotions also came around the same time Coppolella and Hart had barged into Snitker's office and yelled about Jim Johnson being used in a high-leverage situation. A month later, the GM made a spectacle in front of the press box elevator about Snitker not pinch-hitting for Matt Kemp in the ninth inning of a meaningless game in Miami.

Of course, this was also the night before Coppolella was ordered to return to Atlanta to talk to MLB investigators. Rome was burning, but few knew how serious this truly was. It was far more serious than that summer's speculation that he had tampered with the Rockies or twice had lunch with Dodgers assistant hitting coach Tim Hyers.

Coppolella, Hart and Blakeley had to pay for transgressions committed regarding both the international market and the MLB draft.

The Braves lost 13 of the prospects signed from that "great" 2016 international class, which was primarily filled with busts. They also faced significant restrictions on the international market for three years and lost their third-round pick in the 2018 draft.

Blakeley was given a one-year suspension. Coppolella was given baseball's harshest penalty, as he was placed on the permanently banned list. The stiff penalty was influenced by the fact that he lied and misled investigators, seemingly in an attempt to protect the Braves and others. He was reinstated in 2023, but has not regained a role in baseball.

Blakelely and Coppolella resigned from their roles on October 2, but Hart remained with the organization even after the investigation was announced. There was always reason to wonder whether Hart knew what was happening or if he truly was oblivious.

Either way, he was guilty of ignoring his responsibility to guide Coppolella, who was an incredibly intelligent and diligent individual who was swimming in water he couldn't handle.

Knowing where the Braves were at the end of the 2017 season makes it easy to understand why McGuirk has said the 2021 World Series title was more enjoyable than the one the team captured in 1995.

7

Hiring Alex

THERE WAS SPECULATION BRAVES GENERAL MANAGER JOHN Coppolella might face punishment once the 2017 season ended. The Rockies were upset about potential tampering and the Dodgers weren't happy to hear Coppolella twice had lunch with their assistant hitting coach Tim Hyers, a Georgia native who was interested in a roving hitting instructor role.

But nobody was expecting what actually transpired.

Freddie Freeman didn't have a clue as he had breakfast with Coppolella at the team's Miami hotel on September 30, 2017. The meal was interrupted by MLB officials calling to inform Coppolella he needed to return to Atlanta immediately to speak to investigators.

Coppolella resigned two days later, after MLB announced it had found infractions committed within the international market. The team's punishment included fines, the loss of prospects and significant limitations regarding the pursuit of international players.

As for Coppolella, he was placed on the permanently banned list and he remained on that infamous list until being reinstated in 2022.

Needless to say, the Braves were at one of the lowest points in club history. A major rebuild had started in 2015. So, the pieces were in place to be successful within the very near future. But the club needed to find the right guy for the job.

Remember how McGuirk and Kasten played a part in bringing Schuerholz to Atlanta? Well, they also both influenced Alex Anthopoulos' arrival in Atlanta.

Anthopoulos was hired as the Blue Jays GM after the 2009 season, and he remained in that role until he guided them to an American League East title in 2015. His exit came after his power seemed to be weakened by the club's decision to hire former Cleveland GM Mark Shapiro as the team's president.

After declining multiple requests to remain in Toronto with a multimillion-dollar deal, Anthopoulos took a job with the Los Angeles Dodgers. This is when he joined Andrew Friedman's team of hot-shot baseball executives.

Anthopoulos' move to California introduced him to Kasten, who became the Dodgers president and CEO after leaving Atlanta to spend some time as the Washington Nationals president.

After working together for two seasons, Kasten knew Anthopoulos would be a great fit in Atlanta.

"He had other opportunities when he was here and I'd say, 'That's not the right one, just wait for the right one,'" Kasten said. "When this one popped up, I said, 'Yes, this is the one that you want.'"

The Braves' search coincided with the Dodgers playing the Astros in the 2017 World Series. Anthopoulos accepted the Braves' offer to spend the off day between Games 5 and 6 in Atlanta instead of Los Angeles.

So, instead of heading home on the team charter, Anthopoulos went to Georgia, where he had dinner with Terry McGuirk, Bobby Cox, John Schuerholz and John Hart, who temporarily still had held a position within the organization, despite being Coppolella's boss.

"That dinner was two or three hours long and I felt good about it," Anthopoulos said. "I felt comfortable. It felt like the right place for me."

Other candidates included former Cubs GM Jim Hendry and Royals GM Dayton Moore, who had been raised within the Braves organization. Had the Royals allowed Moore to pursue an opportunity, he may have ended up with the job. But the fact is, Anthopoulos made a great first impression during this hastily scheduled dinner.

"We didn't give him the job for two more weeks," McGuirk said. "We had some more discussions. He was so good, he caused me to want to test whether he really could be this good."

Anthopoulos grew weary over those next two weeks. He hadn't been actively pursuing a job. But that one night he had spent in Atlanta had given him reason to believe this was the right fit. He'd have the opportunity to report directly to the control person (McGuirk) and he was comfortable with the people who would surround him.

McGuirk may have unknowingly provided a clue of which way he was leaning. As he used a golf cart to transport Anthopoulos to the Omni Hotel, located adjacent to Truist Park, he told Anthopoulos he'd show him another portion of the stadium during his next visit to Atlanta.

Anthopoulos learned the job was his on November 12. He traveled to Atlanta the following day for a press conference and then headed straight to Orlando, where the General Managers Meetings had already started.

"When I got to Atlanta, I walked in Terry's office and said, 'I was really hoping I was going to see this office again,'" Anthopoulos said.

It's safe to say Anthopoulos continued to pass the tests after getting the job. The Braves surprised most, including themselves, when they won the 2018 National League East title. They showed great signs of improvement in 2017 and Ronald Acuña Jr. arrived in 2018. But this division crown came at least a year earlier than expected.

Less than a calendar year after seemingly hitting rock bottom, the Braves were making their way back to the top. Anthopoulos' arrival brought the franchise the advanced analytics approach it needed. One of the immediate benefits was improved defensive positioning, which allowed Nick Markakis to immediately transform from average outfielder to Gold Glove right fielder in 2018.

At the same time, Anthopoulos proved to be a tireless worker who repeatedly made highly valuable trade deadline deals.

With the Braves proving they were contenders in 2018, Anthopoulos added bullpen depth, gained long-term value via Adam Duvall and acquired Kevin Gausman, who proved effective long enough to be a difference maker.

Anthopoulos completely reconstructed the back end of his bullpen with the 2019 trade deadline acquisitions of Mark Melancon, Will Smith and Shane Greene, a trio of relievers, whose impact extended into the team's run to the 2020 NL Championship Series.

But Anthopoulos' greatest act was securing what might have been the most impactful trade deadline haul in baseball history.

After Acuña was injured two days before the 2021 All-Star break, Anthopoulos spent the final two weeks of July acquiring outfielders Joc Pederson, Jorge Soler, Adam Duvall and Eddie Rosario.

Pederson brought an edge to the clubhouse. Duvall provided consistent power over the regular season's final two months. Rosario was named the NLCS MVP and Soler was the World Series MVP.

Given the World Series title that came with it, that trade deadline haul might have alone been enough to warrant placing a statue of Anthopoulos outside Truist Park.

PART 2

THE LEGENDS

8

Hank Aaron

HANK AARON WAS FAR MORE THAN JUST BASEBALL'S HOME Run King.

"I think he might be the best role model in all of the game," Andruw Jones said. "You know all that he went through when he was chasing [Babe Ruth's home run] record. Jackie Robinson gave everybody a chance to play baseball. But after that Hank also took a lot of heat from writers and fans about race and everything else. Then you look at his numbers and the kind of person he was. He was a great player and a great person."

Aaron established himself as one of the game's best players as he captured a World Series title, was elected National League MVP and collected 11 All-Star selections while playing for the Milwaukee Braves from 1954 to '65. But a better feel for his overall impact on the game and society seemed to come into focus when the Braves moved to Atlanta for the start of the 1966 season.

Having grown up in Mobile, Alabama, Aaron was very familiar with the racial tensions that still existed in this region during the 1960s. He had helped integrate the South Atlantic League in 1953 and now he was the face of the first Major League Baseball team located in the Deep South.

Ambassador Andrew Young remembers the first time he realized the impact Aaron could have in his new city. Young was among the thousands who lined the streets of Atlanta for a welcome parade before the start of the 1966 season. Standing in front of him were what he referred to as a couple "good ol' boys." The stereotypical assumption was they wouldn't be accepting of a Black player playing for their team.

But one of the men said something like, "For this to truly be a major league city, that man [Aaron] has to be able to live wherever he wants."

With this brought some relief. Aaron would be accepted by most within his new hometown and the acceptance would grow as he spent the next nine seasons capping one of the greatest careers baseball has ever seen.

"Bringing people together is one of the things baseball is appreciated for," Aaron said. "You could have all kinds of disagreements, no matter what it would be about. But then you went to the ballgame, and everybody was rubbing shoulders and rooting for their team. Baseball, and sports in general, really helped bring people together."

Aaron owns MLB's all-time records for RBIs (2,297) and total bases (6,856). His 755 home runs stood as the record until Barry Bonds passed that mark while being questioned about steroid use during his final years. Aaron also ranks fourth in runs (2,174) and third in hits (3,771).

Many have said their favorite Aaron stat is that he would still have 3,000 hits if you took away each of his 755 home runs.

So, while Aaron might still be viewed by some as the true home run king, he was far more than just a home run hitter. His proudest accomplishment was owning the RBI record.

"I happen to think Hank Aaron was the greatest player of our generation," former MLB commissioner Bud Selig said. "I know a lot of guys say Willie Mays and I get all of that. But Henry played in Milwaukee and Atlanta. He was a quiet and thoughtful guy who didn't seek attention."

Playing in Milwaukee and then moving to what would now be an unrecognizably smaller version of Atlanta was likely the primary reason Aaron ended up winning just one NL MVP Award. He gained that honor in 1957, when he helped the Milwaukee Braves beat the New York Yankees in the World Series.

Aaron hit .323 with 385 homers, 1,236 RBIs and a .955 OPS from 1955 to '65. He led all MLB players in RBIs and ranked among the top four in each of the other three categories. He won a pair of batting titles, led the league in homers twice and led the league in RBIs three times. He finished in the top 10 in MVP balloting nine of those 11 seasons. But he certainly may have added a couple more MVP plaques to his collection if he were playing in a bigger market.

Or maybe if he were receiving proper appreciation from guys like former Braves broadcaster Milo Hamilton.

Aaron didn't have much fun during the 1967 season, which was the first he played without his longtime teammate Eddie Mathews, who had been traded to the Houston Astros. Coincidentally, the Braves were no-hit in Houston that same year. A few hours later, on the team's charter flight to Los Angeles, Aaron came to blows with Rico Carty, who had instigated the incident using a racially insensitive term.

Aaron, Mays and Roberto Clemente were elected to serve as the NL's starting outfielders during the 1967 All-Star Game. Aaron agreed to play left field. But when the Pirates were in town for a luncheon, Hamilton announced Clemente as the man who beat out Hank Aaron as the NL's starting right fielder.

This enraged Aaron, who had received more votes than either of the other two outfielders. The next day, he went 4-for-4 with a pair of two-run homers. He also threw out Clemente as he attempted to go first to third.

In his autobiography *I Had a Hammer*, Aaron said he confronted Hamilton in the team's New York hotel and then continued to get wind of what the broadcaster was saying about him on air.

"I kept getting angrier," Aaron wrote. "In one game in Atlanta, I singled to right and watched Clemente pick up the ball. He had a habit of dropping his arm before he threw the ball back to the infield. I waited for him to do that, then broke for second. I slid in before he got the throw to the bag. I dusted myself off and then looked up to the radio booth and flipped Milo the bird."

When Aaron arrived in Atlanta, he was 32 and still at the top of his game. He led the league in home runs in the team's first two seasons in Georgia. In fact, he totaled a MLB-leading 315 homers from 1966 to '73, his 32- to 39-year-old seasons. Willie Stargell ranked second within this span with 262 home runs.

So, as Aaron neared his forties, he was undoubtedly the game's best home run hitter. The only other players to total more than 300 homers from their age 32–39 seasons were Ruth, Bonds, Rafael Palmeiro and Mark McGwire. Ruth and Aaron were the only members of this group never linked to illegal performance-enhancing drugs.

This late-career power surge set the stage for Aaron to hit his historic 715th home run on the night of April 8, 1974. His homer off Al Downing broke what was once viewed as Ruth's unbreakable home run record.

Aaron would hit 40 more home runs during the remainder of his career, which concluded where it began, in Milwaukee, during a two-year stint with the Brewers, who came into existence after the Braves moved to Atlanta.

"Milwaukee was really good to Henry," Selig said. "I would say of all the great players we've had like Robin Yount and others, Hank Aaron is still, to Milwaukee, their favorite and greatest player."

Once Aaron returned to Atlanta, he began working with Bill Lucas, his former brother-in-law, who was serving as the Braves' general manager, despite Ted Turner never giving him the title.

Aaron served as a father figure to many different Braves prospects and helped launch Brian Snitker's career by transitioning him from backup catcher to coach within a span of a week. By the mid-1980s he was venturing toward the business world, where he would own restaurants and car dealerships.

Still, he always had an office at the stadium and found time to talk to players whenever necessary.

"We never really talked about baseball," Jones said. "We'd talk about family. He'd tell me to always check on my parents and be the great person they wanted me to be. He'd always say, 'You won't always be a great player, but you can always be a great person.'"

Dusty Baker and Ralph Garr received similar messages, as they had the good fortune of having Aaron serve as their mentor during their early years with the Braves.

"The first thing he'd do is say, 'Calling Mr. Dusty Baker,' and then he'd start laughing," Baker said when asked what Aaron would have thought leading up to the Braves playing the Astros in the 2021 World Series. "I don't know what the conversation would be. We probably wouldn't talk much baseball. The first thing he would have asked about is my mother. He promised my mom [he'd take care of me] when I was 18 years old."

Aaron took care of Snitker a few years later and thus would have taken great pride in having served as a positive influence for the opposing managers in that 2021 Fall Classic.

Unfortunately, Aaron died in January 2021. His death came a couple months after Freddie Freeman had been named the NL MVP. Asked who his favorite player was while he was at the Braves spring training facility in February 2020, Aaron said Freeman.

Aaron's passing also came during the same year one of his closest friends (Baker) battled the Braves in the World Series. It was almost like it was meant to be, as the Braves honored their most significant star by winning it all the same year the baseball world took time to celebrate Aaron's incredible life.

Unfortunately, the baseball landscape was much different during Aaron's final full year on this earth. The COVID pandemic prevented him from occasionally attending games. He watched nearly every game on television. But that 2020 regular season lasted just two months.

"I sit there sometimes and I shed a tear about it," Aaron said during the early days of the pandemic. "I don't cry that much. But I shed some tears about it, and I wish things would be a little bit better."

Aaron made this world a better place and he seemingly died happy with what he experienced here on Earth.

"The good Lord plays the game the way he wants it played," Aaron said. "You do things the way you think you can do them. But after all, you have to wait and do them the way the good Lord intended."

9

Chasing Babe

To best appreciate the significance of Hank Aaron breaking Babe Ruth's unbreakable home run record, it's best to go back to 1949, when Jackie Robinson and Roy Campanella visited Atlanta and became the first Black players to ever play in an integrated professional game in the Deep South.

Remarkably, this occurred on April 8, exactly 25 years before this date became widely recognized as the one during which Aaron broke Ruth's record.

Racial tensions were still high when Robinson, Campanella and their Brooklyn Dodgers teammates came to play a three-game exhibition series against the Atlanta Crackers at old Ponce de Leon Park. Robinson had broken baseball's color barrier just two years earlier.

"It was more than a game. It was definitely an event," said longtime Braves usher Walter Banks, who was a nine-year-old Atlanta resident when Robinson came to town. "I've been so proud of it over the years because things like that just didn't happen."

The Ku Klux Klan objected to this planned event, arguing the staging of interracial games went against Jim Crow laws, which mandated racial segregation in all public facilities within former Confederate states.

Fortunately, Dodgers owner Branch Rickey received assistance from many of Georgia's progressive politicians, including mayor William Hartsfield. Atlanta police chief Herbert Jenkins began a vigorous reform plan when he assumed that role in 1947. He abolished what was considered a Klan-dominated union and integrated the police force in 1948.

"When I was in the sixth grade, we went to Washington, D.C., and police chief Jenkins was on the train with us," Banks said. "When I saw him, it was like I saw a rock star. That's how I felt about him because he always had such a good reputation about race relations."

According to author Tim Darnell, who wrote *The Crackers: Early Days of Atlanta Baseball*, Jenkins quickly quelled the death threats Klan members were directing toward Robinson, Campanella and Earl Mann, who owned the Crackers.

"It just so happened Jenkins was sitting at Mann's house having dinner that night the Klan's Grand Dragon called," Jenkins said. "So Mann said, 'Hold on a minute. I'm going to let you tell Atlanta's police chief what you just told me.' The Grand Dragon hung up and they never heard from him again."

Historical accounts indicate some protesters stood outside the Dodgers' downtown Atlanta hotel and voiced their displeasure while attending the three games. But the exhibition series was completed without incident and a majority of the fans showed their appreciation for Robinson and Campanella.

According to Atlanta sports author and historian Jim Weathersby, before the series, Robinson, a native of Cairo, Georgia, said, "This is the most thrilling experience of my life. It's the most wonderful thing that ever happened to me. It's great to feel that I am playing a part in breaking down the barriers against the people of my race."

Per the Georgia Historical Society, more than 25,000 fans filled the 15,000-seat Ponce de Leon Park, which was located across from where Ponce City Market currently sits. Though the fans were still segregated, with most of the Black fans forced to sit in the outfield, the progress made that weekend helped set the stage for Aaron and the Braves to move from Milwaukee to Atlanta in 1966.

Just 25 years and approximately three miles separated that moment of progress from the moment of triumph Aaron created on April 8, 1974, when he hit his 715th and passed The Babe on baseball's all-time home run list.

To put that in perspective, 26 years elapsed between the World Series titles the Braves won in 1995 and 2021.

So, while racial tensions might have lessened, Aaron still felt some hate, especially as he neared the home run record.

Braves longtime clubhouse and travel director Bill Acree remembers Aaron as being "one of the most normal guys in the clubhouse you would have ever seen." But Acree also has memories of how the legendary slugger was denied the opportunity to continue laughing and interacting with his teammates over the last year before he broke Babe Ruth's home run record.

Once it became apparent that he might pass Ruth's mark, Aaron was besieged with media attention and threats made against him and his family. In response, he was placed under the watchful eyes of a bodyguard and forced to stay at a different hotel than his teammates.

"It wasn't a lot of fun for him," Acree said. "It was fun for the people around it. It wasn't fun for the people in the middle of it."

Aaron's personal assistant, Carla Koplin Cohn, sorted through the enormous about of fan mail sent to the slugger. The United States Postal Service estimated Aaron received 930,000 pieces of mail, 870,000 pieces more than any other person in 1973.

Many of the notes were supportive. Cohn filtered many of the hateful ones, allowing Aaron to only see some. Some were threatening enough to require analysis by the FBI.

All of this added incredible stress to what was supposed to be an enjoyable experience. Aaron's hope of ending this madness in 1973 faded as he ended up with 713 home runs, one short of Ruth's record.

As the Braves opened the 1974 season in Cincinnati, thoughts of keeping Aaron out of the lineup to ensure he broke the record in Atlanta were trumped by then Commissioner Bowie Kuhn's edict that Aaron play in at least two of the three games scheduled that opening week against the Reds.

Aaron matched Ruth's record when he hit his 714th career home run during his first plate appearance on Opening Day. As fate would have it, he did not go deep during the other five at-bats he recorded in Cincinnati that week.

So, the scene was set on April 8, 1974, as the Braves welcomed the Dodgers to Atlanta for their home opener. Aaron's dad threw out the ceremonial first pitch. Sammy Davis Jr. and Georgia Governor Jimmy Carter, who was two years from becoming the United States President, were present.

Aaron showed his sense of humor in his autobiography *If I Had a Hammer* when he wrote, "It seemed like the only people who weren't there were the President of the United States and the Commissioner of Baseball. Nixon had a pretty good excuse. Congress was on his back to produce the Watergate tapes."

Many years and interactions would pass, but Aaron never forgave Commissioner Bowie Kuhn for not attending that night's game.

Aaron walked against Al Downing without even swinging his bat in the second inning. He came around to score what was a historic run. More than 54,000 fans in attendance and a nationwide television audience were watching to see him hit his 715th homer. As an added bonus, they saw him break Willie Mays' National League record for runs with his first trip around the bases.

Dusty Baker said Aaron told him he was going to homer as he strolled toward the plate to face Downing in the fourth inning. While he proved prophetic, Aaron was not making a boastful prediction. He was simply determined to end the mentally draining stretch during which he felt isolated and fearful of what could happen to his friends and family members.

"I think I made that remark to Dusty maybe three or four times," Aaron said. "I just felt within myself that before the night was over, I was going to hit a home run."

Aaron strolled to the plate with the Braves trailing by two runs in the fourth inning. He looked at a ball low and heard the crowd express its displeasure, which was influenced by the second-inning walk. Those same fans roared a few second later, when the man they came to see belted his record-setting home run over the left-center field fence.

After sharing his memorable trip around the bases with a couple college kids who had entered the field, Aaron was greeted at the plate by a mob of teammates. His father reached his arm into the crowd and his mother provided a long, loving embrace.

As this scene was being shown nationwide, legendary broadcaster Vin Scully could be heard saying, "What a marvelous moment for baseball. What a marvelous moment for Atlanta and the state of Georgia. What a marvelous moment for the country and the world. A Black man is getting a standing ovation in the Deep South for breaking the record of an all-time baseball idol."

When Robinson and Campanella had visited 25 years earlier, this might have seemed impossible. But Aaron spent a career doing the impossible, including breaking what at the time was baseball's most sacred record.

10

Chipper Jones

CHIPPER JONES TAKES GREAT PRIDE IN JOINING KEN GRIFFEY JR. as one of the only players to be elected to Baseball's Hall of Fame after being selected with the first overall selection in the MLB draft. He also vividly remembers the extra challenges that come with being taken No. 1.

"Everything you do is under a microscope," Jones said. "You're expected to never make it out. You're expected to never make an error. You're supposed to be this Johnny-Be-Good, All-American boy that does no wrong. It's hard to be perfect. It's impossible to be perfect. And whenever you're not, which I was a lot in my first year, you get scrutinized for it."

Raised in Pierson, Florida, a three-stoplight town between Orlando and Daytona, Jones was a tremendous athlete, whose success at Jacksonville's Bolles Academy drew interest from Florida State's football team and the University of Miami's baseball team. Both programs were at an elite level when the multisport star graduated from high school.

But once the Braves came calling and made him the top pick in 1990, it was time to pursue that baseball dream he had developed as the only son of Larry and Lynne Jones. His first assignment was with the Braves' Rookie Level Gulf Coast League team. He hit .229 with one homer and a .529 OPS over 164 plate appearances. He was also charged with 18 errors in 44 games.

"You're getting everybody's best," Jones said. "Not only that, people try to send a message that they don't think you're very good. They got no problem dotting you between the one and the zero and sending you down to first base. I got hit a ton early on in my career."

Those first couple years in professional baseball certainly weren't easy, but Jones found a couple great mentors in Willie Stargell, who was about a decade removed from his Hall of Fame career with the Pittsburgh Pirates, and Frank Howard, who enjoyed a long coaching career after hitting 382 homers in the big leagues.

Stargell immediately lobbied for Jones to begin swinging a Louisville Slugger K44 that was 36 inches and 36 ounces. This was one of the heaviest bats you could find, and it became the one this 18-year-old prospect began swinging two days into camp.

Jones describes Howard as being "the hardest-working man on the planet." The 6'7", 290-pound coach was an imposing figure who instructed his new switch-hitting prodigy to take twice as many swings from the left side as he did from his natural right side.

"Not only do I have the guy making me swing logs and telling me I'm going to hit 30 home runs in the big leagues, while I roll my eyes and think, 'yeah right,'" Jones said. "But I also have Frank Howard telling me I'm going to take twice as many swings as everybody else with that big bat."

Jones viewed his ability to swing this big bat as a bit of a status symbol. Not everyone could swing a bat that size, especially from both sides of the plate. The success didn't come immediately, partly because he broke his hand when he punched a jealous high school teammate near the end of his senior year.

But the struggles he endured during the introduction to pro baseball in 1990 proved to be quite beneficial.

"I think it took that experience in Rookie Ball and everybody saying, 'Man, that guy is the number-one pick?' for me to go home and say, 'Alright, I'm playing with grown-ass men now, I got to get bigger, stronger and faster'," Jones said. "I think without that motivation, maybe I don't have the year I had in Macon [Georgia] in 1991. I went from being a guy who was passive and laid back and watching what everybody does to being like, 'Screw them, I'm playing with a chip on my shoulder now.'"

When Jones arrived to play for Class A Macon, he was introduced to his new hitting coach, a 35-year-old Brian Snitker. Neither had a clue they were destined to become two of the most successful individuals in franchise history.

"You go back and look at those numbers," Snitker said. "It was just stupid what he did that first full year. It was crazy."

Jones hit .326 with 15 homers, 40 stolen bases and a .925 OPS during his first full professional season. One year removed from high school, he was already looking far different than the ordinary prospect. The only knock against the 19-year-old shortstop was the 56 errors he committed in 135 games.

"He could flat-out hit and he was a great athlete," Snitker said. "He made a bunch of errors. But when you thought back, none of them beat you. He was just a ballplayer. It was great to see."

What does Jones remember about working with Snitker that year?

"Him working my [butt] off," Jones said. "We were still in Low-A ball. We were still kind of bootcamping it before games. It was ground ball after ground ball after ground ball. [Glenn Hubbard] watching every single move I made there at shortstop. Not much has changed. It's the same temperament [Snitker] has always had."

Jones advanced to the Double A level by the end of the next season and hit .346 with a .961 OPS over 285 plate appearances. He and Javy Lopez both moved to Triple A Richmond (Virginia) the following year and became teammates with Ryan Klesko. This trio brightened the future of an Atlanta club that had won the past two NL pennants.

After hitting .325 with an .887 OPS against Triple A pitchers, Jones got his first taste of the majors. How did he begin his Hall of Fame career? As a pinch runner and late-inning sub. His first big-league experience came when he entered to play shortstop during the ninth inning of a 13–1 win over the Padres on September 11, 1993.

Jones was used as a pinch runner the following night. He finally got his first plate appearance on September 14. He tallied a single off Kevin Wickander in a 10–3 win over the Cincinnati Reds. His first extra-base hit came a week later, when he doubled against Mel Rojas in the eighth inning of an 18–5 win over the Expos.

Though Jones tallied just four plate appearances in 1993, he gained valuable experience during an epic pennant race. This was the year they won 104 games, but won the NL West by just one game over the San Francisco Giants. He also got a taste of the postseason scene, as he was part of the traveling party for the NL Championship Series against the Phillies.

Everything seemed to be progressing smoothly. Jones was set to begin the 1994 season as Atlanta's left fielder. He was raking throughout the Grapefruit League season.

But his dreams were halted during an exhibition game against the Yankees on March 18 in Fort Lauderdale. This is when he tore his left anterior cruciate ligament while running to first base on a ground ball to shortstop. The throw took the Yankees first baseman up the line slightly, leading Jones to attempt to avoid the tag. Immediately, he felt a pop and had to be helped off the field by first base coach Pat Corrales and longtime athletic trainer Jeff Porter.

With team president Stan Kasten serving in that same role for the NBA's Atlanta Hawks, Jones had a chance to talk to Doc Rivers and Danny Manning, basketball players who had both recovered from this same injury. He also got tremendous support from many teammates, including Terry Pendleton, who visited the hospital the night of the injury.

"Once I came to the realization that no matter what I was going to do, I wasn't going to play in 1994," Jones said. "That was devastating. I'm 22 years old. I'm having a great spring training. I've got the team made. And then, it all comes to a crashing halt."

A full year of recovery, rehab and preparations followed. With Pendleton having exited via free agency, the third base job now belonged to Jones. However, another delay came in the form of the work stoppage that prematurely ended the 1994 season and delayed the start of the 1995 season.

Accounting for all this information, it's a little easier to understand Jones' overanxious response to a fly ball in the first inning of an Opening Day game against the Giants.

Maddux was making the first start of what would become his fourth consecutive NL Cy Young Award–winning season. He ended the first inning by getting Barry Bonds to hit a popup that would have seemed quite routine had an eager Jones not collided with the veteran pitcher as first baseman Fred McGriff was securing the catch on the right side of the mound.

As Maddux casually got out of McGriff's way, his right calf was impacted by Jones' left knee. Both players fell to the ground before getting up to head to the dugout for the bottom half of the inning.

"I think I called him a piece of s—t rookie and said something like, 'You know, we have 161 more of these to play, so relax,'" Maddux said. "He was trying to do something so good. He was trying to take balls away from the first baseman. Not the shortstop, the first baseman. He was a little eager to do something good. It wasn't funny then. But it's funny now."

Jones gathered himself quickly and drove in the season's first run with a first-inning single against Terry Mulholland. He tallied another RBI single in the eighth inning to record the first of his 763 multi-hit games. Hank Aaron is the only other player in Braves history to record more.

The first big milestone moment was experienced on May 9, 1995, at Shea Stadium. But many of Jones' teammates didn't initially realize the significance of the moment.

This was the night Jones hit his first career homer. It was a go-ahead homer in the ninth inning against the Mets' Josias Manzanillo.

"When I got back to the dugout, I had to go down the stairs and compose myself," Jones said. "When I got back to the bench and told some of the guys it was my first, they were like, 'No way.' I'd been called up in September in 1993 and I was with the team [while recovering from knee surgery] all of '94. So, they just assumed I had already hit one."

Braves broadcasters Pete Van Wieren and Joe Simpson took a little more than a moment before realizing they had just seen a first.

Jones had already rounded third base and was nearing the plate before Simpson said, "I think that was Chipper Jones' first big-league home run." Van Wieren then calmly added, "It is."

"I think it's one of those things we had taken for granted," Simpson said. "It felt like he had already hit 25 home runs because that's how good he was. I think we had assumed he'd already hit one."

Jones ended up hitting .265 with 23 homers and a .803 OPS during that rookie season. He again showed his clutch gene produced a multi-homer game in his postseason debut. He hit a solo shot off Kevin Ritz in the sixth inning and then damaged Curt Leskanic with a go-ahead, two-out, ninth-inning homer that gave the Braves a 5–4 win over the Colorado Rockies in Game 1 of the 1995 NLDS at Coors Field.

The Braves moved past the Rockies, swept the Cincinnati Reds in the NL Championship Series and then beat the Cleveland Indians to win the World Series. Jones hit .364 with three homers and a 1.064 OPS during that postseason.

"It was very satisfying from a team standpoint," Jones said. "We set out for a goal to be the last team standing and we were at the end of the season. But I was nowhere near satisfied with the year I had. Did I contribute and was I a major cog? Yes. But I knew there was a lot more."

There certainly was. Jones finished second to Hideo Nomo in balloting for the 1995 NL Rookie of the Year Award. He then finished among the top 11 in NL MVP balloting each of the next seven seasons. He won the top award during his great 1999 season, which enriched the love-hate relationship he would always have with Mets fans.

Using then general manager John Schuerholz's words, the Braves tried to invigorate their coaching staff after the great 106-win 1998 season ended with a loss to the Padres in the NLCS. This included replacing longtime hitting coach Clarence Jones with Don Baylor, who had recently been fired as the Colorado Rockies manager.

Baylor's arrival changed everything for Jones, whose focus on improving his swing from the left side had adversely affected his production, especially from a power standpoint, from the right side.

"I think it's about getting a hitting coach that you just click with," Jones said. "Don Baylor was that guy for me. Having a guy like Don in your ear who was going to put a chip on your shoulder is invaluable. He didn't let you give away a single at-bat. If you do, you're going to hear about it. During spring training, he told me, 'You hit third and play third for the best team in the National League, people need to fear you right-handed.'"

Baylor motivated Jones by making it clear he and other opposing managers never had a problem pitching to him right-handed. The Braves third baseman had hit .281 with 12 homers and a .762 OPS over the 769 plate appearances he collected right-handed from 1995 to '98. He hit .303 with 96 homers and a .935 OPS batting from the left side within this same span.

"He said we're going to do damage right-handed," Jones said. "I want you to come out of your shoes. I was a 30-homer guy, and he took me to a 40-homer guy strictly because of a change in mindset."

Jones hit .319 with 45 homers, 25 stolen bases and a 1.079 OPS during what proved to be Baylor's only season on Atlanta's coaching staff. He hit .308 with 30 homers and a 1.035 OPS in 530 plate appearances from the left side. He hit .352 with 15 homers and a 1.190 OPS over 171 plate appearances from the right side. He homered once every 56.4 at-bats as a right-handed hitter during his first four full big-league seasons and then homered once every 9.46 at-bats from that side in 1999.

Baylor impacted Jones' rise toward Hall of Fame status and then became the Cubs' manager the following season.

"From a selfish standpoint, I'd have liked to have seen what the next few years would have looked like had he stayed my hitting coach, because nobody rode me like he did," Jones said. "He never let up."

Jones caught fire in June and cemented the MVP Award when the Mets came to Atlanta in late September with a chance to end Atlanta's run of consecutive titles at seven.

The Mets came to Atlanta just one game back in the division standings. But Jones set the tone for the series when he hit a pair of homers to give the Braves a 2–1 win in the September 21 series opener. He homered in the first inning off Rick Reed and then added a decisive eighth-inning homer off Dennis Cook. Jones homered once in the next two games and the Braves ended up finishing eight games in front of the Mets.

"This was a pretty even series except for him," Mets third baseman Matt Franco told reporters after the game.

When the Braves faced the Mets a couple weeks later in the NLCS, Jones heard those "Lah-REE, Lah-REE" chants grow louder. And when Atlanta won that series, Jones fueled the hatred by saying, "Now all the Mets fans can go home and put on their Yankees gear."

John Rocker became public enemy number one when he offended multiple races, religions and origins in a *Sports Illustrated* article that winter. As for Jones, he was the guy

Mets fans hated in the heat of battle and respected for the tremendous player he was.

Jones' 49 homers against the Mets are tied for the most he has hit against any club. The only player to hit more is his former mentor, Stargell (60).

"My dad always said if you can perform on that stage in New York, you can perform anywhere," Jones said.

Jones followed his 1999 MVP season by delighting the hometown fans with a two-hit performance in the 2000 All-Star Game at Turner Field. He singled in the first inning and then smacked a two-out solo homer in the third against James Baldwin. Coincidentally, Hank Aaron also homered in front of his hometown fans when Atlanta had previously hosted the All-Star Game in 1972.

As Jones progressed through the first half of his career, he strengthened his place among the game's elite. The 46.3 FWAR (Fangraphs' Wins Above Replacement Model) he produced from 1996 to 2003 ranked fourth among all MLB players, trailing only Barry Bonds, Alex Rodriguez and Jeff Bagwell.

Unfortunately, foot and leg issues diminished Jones' playing time over the next few years. He agreed to move to left field to accommodate Vinny Castilla, who was signed to a two-year deal before the 2002 season. He moved back to third base after Mark DeRosa struggled to hold the starting role after a couple months in 2004.

Those seasons in the outfield took their toll, as Jones hit just .248 in 2004 and tallied just 21 homers in 2005. But this rough stretch wasn't the beginning of the end. In fact, these seasons just made the end of his career that much more impressive.

From 2006 to 2008, Jones' 34- to 36-year-old seasons, he hit .342 with 77 homers and a 1.027 OPS over 1611 plate appearances. He is just one of two players to hit .300 with 70-plus homers and a 1.000-plus OPS over 1,600-plus appearances from 34 to 36. The other was Babe Ruth.

Jones finished 20th in NL MVP balloting in 2006, sixth in 2007 and 12th the following year. He hit .364 and won his only batting crown at 36 years old in 2008. His on-base percentage that season was an insane .470.

"To come out and contend for a batting title and then ultimately win one, it was really gratifying," Jones said. "I knew who I was as a baseball player, and it just felt like everything came together. It was crazy. I remember having conversations with my dad, driving home after games, and I'm like, 'Nobody can get me out. I don't care who is on the mound, I'm getting at least two [hits] every night.' To have that feeling for basically two years at my advanced age, that was extremely gratifying."

Jones' production began to decline in 2009 and he actually contemplated retirement when his struggles progressed through the first three months of the 2010 season. But he got back on track and was playing well before he tore his left ACL yet again while making a play near the third base line during an August 10 game in Houston.

Sixteen years later, Jones was forced to recover from the exact same left knee ailment that delayed the start of his days as an everyday cog in Atlanta's lineup. But instead of calling it quits, he recovered, rehabbed and earned two more All-Star selections during his final two seasons.

Jones' final home run was fittingly of the clutch variety. He capped a five-run ninth inning with a three-run walk-off homer against Phillies closer Jonathan Papelbon on September 2, 2012. Twenty-two years after being selected with the top overall pick, Jones was helping the Braves advance to the postseason for the 16th time in 21 seasons.

"Nothing beats that," Jones said after hitting the last homer. "That's as good as it gets for a baseball player, to walk off the field—especially in that situation, where we were really down and out."

Jones' first and last career homers gave the Braves a lead in the ninth. He totaled nine walk-off homers. Two were tallied in his rookie season and two more were recorded in his final season. He spent nearly two decades entertaining Braves fans and establishing himself as one of the greatest switch hitters of all time.

"It was great to see him grow as a hitter," Maddux said. "He had incredible memory. He knew all of the pitchers and he'd give us a quick scouting report as we were pulling into a city on the bus. He'd know who the other team was starting, and he'd know something about the guy none of us had heard of. He'd be like, 'Yeah we faced him in the fourth inning of that [spring training] game in Kissimmee. He's got a tired fastball and a lazy slider.'"

While playing the entirety of his professional career with the Braves, Jones had a .303 batting average with a .401 on-base percentage, a .529 slugging percentage, 468 home runs, 1,623 RBIs and 1,619 runs. He earned eight All-Star selections, garnered the one MVP Award and proudly retired having struck out fewer times (1,409) than he walked (1,512).

Jones joins Ruth, Stan Musial, Lou Gehrig, Mel Ott and Ted Williams as one of only six players in MLB history to record a .300 batting average, a .400 on-base percentage, a .500 slugging percentage, 450 home runs, 1,500 walks, 1,600 RBIs and 1,600 runs.

"I didn't work every game, but I virtually saw every at-bat of Chipper's career," Braves broadcaster Joe Simpson said. "That's a wonderful thing to be able to say. You see the changes he went through and the injuries he had to deal with, and you realize the numbers he could have piled on to what he accomplished. But that was a privilege to see what he accomplished on a nightly basis."

Baseball's Hall of Fame welcomed Maddux, Cox and Tom Glavine in 2014. John Smoltz entered in 2015. John Schuerholz gained this honor in 2017 and Jones joined this group when he became eligible in 2018.

This made the Braves the first team in history with four first-ballot teammates who spent 10-plus years with the same club. Jones was the kid when he joined Maddux, Glavine and Smoltz as a mainstay in Atlanta in 1995.

But by the end of his career in Atlanta, he was widely considered to be The Man.

"From the first time you saw him, you knew he was going to be something special," Smoltz said. "He's the most gifted hitter I ever played with. He could do about anything he wanted to. Guys like him don't come around too often."

11

John Smoltz

WHEN EVALUATING JOHN SMOLTZ'S HALL OF FAME CAREER, it makes sense to focus on the great turnaround he enjoyed midway through what proved to be a magical 1991 season for him and the worst-to-first Braves.

Smoltz debuted with the Braves during the second half of the 1988 season, earned his first All-Star selection the following season and posted a 3.84 ERA while making 34 starts in 1990. All seemed to be going well right before the right-hander experienced his first contract dispute with John Schuerholz, the veteran executive who had come from Kansas City during the offseason to become Atlanta's new general manager.

"I allowed an offseason negotiation with a new general manager really get me sideways," Smoltz said. "I was 14–11 on a [1990] team that lost 97 games. I was close to arbitration and here comes a new general manager setting his boundaries and standards."

Smoltz asked for $460,000 and was assigned a $360,000 salary. Suddenly, instead of being the good-natured teammate who wore his emotions on his sleeves, he was less energetic both on and off the mound. As a result, he posted a 5.16 ERA over 18 starts before the All-Star break. The Braves won just three of those 18 games.

"I literally went out to prove him wrong, every start that I made, and that obviously didn't go well," Smoltz said. "We always talk about physical slumps, and we rarely talk about mental slumps. So here's my desire to show him and everybody that I was going to win 35 games. Next thing you know, I'm 2–11 at the All-Star break."

Many people might remember sports psychologist Jack Llewellyn getting credit for the great turnaround Smoltz experienced in the second half. But before getting the pitcher's take on this assessment, it's best to know about a fishing trip he took with catcher Greg Olson during the All-Star break.

"We went on a fishing trip on a pontoon just to get away," Smoltz said. "The Braves were nine games back and I was nine games under .500. It doesn't take a genius to see how those numbers match. He was an experienced fisherman, and I wasn't at the time. You're not supposed to troll in a pontoon boat and catch the kind of bass we were trying to catch. I must have rolled over a nest or something and I caught a whopper while trolling with a worm. He turned to me and said, 'You're going to have a great second half.'"

Olson certainly proved to be right, as Smoltz posted a 2.63 ERA in 18 starts after the break. The Braves went 15–3 in those outings, the inverse of Smoltz's record on the mound during the first half. So how did Llewellyn help from a mental perspective?

"We rarely talked about baseball and it's not like I was laying on a couch and he was using a wristwatch to turn me into a baseball player again," Smoltz said. "What it came down to was a two-minute video he put together to show me my best pitches to every right-hander and every left-hander. It clicked because I'm a visual guy. It was that simple. We didn't really talk again."

This is why Smoltz was caught off guard during the postseason when fans were asking him about Llewellyn wearing a red shirt in the stands. He had no clue the sports psychologist was doing this in case the pitcher ever felt like he was in trouble on the mound and needed some reassurance.

The unrelenting support Cox showed to a struggling pitcher certainly paid off as Smoltz posted a 1.52 ERA in four starts during the 1991 postseason. He tossed a six-hit shutout in Pittsburgh in Game 7 of the NLCS and then tossed seven scoreless innings in Game 7 of the World Series in Minnesota.

When Smoltz left his Pittsburgh hotel to prepare for the first Game 7 of his career, he grabbed a taxi being driven by a die-hard Pirates fan. The cabbie asked where his patron was from and responded, "Atlanta's run ends tonight. The Pirates are going to beat that Smoltz guy."

Somewhere over the next five hours the cabbie might have realized he may have given Smoltz a little more motivation.

"I was calm before the biggest games," Smoltz said. "I felt like that's where I wanted to be. I can really attribute that to my childhood, when I just had an incredible imagination to put myself in those situations all the time. I wanted the ball. I wanted the last shot. I wanted the ball on the mound."

The Braves actually got their first glimpse of this clutch gene as Smoltz posted a 1.38 ERA over his final eight postseason starts. He fittingly started the game that allowed the Braves to clinch the NL West with one remaining game.

Once Steve Avery guided the Braves to a Friday-night win, Smoltz knew he would have a chance to help clinch the title if the Dodgers lost to the Giants. In these pre-internet days, knowing what was occurring in the West Coast games often had to wait until the newspaper arrived the following morning.

Smoltz tried to stay awake to watch the game on ESPN, but he decided it was best to just go to sleep. He woke up, saw the Dodgers lost 4–1 and said, "It's over."

A few hours later, Olson started a mini tradition by jumping into Smoltz's arms. Smoltz allowed two runs over nine innings against the Astros and created the opportunity for him and his teammates to celebrate the NL West title once they gathered in the infield to watch the stadium's video board show the conclusion of the Dodgers' second straight loss to the Giants.

Fast-forward to Game 7 of the NLCS in Pittsburgh. After getting a ride from the die-hard Pirates fan, Smoltz was so relaxed he took a nap inside the visitors' clubhouse at Three Rivers Stadium. The Braves scored three runs in the first inning and the Pirates nearly answered when Andy Van Slyke flirted with a three-run homer in the bottom half of the inning.

"Olson came out after Van Slyke flew out and said, 'Are you alright?' Smoltz said. "I said, 'It's over now.' He said, 'Why is it over now?' I said, 'They had their chance. They won't score now.'"

Eight innings later, Smoltz had notched a shutout in his first career Game 7 start. His next Game 7 assignment came in the World Series just 10 days later, when he experienced the thrill of matching up against his childhood idol Jack Morris.

Smoltz again proved up to the challenge as he tossed 7⅓ scoreless innings and then exited after the Twins tallied a pair of eighth-inning singles. His effort wouldn't be enough, as

Morris threw 10 scoreless innings and the Twins won 1–0 on Gene Larkin's one-out single in the 10th.

This will forever be considered one of the greatest pitchers' duels in World Series history. The effort helped Morris eventually gain election to the Hall of Fame. For Smoltz, this was just the beginning. Or you could say it was an incredible conclusion to a season that had started as miserably as he or anybody else could have imagined.

"Wanting to be in that spot doesn't guarantee success," Smoltz said. "But it's a precursor to success."

Smoltz earned a pair of All-Star selections and notched consecutive 200-strikeout seasons the next two years. He produced a respectable 3.18 ERA over 29 starts while helping the Braves win the 1995 World Series. He exited that Fall Classic having posted a 2.76 ERA over 13 career postseason starts.

Still, it felt like it was always (Greg) Maddux, (Tom) Glavine, Smoltz or Glavine, Maddux, Smoltz. It was seldom Smoltz, Maddux, Glavine. Glavine won the 1991 National League Cy Young Award and Maddux won each of the next four, including each of his first three seasons with Atlanta.

There was never a sense of jealousy between these three iconic teammates. But whether on the mound or the golf course, they were all highly competitive, especially Smoltz, who entered 1996 as a man on a mission.

"I told [heralded sports journalist] Peter Gammons he had to stop picking me to win the Cy Young because I was ruining his credibility," Smoltz said. "I kept hearing, 'Here is the guy with all the stuff, why can't he win 20 games?'"

When Smoltz arrived at the West Palm Beach complex for spring training in 1996, he approached the coaches and said, "Maddux's run is over."

"They said, what do you mean?" Smoltz said. "It's my turn. I'm going to win the Cy Young this year. I was healthy and I was confident. I became a Christian in 1995. I didn't tell any of the reporters, but my faith was important to me in determining this up-and-down career I was having. But I did tell them, I might lose my first game and win my next 14 and you won't see any difference in me this year."

Smoltz proved prophetic once again. He gave up six runs over 6⅓ innings while losing his first start to the Giants. But he proceeded to go 14–0 with a 1.91 ERA over his next 15 starts. Suddenly, the buzz was it was his Cy Young Award to lose.

Around this same time, Smoltz began nagging longtime clubhouse and equipment manager Bill Acree about changing his jersey number. He didn't think 29 wins was attainable, so he wanted something more realistic. Mark Lemke was wearing No. 20 and Warren Spahn's No. 21 was retired. No. 22 was available. But there was never any real attempt to make an in-season change.

So Smoltz finished the regular season 24–8 with a 2.94 ERA. He then went 4–1 with a 0.95 ERA in five postseason starts. That's a total of 28 wins.

But after the season concluded, Acree reminded Smoltz he had got the win in the All-Star Game. So, he said, "There's your 29."

Smoltz won the 1996 NL Cy Young Award. This marked the sixth straight year either he, Glavine or Maddux had captured this honor. But instead of savoring this accomplishment, Smoltz entered the offseason distraught about the fact the Braves had blown a 2–0 lead over the New York Yankees in the World Series. He was on the wrong end of a 1–0 loss in his Game 5 matchup against Andy Pettitte. An unearned run accounted for the game's scoring.

"That year was pretty gratifying to say the least," Smoltz said. "But then we were left with this empty hole because we didn't win the championship. I mean, I'm the guy that if I went 12–20 and we won a championship, I'm ecstatic. But I couldn't fully enjoy that season when we didn't win the World Series."

Smoltz posted a 3.02 ERA while completing a career-high 256 innings in 1997 (three more innings than his 1996 total). He finished fourth in Cy Young Award balloting after going 17–3 with a 2.94 ERA in 1998. Still, the wear and tear was catching up to him. When he underwent arthroscopic surgery for the second time in his career on his right elbow after that 1998 season, he was told the next procedure would be Tommy John surgery.

This wasn't surprising to Smoltz, who had known his ulnar collateral ligament had been torn to some degree for at least three years. It was just a matter of when the pain would reach a point where couldn't continue to pitch.

Instead of shutting down, Smoltz reinvented himself by throwing sidearm and adding a knuckleball to his arsenal. He took a couple weeks off in July of 1999 and then posted a 2.87 ERA over his final 14 starts. He wasn't at full strength, but knowing his elbow was about to blow, he let it all go during that postseason.

Smoltz made just one start during the NL Division Series against the Astros and then came out of the bullpen to record a save in Game 2 of the NLCS against the Mets. Three days later, he threw 7⅓ innings in a Game 4 loss at Shea Stadium. He tweaked his arm in that outing and dealt with pain over the days and weeks that followed.

Still, despite initially making it clear he wasn't physically capable of pitching out of the bullpen in Game 6, he ultimately relented and allowed Mike Piazza to hit a game-tying home run in the seventh. The Braves had had a 3–0 lead in this best-of-seven series and were now looking at the possibility of having to play Game 7.

"I was like, this was the lowest moment of my career if we end up losing this game and blow a 3–0 [series] lead," Smoltz said. "I wouldn't have been able to live with myself."

Smoltz's mood was brightened about an hour later when Andruw Jones drew a bases-loaded walk in the 11th inning. The Braves were headed to the World Series for the fifth time during the 1990s and Smoltz was going to get one more start.

Unfortunately, the Yankees held a 3–0 series lead by the time Smoltz was available to pitch. He struck out 11 over seven innings, but the Braves bid adieu to the 1999 season with a 4–1 loss at Yankee Stadium.

"I threw like six or seven knuckleballs in that game," Smoltz said. "Chipper [Jones] always laughs because I would scream in my glove, 'That's a knuckleball. Take that.' I was pretty frustrated."

Instead of undergoing Tommy John surgery during the off-season, Smoltz came to camp in 2000 determined to prove he could get by throwing just knuckleballs and fastballs. The slider was what most bothered his elbow.

So Smoltz told Cox he was going to throw this "nasty knuckleball" that wasn't like "your average knuckleball." Catchers Eddie Perez and Javy Lopez quickly agreed.

Perez wore a welt on his right biceps muscle after he whiffed while trying to catch one of these knuckleballs in the bullpen. Lopez was charged with a couple passed balls when Smoltz made his first spring training start that year.

Smoltz walked away from that outing feeling good about where he was heading. All seemed to be fine until he couldn't lift his fork while having dinner with his family that night. A quick call to team orthopedist Dr. Joe Chandler led to an MRI, which led to Dr. James Andrews performing Tommy John surgery the following week.

Before the surgery, Smoltz received a call from Tommy John, the man who underwent this elbow ligament procedure in 1974 and then pitched another 14 seasons. His successful recovery has since prolonged the careers of countless pitchers.

"He goes, 'John, this is Tommy John,'" Smoltz said. "I'm like, really? I'm sure it's one of my friends. But he goes, they've got this thing, and it will work. Once I hung up, I was all in. I went to Birmingham and had all the trust in the world in Dr. Andrews and Dr. Joe Chandler, who I trust more than anybody in the world. From that moment on, there wasn't a doubt in my mind I was going to pitch again."

Smoltz returned about six weeks into the 2001 season and was efficient in three of his first five starts. But after lasting just three innings in that fifth start, he returned to the Yankee Stadium clubhouse, tore his jersey off, threw it to the ground and said he was done. Once his anger subsided, he returned to Birmingham, where he was convinced he was simply dealing with tendinitis.

But Smoltz knew he couldn't get where he needed to be as a starter that year. So, he told Cox he wanted to go to the minors to learn how to work out of the bullpen for the remainder of the 2001 season.

It was a successful transition. Smoltz rejoined Atlanta's pitching staff after the All-Star break and worked as a middle reliever and setup man for about a month. He spent most of the season's final six weeks serving as the closer. He posted a 1.59 ERA over 34 innings and converted 10 of 11 save opportunities.

Now came the interesting development. Smoltz made himself a reliever because he knew that was the only way he could be valuable in 2001. He didn't think about possibly returning to that role until he entered free agency and began receiving offers.

"Those same negotiations that went bad in 1991 were remembered again," Smoltz said. "The only thing discussed by the Braves was that I would be the closer and I'd be getting a closer's contract. I wasn't given a choice. I was offered a monster contract to go to the New York Yankees as a starter and I wasn't offered nearly close, not even remotely close to the same to remain a closer for the Atlanta Braves."

Smoltz passed on the Yankees' three-year, $52 million offer to accept the three-year, $30 million deal that allowed him to continue playing for Cox and extend his desire to spend his entire career with the Braves.

Though serving as a reliever might not have been his cup of tea, Smoltz quickly proved masterful in that role. He set a new NL record with the 55 saves he tallied in 2002 and set a franchise record with the 154 saves he compiled through the end of the 2004 season.

Smoltz was doing his job out of the bullpen. But while one of the best postseason starters in baseball history sat in the bullpen, the Braves lost three consecutive years in the NLDS. The starter-turned-closer got two save opportunities within the 15 playoff games played during this span.

"If we would have won championships, I would have never gone back to starting," Smoltz said. "I wanted to win championships. I'm bold enough to say if you give me 11 chances during the postseason, we're World Series champs. There's no doubt in my mind."

With this logic, Smoltz convinced the Braves to move him back to the rotation in 2005. They did this by acquiring closer Dan Kolb from the Brewers.

Kolb was an immediate bust. After a couple months, Cox playfully asked, "Do you guys also boo me when I bring Kolb in the game?" But the Braves found solutions for the ninth inning and Smoltz again established himself as one of the game's top starters.

Smoltz was 38 years old when he returned to the starting role. He earned an All-Star selection in 2005 and had top-10 NL Cy Young Award finishes in 2006 and '07. Twenty years after being acquired for Doyle Alexander, the determined hurler was still providing the Braves value.

When Smoltz spent those years recovering from Tommy John surgery and working out of the bullpen, he bid adieu to hopes of joining Glavine and Maddux in the 300-wins club. But he did experience the thrill of collecting his 200th win. It coincidentally came as he squared off against Glavine in a 2–1 win over the Mets on May 24, 2007.

Smoltz recorded his 3,000th strikeout in 2008, before under-doing season-ending shoulder surgery. The Braves said they offered him a $14 million salary for 2009 if he wanted to return. He pointed out the base salary was $1 million, and he would have needed to throw 240 innings to earn that amount.

So, he ended up spending his final season with the Red Sox and Cardinals. But he's mended his fences with the Braves, who put him in the team Hall of Fame in 2012.

Smoltz might forever remain the only pitcher to ever record 200 wins and 150 saves. He tallied 15 postseason wins and he stands with Justin Verlander, Pettitte and Glavine as the only pitchers to ever complete at least 200 innings in the postseason. Smoltz (2.67) is the only member of this group with a sub-3.00 ERA in the playoffs.

His career played out much like he had envisioned when he put himself in big-game situations while throwing a ball against a wall during those childhood days in Lansing, Michigan.

"In my mind and in my own cathedral, I played it out," Smoltz said. "Ernie Harwell was doing the announcing and I was doing the pitching. As far as I was concerned, it was a fun ride. Getting to do that for real was just unreal."

12

Tom Glavine

WHEN TOM GLAVINE AWOKE ON OCTOBER 28, 1995, HE KNEW what awaited him that evening. So, as Braves fans stirred, excited about the possibility of winning a World Series that night, the Game 6 starter tried to do whatever he could to take his mind off the task at hand.

"It was a fairly normal morning, except it wasn't," Glavine said. "I never I never slept great on a game night, and that night was no different. I think that forced myself to stay in bed and get some sleep, so to speak, but it wasn't easy to do."

Glavine spent time with visiting family members, played with his daughter and tried to subdue the nervous energy. But once he got in the car and began driving toward Atlanta-Fulton County Stadium, he was locked in on facing the best lineup he ever encountered during a 22-season big-league career.

With Albert Belle, Manny Ramirez, Eddie Murray and Jim Thome highlighting the lineup, the Cleveland Indians entered the 1995 World Series as heavy favorites. But Greg Maddux limited them to two unearned runs over nine innings in Game 1 and Glavine allowed just two runs over six innings as the Braves won Game 2.

The Indians exacted some revenge when they tagged Maddux for four runs over seven innings in Game 5. But they wouldn't be as fortunate during this second chance against Glavine.

"It's not like I hadn't had incredible admiration for him before, but my admiration for him went up that night," Braves Hall of Fame executive John Schuerholz said. "He was really a bulldog that game. Of all the games I remember with big circumstances, he really came to the fore that night."

Glavine worked a 13-pitch perfect first inning and then might have really found his groove. He walked Belle to begin the second inning and then picked him off before striking out the next two batters. He retired eight straight before pitching around a Belle walk in the fifth.

The Braves squandered a David Justice double in the fourth. It was around this same time that Glavine came in the dugout and famously yelled, "Just get me one run because they aren't getting any."

Tony Peña broke Glavine's no-hit bid with a soft leadoff single in the sixth. But what really mattered was what happened in the bottom of the inning, when Justice homered off Jim Poole.

Glavine got his run and he proved to be a man of his word. He surrendered just the one hit over eight scoreless innings and then watched Mark Wohlers pitch a perfect ninth. The Braves were World Series champions and Glavine was forever a legend in Atlanta.

"For Glavine to go out there and be the face of the organization and somebody who came up through the team's minor league, it was just a great story to see what he did in Game 6," Maddux said. "If you're ever going to watch a Disney movie of a kid getting drafted out of high school and being with the organization for a long time before winning the big game for his team and city, you could just go with Glav's story."

Glavine's journey toward that triumphant moment began when the Braves selected him in the second round of the 1984 MLB Draft. A few days later, the National Hockey League's Los Angeles Kings drafted him in the fourth round. He was selected ahead of future hockey Hall of Famers Brett Hull and Luc Robitaille.

But Glavine put his hockey stick away and began his march toward Baseball's Hall of Fame.

Glavine shot through the lower minor league levels and ended up with Triple A Richmond by the end of the 1986 season. He began the following season with Richmond, but was called up to Atlanta in August. He showed the signs of youth as he alternated good and bad starts while introducing himself to the big-league scene near the end of 1987.

Some success was tasted in 1989, but Glavine spent much of his first three full seasons dealing with growing pains. But everything changed in 1991, when Glavine was gifted with a much-improved defense. Rafael Belliard was at short. Sid Bream and Terry Pendleton were at the corner infield spots and Otis Nixon was in center field.

"I was a much more complete pitcher in 1991," Glavine said. "Obviously, a lot of that had to do with the team that was behind me. It's a lot easier to buy into the notion of throw more strikes, pitch to contact and let your guys behind you make plays when those guys behind you are actually making plays.

"I think secondarily for me was the confidence in my changeup. In 1988 and '89, when I went out there with my A stuff,

I could compete even when we didn't have great teams. I think the difference became I learned how to win or at least stay in the game with my B stuff and eventually my C stuff. I couldn't do that before 1991."

Glavine went 20–11 with a 2.55 ERA in 1991 and won the first of two National League Cy Young Awards. This was also the first of three straight 20-win seasons. There's a chance he could have tallied four or five straight had the 1994 and 1995 seasons not been shortened because of a work stoppage.

Suddenly, Glavine was one of the game's top starters and Smoltz also started making his way to this elite level during the second half of 1991. By the time the 1993 season arrived, Glavine, Smoltz and Maddux were all part of the same rotation.

Glavine won the 1991 and 1998 NL Cy Young Awards. Maddux captured this honor four straight times from 1992 to '95 and Smoltz grabbed the trophy in 1996. So, these three men, who spent a decade together within the same pitching staff, captured seven Cy Young Awards within an eight-year span.

"There was a genuine respect, and I'll say love for one another as teammates," Braves broadcaster Joe Simpson said. "They were proud of each other and what they were able to accomplish. But certainly there was a competition because they were competitors. Was there ever any one-upmanship? Sure. They wanted to be better than the guy was last night. That's kind of one of the things that I always felt like drove them to be so good."

Smoltz had tremendously powerful stuff that provided him the ability to compile high strikeout totals on a consistent basis. Maddux had incredible control and the ability to baffle opponents with movement. As for Glavine, he could methodically master his opponents.

"Glavine had this amazing way to pitch to hitters that frustrated them to no end," Simpson said. "He knew how to pitch. He knew how to mentally get in people's heads."

Glavine posted a 3.15 ERA and had a 134 ERA+ from 1991 to 2002. Among all pitchers who totaled at least 1,500 innings within this span, Glavine ranked fifth in ERA+. The only pitchers with a better mark were Pedro Martinez (172), Greg Maddux (164), Randy Johnson (155) and Roger Clemens (140).

Glavine finished second in Cy Young Award balloting after he notched his fifth 20-win season in 2000 and he earned his ninth All-Star selection in 2002. But at the end of that season, he ended up being the odd man out.

The rotation looked different at this point. Smoltz was now serving as the closer because of the difficulty he experienced recovering from Tommy John surgery. Maddux was still pitching like a frontline starter and Kevin Millwood had bounced back from a couple of rough seasons.

Still, with Jason Marquis and Damian Moss filling out the rotation's other two spots, the rotation had a lot of uncertainty beyond Glavine and Maddux.

Thoughts that Glavine might have some leverage quickly dissipated when he signed with the Mets. He received a three-year, $35 million contract, which had an option that would make it a four-year, $42 million deal.

"I think my only ill will toward that was the perception was I left Atlanta for more money," Glavine said. "While that was ultimately true, that wasn't the process and I think that is how it was portrayed. I never changed in terms of what I wanted from the Braves. That never changed even after I went out on the open market and got more. I never asked them to match what I was getting from somebody else."

Glavine just wanted the same three-year, $30 million deal Smoltz got after the 2001 season.

"We just never got there for whatever reason," Glavine said. "I don't know why. I really don't. I didn't think it was very out of line what I was asking for. I just got a sense I didn't fit in their plans anymore or they were just expecting me to take a super home discount."

With the perception he chased more money to join the hated division rival Mets, Glavine was loudly booed when he returned to Turner Field. This certainly seemed unfair, given that he had established himself as one of the most successful and influential players in Braves history.

It took Glavine approximately a year to stop feeling the anger that consumed him after leaving the Braves.

Glavine ended up winning his 300th game while playing for the Mets, but he returned to the Braves at 42 years old in 2008. Three of his first four starts were solid. Within this stretch, he threw 6⅓ scoreless innings at Coors Field. Game time temperature was 41 degrees. He never publicly told anybody, but the wintry conditions that night led to the start of the elbow issues that ended his career.

Signs of age started to show again during Glavine's next start at Nationals Park. He exited with a hamstring strain in the first inning. He went on the injured list a few days later for the first time in a career that had consisted of 669 starts to this point.

Glavine's elbow became an issue again in June and continued to give him problems when he made one final start in April. He attempted to return the following year, but again experienced what seemed to be a rude goodbye.

The Braves had Glavine make all his rehab starts leading up to what was expected to be a return in June. His presence at each of these minor league parks increased attendance, which enhanced the team's revenue.

Nothing changed in terms of health or performance. Glavine finished his rehab assignment by tossing six scoreless innings for Class A Rome. But instead of being activated to start the next weekend against the Brewers, he was released to make room for the promotion of top prospect Tommy Hanson.

Glavine was livid with general manager Frank Wren. He scheduled a press conference at a local radio station the next day and aired his grievances. Again, the guy who had given this organization so much felt disrespected.

But time has healed all wounds and Glavine is again a happy member of the Braves family. He takes great pride in the fact that he was a key figure during what was the franchise's greatest era.

"It makes me extremely proud to know that I was a part of that group that essentially put baseball back on the map in Atlanta," Glavine said.

13

Dale Murphy

AFTER PASSING ON THE OPPORTUNITY TO PLAY FOOTBALL AT Arizona State University, Dale Murphy left his native Oregon and travelled to Kingsport, Tennessee, to begin his professional baseball career for the Braves' Rookie Level affiliate. He was a homesick 18-year-old catcher who appreciated the easy-going nature of his manager, Hoyt Wilhelm, whose 21-season big-league career included more than 2,200 innings pitched.

The Braves took Murphy with the fifth overall selection in the 1974 MLB Draft. The early reviews were encouraging, especially from the defensive perspective.

Wilhelm told *The Atlanta Constitution*, "He throws better than any catcher I've ever seen and I've seen a few in my time."

Over the next few years, that great throwing arm would become erratic and force a position change. This proved to be a very beneficial transition for Murphy, who ranks with Hank

Aaron and Chipper Jones as the most beloved players in Braves franchise history.

Long after Murphy won consecutive National League MVP Awards, earned seven All-Star selections and won five Gold Gloves as an outfielder, longtime Braves coach and instructor Bobby Dews told Murphy, "I hear you give Bobby Cox all the credit for moving you to the outfield, but I just want you to know, that was my idea.'"

This was Dews at his finest. He seemed to always find a way to stir a laugh at the ballpark. He used to get a kick out of telling people he once lived with the Georgia Peach. When they would respond, "Ty Cobb?" He'd say, "No, this lady who was a stripper at a place down on Peachtree Street."

"Bobby Dews was just the perfect fit for me," Murphy said.

Murphy's first full professional season was spent playing Dews at Class A Greenwood (S.C.). The team was filled with a bunch of players just a year or two out of high school.

This certainly wasn't an easy year for Murphy, who hit just five homers and had an abysmal .597 OPS in 491 plate appearances. One day Dews told his players he was sick of the lolly-gagging. So, he told them they needed to remove themselves from the game if they ever found themselves not hustling.

A few hours later, a frustrated Murphy hit a high fly ball to the right of the mound and jogged down the first base line. Knowing what he had done, he returned to the dugout and sat quietly on the bench.

Recognizing his catcher wasn't getting ready when the half-inning ended, Dews said, "What are you doing?" Murphy replied, "I didn't hustle down the line." This led Dews to exclaim, "I didn't mean you."

Even though Murphy struggled at the plate, the Braves moved him to Double A Savannah (Georgia) the next year. This is where he spent the first of two straight years with Tommie Aaron as his hitting coach. Aaron, who was Hank Aaron's younger brother, helped mold the young catcher's swing as he started to benefit from physical maturity.

Murphy hit 12 homers over 104 games for Savannah and then enjoyed a short stint with Triple A Richmond before getting his first call to the majors when the major league rosters expanded in 1976. He hit .262 with no homers and a .687 OPS over 72 plate appearances for Atlanta.

Just 20 years old and two years removed from high school, Murphy had reached the majors. One of his first great thrills was being behind the plate when Phil Niekro carried a no-hitter into the ninth inning against the Reds on October 2, 1976. Cesar Geronimo ended the bid with a one-out, opposite-field double.

This link to Niekro would prove significant again just a few years later, when Murphy's days behind the plate ended.

Murphy got a taste of first base as he belted 22 homers while producing an .884 OPS over 127 games for Richmond the following summer. But he was still primarily being used as a catcher, even when he returned to Atlanta's roster for a second straight September.

Though owner Ted Turner assigned himself the general manager title, Bill Lucas handled the GM responsibilities. Lucas visited Murphy during the winter after the 1977 season, gave him a $2,500 bonus and told him he was happy with his progress. It has been reported Murphy refused the check. But he actually just said, "Are you sure you want to do that?" before accepting the money.

Humility has always been one of Murphy's top qualities. Hailed as one of the most genuinely friendly individuals to ever grace the professional sports world, he was named a *Sports Illustrated* Sportsperson of the Year in 1987.

As he progressed through the minors and proved himself as the 1980s arrived, Murphy never lost sight of his desire to play for the folks who had believed in him, going all the way back to the day he was drafted.

"All those years in minor leagues and then those years trying to find myself, Bill [Lucas], Tommie Aaron, even Ted [Turner], Bobby Cox, Dewsy [Bobby Dews], they were all pulling for me," Murphy said. "Those relationships were really meaningful to me, and they really motivated me to make something more of myself."

Braves fans didn't know what they were witnessing in 1978, when Murphy finally got to spend a whole season at the big-league level. This is when he met Cox, who had just come over from the Yankees to begin his big-league managerial career in Atlanta.

Murphy and Cox would become iconic Braves. But when they met during that first season together, they were both far from finished products.

With Cox running the show, Murphy found himself as Atlanta's primary first baseman. He played 129 games at that position and was behind the plate for another 21 games. He committed 20 errors as a first baseman but denied 12 of 25 stolen base attempts against him. There still seemed to be some hope behind the plate.

But the following year, while attempting to catch Niekro's knuckleball, he felt a pop in his knee. This may have influenced some of the errant throws that ended his catching career. But it definitely marked the start of the knee issues that prematurely slowed his production and ultimately, hurt his Hall of Fame résumé.

"I loved to catch, and I liked first base," Murphy said. "But in the back of my mind, I was thinking we're not competitive now, so I know they're giving me a chance to get my feet wet and try to find a position. But I was also wondering when we got competitive, how it would work out at first base or catcher, because I didn't do well at either position."

When Murphy arrived at spring training in 1980, he became a full-time outfielder. Dews worked with him every day and tried to help develop an outfielder's mindset. The first assignment in spring training was left field, and it didn't take long for the quick study to pass the test.

It all seemed to click during a spring training game that year, when Murphy fielded a ball along the left field line, turned and threw the hitter out at second base.

"I hadn't felt like that in a few years," Murphy said. "I was like, 'Oh my, that was fun.' That's what happened to me mentally. It was like, 'I'm going to contribute defensively instead of being, like, a project, which was what I was at catcher and at first base. I was hitting 20 home runs, so they tried to hide me at first base. But you can't hide anybody there. In the outfield, I felt like I had a shot to be a pretty good defensive player.'"

No longer stressed by his defensive limitations, Murphy became a better offensive threat. And his adaptation to the outfield was successful enough that he spent the 1980 season as a center fielder. He hit 33 homers, earned his first All-Star selection and finished 12th in balloting for the NL MVP Award.

Murphy struggled during the strike-shortened 1981 season. He fared better when play resumed in August, after a two-month stoppage. But it was still hard to see what was coming.

Joe Torre replaced Cox as the Braves' manger after the 1981 season and inherited a team that was ready to win. Atlanta set an MLB record by claiming 13 straight wins to begin the 1982 season. This was the first sign that this could be a special season for both Murphy and the team.

Murphy started the season on fire, posting a 1.002 OPS in April and a 1.001 OPS in May. He was the clear-cut early season favorite for the NL MVP Award. He held that distinction until his offensive production began to dip during the season's final two months.

"[The MVP] hadn't been a consideration for me earlier in my career, so I didn't know what to think about it," Murphy said. "When somebody would ask you, I'd give the typical, 'I'm just thinking about tonight's game,' but it was going on in my mind for sure."

Murphy hit .281 with an .885 OPS, while leading the NL with 36 homers and 109 RBIs. He would have more productive seasons. But this one would be forever special. He won the NL MVP and his first Gold Glove Award. His production helped the Braves surprise the baseball world by winning the NL West.

"I knew I was in the running, but without the internet or anything like that you really don't know what's going on," Murphy said. "Then one day I get a phone call from Jack Lang, the president of the Baseball Writers Association [of America], and he told me I had won.

"Emotionally, mentally and professionally it just finally all fit together. It was fun playing with the guys out there. We were winning and I just felt comfortable and confident out there."

Murphy's success extended into the 1983 season, which may have been the most productive of his career. The center fielder hit .302 with 36 homers, 30 stolen bases, 121 RBIs and a .933 OPS.

This was a uniquely successful campaign. It marked just the 11th time an MLB player had hit 30-plus homers and recorded 30-plus stolen bases in the same season. At that point, the only other players who had done this were Bobby Bonds (five times), Willie Mays (twice), Tommy Harper, Hank Aaron and Ken Williams.

So, it was no surprise when Murphy won a second straight NL MVP Award. At the time, he stood as he just one of nine players who could lay claim to earning the honor in consecutive years.

Murphy has spent plenty of time reflecting on how fortunate he was to have played within a span that created the opportunity for him to be deemed the best player two straight years. Hank Aaron stands as one of the greatest players to ever step on a diamond. But he won just one MVP Award.

"I'm very grateful, but it's all kind of subjective and has a lot to do with timing," Murphy said.

Murphy spent the earliest years of his career trying to prove the Braves were wise to take him with their first draft pick in 1974. Now, he had the challenge of proving he could maintain his status as one of the game's elite players.

"Going into spring training in 1984, I was thinking, you've won a couple really cool awards, how are you going to follow this up?" Murphy said. "What is going to motivate you? I just used the old thought about how you can't read the old press clippings or rest on your laurels. It was really motivating to me to be in good shape and to work hard and to keep grinding. I wasn't getting hurt."

One of the keys to Murphy producing such impressive numbers during the 1980s was his desire and ability to play on an everyday basis. This certainly wasn't easy during an era when quite a few NL parks had an artificial surface.

Still, Murphy managed to play 740 consecutive games from September 26, 1981, until July 8, 1986. The only players to amass a longer such streak since the completion of Murphy's were Cal Ripken (2,632 games) and Miguel Tejada (1,152 games).

Ripken's record-setting streak was at 686 games when Murphy's streak ended.

Murphy's streak ended unceremoniously. He needed a break physically and mentally. At the same time, he knew manager Chuck Tanner would be more comfortable not having to play him every day just to keep the streak alive.

"Murphy can be like everybody else now," Braves third baseman Bob Horner told the *Atlanta Journal*. "People forget he is only human."

The only thing separating Murphy from six consecutive 30-homer seasons was the fact he hit just 29 homers during the 1986 season. His production dropped slightly that year, but he came back to hit 44 homers and produce a .997 OPS during the 1987 season.

Murphy hit his 300th homer against the Pirates' Brian Fisher on August 21, 1987. He was just 31 years old and in the midst of a six-season stretch during which he averaged 36 homers per season. It looked like he had a chance to join the exclusive 500-homer club. But chronic knee issues took a toll as the slugger's production significantly declined over the next few years.

There was a time when it seemed Murphy was a lock for the Hall of Fame, but his candidacy weakened when he hit just .238 with 86 homers and a .715 OPS from 1988 to '91. He underwent knee surgery to repair structural damage after the 1989 season and then dealt with a blood infection that caused further deterioration.

Murphy gained a sense his time in Atlanta might be done as the 1990 season progressed. David Justice, who would win NL Rookie of the Year that season, had arrived. So, too, had Ron Gant to fill another of the outfield spots.

The Braves were getting younger, and Murphy was getting older.

Knowing the Braves were in a tough spot, Murphy went to Bobby Cox, who was serving as both GM and manager at this time, and told him he planned to sign elsewhere during the offseason. Suddenly, Cox could make the trade without feeling like he had disrespected one of the most beloved players in franchise history.

Had he felt comfortable a year or two earlier, he could have garnered a much more significant return.

Nevertheless, August 3, 1990, proved to be a very sad day for countless Braves fans and employees. This was the day Murphy was traded to the Philadelphia Phillies for three players who were long gone by the end of the next season.

"If you're unemotional about this, this is clearly the thing to do," Braves president Stan Kasten told the *Atlanta Journal and Constitution* after the trade. "But emotions are a part of it. I mean Dale Murphy isn't just another guy."

Eddie Mathews, Warren Spahn and Hank Aaron were Braves legends who grabbed headlines across the country throughout their respective careers. The nation had the opportunity to see Aaron break Babe Ruth's home run record as he neared the end of his iconic career.

But Murphy was the first Braves legend whose career played out on television screens across the country. He was one of the most feared sluggers of the 1980s and one of the kindest souls to ever play professional sports.

"I don't regret moving on, I really felt like it was time," Murphy said.

Murphy was on a team that produced a winning record during just three of the 15 seasons he spent on the Braves' big-league roster. But things quickly changed.

The Braves won the first of their 14 consecutive division titles in 1991 and won the World Series in 1995. They captured five NL pennants in the 1990s.

"It's like leaving Apple after spending a few years building computers in a garage, and then the very next year it becomes the Apple we know," Murphy said. "Not in 20 years, the very next year. They went to the World Series the very next year. I'm like, 'This team is amazing,' and I'm not a part of it. You move on. Do you feel envious and jealous? Yeah, certainly.

"I tried to put on a good face. But deep down inside, [my wife] Nancy and I would look at each other, like 'What is going on?'"

Murphy hit .265 with 398 homers and a .815 OPS over an 18-season career that concluded with stints with the Phillies and Colorado Rockies. He finished in the top 10 in MVP voting in four consecutive years (1982–85) and his 32.4 fWAR (Fangraphs' Wins Above Replacement Model) ranked ninth in MLB from 1982 to '87.

All of the eight players who ranked ahead of him are Hall of Famers—Wade Boggs, Rickey Henderson, Cal Ripken, Mike Schmidt, Tim Raines, Gary Carter, Eddie Murray and Alan Trammell.

Murphy produced the second-most home runs (308) and RBIs (929) during the 1980s. Schmidt hit the most home runs, with 313, and matched Murphy's RBI total, which was trumped only by Murray's 396.

At the end of the 1987 season, Murphy was 31 years old with 310 homers and a .862 OPS over 6,383 plate appearances. He averaged 36.3 homers from 1982 to '87, but then never again hit more than 24 in a season. Even accounting for a steady decline, it was easy to project that he would easily surpass the 400-homer mark and keep his career OPS around .850.

Each of the 17 players who had hit 400 homers with a career OPS of at least .850 through 1991 are Hall of Famers.

But Braves fans have spent the past couple decades being discouraged by Murphy's Hall of Fame results.

During his time on the official Hall of Fame ballot (1999 to 2013), Murphy never received more than 23.2 percent of the votes, and he garnered as much as 15 percent just three times (1999, 2000 and 2013). He received just seven of the 16 votes cast when he was first placed on the Modern Baseball Era ballot in 2017.

But even that was a disappointing result, given Cox, long-time Braves executive John Schuerholz and longtime Braves broadcaster Don Sutton were on that special committee in 2017. But they couldn't influence the special committee like White Sox owner Jerry Reinsdorf and Tony La Russa were able to do for Harold Baines in 2019.

When you combine talent with character, Dale Murphy might be the greatest individual to ever play a professional sport. This is why there are countless folks hoping he one day finds himself back in Cooperstown, enshrined with the Braves' other greats.

14
1982

THOSE WHO WATCHED THE BRAVES OPEN THE 1982 SEASON with 13 straight wins assumed that season began perfectly. Those who lived this streak know different.

As Grapefruit League season came to a close, the Braves packed all their supplies and headed to Cocoa Beach to play one last game against the Astros. From there, they made the short trek to the Orlando airport, from where they would fly to Seattle for a couple exhibition games.

Because the flight had to go around thunderstorms, there was a need to stop and refuel in Denver. The weather and unplanned stop led the Braves to land in Seattle around 11:30 PM PT, approximately 20 hours after some had started the day at the team's spring training complex.

And to add to the pain, those who had left sunny Florida dressed comfortably were shivering as they got off the plane and quickly learned what 30-degree temperatures felt like in Seattle.

This was quite an introduction for manager Joe Torre, who was back in the organization for the first time since serving as the Braves catcher from 1960 to '68. Torre remembers having lunch with general manger John Mullen before the Opening Day game in San Diego.

After Mullen said something like, 'Well, let's split these two,' Torre responded by saying, 'Why don't we just win both of them?'" The new manager was optimistic. But he had no clue how incredible the season's first two weeks would be.

The Braves opened the regular season with a pair of wins in San Diego and then swept a three-game set against the Astros in Atlanta. This was followed by a 6–0 road trip that included stops in Cincinnati and Houston.

"We were behind in a number of those games," Torre said. "It got to the point that Dale Murphy, he'd be goofy going up and down the dugout saying, 'Guys, they have us where we want them.' It didn't matter who was on the mound, we'd find ways to win. That was special."

All of this was unexpected. The Braves were expected to improve. But this start shocked everybody, including Hall of Fame pitcher Bob Gibson, who had been lured to Atlanta to serve as one of Torre's pitching coaches.

"I remember Gibby getting on the bus one time and under his breath, he said to the driver, 'Make sure these mirrors stay adjusted right because I don't know how we're doing this without them," Murphy said.

Regardless of whether it was smoke and mirrors, this season-opening run of perfection created widespread delight.

Two years removed from his White House tenure, President Jimmy Carter called to congratulate Torre after the team moved to 11–0. The Braves returned to Atlanta and found the city buzzing about this great start.

The Braves went to the playoffs in 1969 and Hank Aaron pursued Babe Ruth's record at the end of 1973 and the beginning of 1974. But there were many other years the club had created this kind of excitement since moving to Atlanta in 1966.

Rafael Ramirez homered and Claudell Washington tripled during a three-run third inning that propelled the Braves to a 12th straight win. Another sold-out crowd filled Atlanta-Fulton County Stadium the next night when the streak reached 13 in dramatic fashion.

How fortunate were the Braves during this stretch? Well, that 13th straight victory came with the assistance of their own baserunning blunder.

With runners at first and second with one out and the Reds winning 3–2 in the ninth, Brett Butler's sharp grounder struck Matt Sinatro's foot as he went toward third base. Butler's speed might have prevented the Reds from turning a game-ending double play. But Sinatro's blunder created a dead ball situation, which prevented any shot of this happening.

Following a wild pitch and intentional walk to Biff Pocoroba, Claudell Washington tallied his game-ending two-run single off Joe Price. Washington had been briefly hospitalized after Price hit him in the head with a pitch the previous week in Cincinnati.

"I was hoping to come back against the Reds," Washington told the *Atlanta Journal*. "After all, they're the ones who kept me out of the lineup and caused me to miss all of the fun this team is having."

It was April. But the nightly celebrations looked and felt much like the ones you'd expect to see in October.

"It was crazy," Murphy said. "It was like our World Series. People ran on the field and everything. It was a really interesting time. There are a lot of great memories. We really gelled during that stretch."

This season was filled with fun. But Torre's bunch certainly didn't just cruise down easy street after becoming the first MLB team to ever begin a season 13–0. In fact, they played just three games above .500 the rest of the season.

The Braves followed 13 straight wins with five straight losses. They lost seven of their final eight games in May and then won eight of their first nine games in June. A couple more good stretches helped create a nine-game division lead on July 29. But this inconsistent bunch lost 19 of its next 21 games. They suffered three straight walk-off losses to the second-place Los Angeles Dodgers during this stretch.

Making matters worse was the fact Murphy appeared on the cover of *Sports Illustrated* a little more than a week into this skid. A potential SI jinx didn't provide any comfort to a team that certainly could have used some.

"It was a roller coaster all year," Torre said.

Speaking of roller coasters, it was the merry-go-round Pascual Perez experienced that helped the Braves escaped that ugly 21-game stretch. The day he kept going round and round on Interstate 285 was the day Torre's bunch righted itself.

Perez was acquired from the Pittsburgh Pirates on June 30, and he was still new to driving. So navigating Atlanta's interstates was a challenge, especially when he didn't realize I-285 was an outer loop. There were no exits that would have taken him directly to the stadium.

So, while the Braves waited for him to make his August 19 start, he was hopelessly driving around and hoping not to run out of gas. He actually borrowed a few bucks from a charitable soul at one point to put some gas in the car.

"Batting practice started and there was no Pascual," Holland said. "Batting practice ended and there was no Pascual. Now, they're either mad at him or worried about him. He could speak a little English, but he wasn't fluent by any means."

Phil Niekro agreed to start on short rest and soon after he began throwing his warm-up pitches, Perez burst through the clubhouse doors.

"He said, 'I'm sorry, I'm sorry,'" Holland said. "I said, 'Where the hell have you been?' He said 285, 285. He was scared to death. He thought they were going to release him."

Niekro took pressure off Perez as he thew seven innings and helped the Braves win that night. Perez showed his appreciation by allowing just one run over 9⅔ innings during a 10-inning win against the Mets the next night.

And the Braves were rolling again. They exited that 21-game skid by claiming six straight wins, two via the walk-off variety.

Nothing came easy for this Braves team. They squandered a chance to clinch the NL West when they lost their regular season finale in San Diego. Now they had to wait to see the result of the Dodgers-Giants game.

Joe Morgan became an instant hero in the Braves clubhouse when he homered to end the Dodgers' bid for a one-game playoff against the Braves. Now, Atlanta had to prepare for a best-of-five NL Championship Series against St. Louis.

Atlanta's coaching staff had strong ties to St. Louis. Torre won an NL MVP Award while playing for the Cardinals and his pitching coach Bob Gibson will forever stand as one of the greatest pitchers to wear a Cardinals uniform.

Just like the regular season, the start of this NLCS was unique. But not in a good way for the Braves.

After Niekro threw four scoreless innings in what was going to be Game 1, a heavy rainfall soaked Busch Stadium and forced the game to be restarted the next day. Gone was the 1–0 lead

Niekro had been given and gone was the magic that had followed the Braves throughout the season.

Perez got hit hard in what became a Game 1 loss for the Braves. Niekro returned to start Game 2. He exited with a one-run lead after seven and watched the Cardinals score a single run in each of the final two innings against Gene Garber. Rick Camp strained a back muscle while celebrating the NL West championship. He declared himself fit to pitch Game 3, but allowed four runs in just one inning.

A great season that started with 13 straight wins ended with three straight losses. Still, the Braves had finally created hope for the first time in more than a decade. Their success during this season was celebrated by the countless TBS viewers who welcomed this team into their living rooms on a daily basis.

There was an early reality television feel to this season, as a young TBS producer named Glenn Diamond spent the year creating a documentary called *It's a Long Way to October*. The behind-the-scenes look at the season was enjoyed by the fans and players alike.

"There was really a star quality to the season," Murphy said. "It was like all of a sudden we were kind of a big deal. We went from relative obscurity to cable TV and then cable TV took off. Then Ted Turner decided to have cameras follow us around for the documentary. There was this little thing going on. I think that was a part of our success. We were all having fun."

With fans stretching from Maine to Hawaii, the Braves had become America's team. Murphy won the first of his two consecutive NL MVP Awards in 1982 and Bob Horner still seemed destined for a great career. There was a lot to like about where this team was heading.

But the Braves fell short of a division title in 1983 and spent most of the remainder of the decade languishing in ineptitude.

Murphy, Horner, Niekro, Washington, Bruce Benedict, Glenn Hubbard and Rafael Ramirez were long gone before the Braves would again be considered winners.

Still, memories of those Baby Blue uniforms bring back good memories to the countless folks who became fans of Murphy, Horner and the TBS-beamed team that entered living rooms with the regularity of *Family Feud* in the 1980s.

15

Greg Maddux

GREG MADDUX WENT TO NEW YORK DURING THE 1992 WINTER Meetings expecting to sign with the Yankees.

"Atlanta is where I wanted to go and [Braves general manager John] Schuerholz said, 'Great, give me like two weeks or 10 days to make a trade. We have to trade a player before we can sign you.' I gave him that time and then he calls back and says, 'We weren't able to trade that player, go ahead and do what you've got to do.'"

So, Maddux and his agent Scott Boras went to New York to be wined and dined by the Yankees. A deal may have been completed had an offer been made. But the reigning National League Cy Young Award winner and Boras left town without a signed contract.

"I had a layover in Chicago, so I talked to Scott, and he said, 'The Braves made you an offer,'" Maddux said. "I said, 'Okay, do your Boras stuff and I'll call you when I land in Vegas. During the three hours I was in the air, the Yankees made their offer. When Scott told me, I said I didn't want to hear it and that was kind of that."

That is how Maddux ended up getting his wish to come to Atlanta. But to fully appreciate how this great union materialized, you have to go back to spring training that year, when Maddux was with the Chicago Cubs, preparing for the first of his four straight National League Cy Young Awards.

After the Braves celebrated their worst-to-first 1991 season, general manager Schuerholz was determined to add more star power to his roster. His first target was the Pirates' Barry Bonds, who won the 1990 National League MVP Award and then finished second to Braves third baseman Terry Pendleton the next year.

Schuerholz arrived at the Braves spring training complex one morning in 1992 prepared to announce Bonds would be joining a lineup that included Pendleton and David Justice. The day before, he had agreed to a deal that would send reliever Alejandro Peña and upcoming outfielder Keith Mitchell to the Pirates in exchange for Bonds.

Pirates GM Ted Simmons agreed to the deal, knowing it was pending Peña's approval. Peña gave the go-ahead, but Pittsburgh manager Jim Leyland didn't.

When Schuerholz called the next day to arrange when the deal would be announced, Simmons informed him there was a problem. Pittsburgh's team president, Carl Barger, nixed the deal after Leyland had barged into his office to complain that morning.

Bonds won the 1992 NL MVP Award, and the Braves killed his World Series hopes by beating the Pirates in the NLCS for a second straight year. Had the trade happened, the Braves may have had the game's best player for the next decade.

Instead, they ended up having the game's best pitcher for that span.

Had the Braves acquired Bonds and re-signed him the following winter, they wouldn't have had the financial flexibility needed to surprise the sports world by signing Maddux during the 1992 Winter Meetings.

As the meetings began, it was assumed Bonds would sign with the Giants, who had long employed both his father, Bobby Bonds, and godfather, Willie Mays. As for Maddux, the general consensus was he would end up with the Yankees.

Maddux won the 1992 NL Cy Young Award after going 20–11 with a 2.18 ERA for the Cubs. He responded to the honor by saying, "I'd trade it all to play for a winner."

He had the opportunity to chase top dollar. But he didn't have the desire. He set his sights on winning a World Series and he determined his best chance to do so would be by joining Tom Glavine, John Smoltz and Steve Avery within Atlanta's rotation.

"We worked hard to get the best hitter in the game, and ended up with the best pitcher in the game," Schuerholz said.

Schuerholz traveled to Louisville for the 1992 Winter Meetings with the impression Maddux would sign with the Yankees. This assumption intensified when then Yankees GM Gene Michael left the meetings to show the pitcher around New York.

But on the final night of the meetings, Schuerholz and then Braves president Stan Kasten negotiated a five-year, $28 million deal with Boras.

As Kasten sat in a suite at the Galt House Hotel, Schuerholz was across the hall trading Charlie Leibrandt to the Rangers. Leibrandt's $2.8 million salary had to be moved to make room for Maddux.

Maddux passed on the Yankees' $34 million offer because he saw a greater chance to win World Series titles in Atlanta. The Braves won the 1995 World Series, captured two other NL pennants and secured 11 of their 14 straight division titles while Maddux was with the team.

The Yankees won four World Series within this span, including two against the Braves. But Maddux never regretted his decision to come to Atlanta, where he had the pleasure of spending time with fellow Hall of Famers Tom Glavine, John Smoltz, Chipper Jones, Fred McGriff, Bobby Cox and Schuerholz.

"Atlanta was 100 percent the right choice for me," Maddux said. "This was 1993. I was going to make enough money. I wanted a chance to win a World Series. If you look at what happened from 1990 to 1993, the Braves were knocking on the door and the Yankees weren't the Yankees yet. The Yankees didn't get good until 1996. Looking back, who knows what would have happened. I never regretted that decision for a second."

Nor did Schuerholz, who shares the belief that this might have been the best free-agent signing of all time.

"Some could argue [signing Maddux] set the fortunes of the organization in place for more than a decade," Schuerholz said.

Adding to the significance of this initial acquisition was the fact that Maddux signed a five-year, $57 million extension two months before his original deal was set to expire. He accepted an arbitration offer to stay in Atlanta for an 11th season in 2003.

Maddux was 32 years old at the start of his second contract in Atlanta. But it still proved to be a wise investment. Pedro Martinez, Randy Johnson and Kevin Brown were the only pitchers to produce a better ERA from 1998 to 2002.

After passing on the Yankees' more lucrative offer, Maddux proceeded to win each of the next three NL Cy Young Awards to become the first pitcher to receive this honor in four consecutive years. He finished in the top five of NL Cy Young balloting in seven of his first eight seasons with the Braves.

When Maddux arrived in Atlanta, the Braves were bidding for their third straight NL pennant. His union with Smoltz, Glavine and Steve Avery created the game's top starting rotation. But this didn't guarantee a third straight trip to the World Series.

Many years later, Maddux talked about feeling the pressure a player feels when joining a new team and introducing themselves to a new city. A teammate standing nearby said, "Yeah, it was so tough for you, you ended up winning the Cy Young."

Maddux allowed one run while totaling 17⅓ innings over his first two starts for the Braves. He allowed four runs in each of his next three starts. But he then proceeded to post a 2.20 ERA over his final 31 starts. He struggled in the decisive sixth game of the NLCS loss to the Phillies. But the next couple seasons would be very impressive.

"I didn't want to be a guy that had one good year," Maddux said. "There's plenty of guys that have had one good year. My goal was to always do a little bit better. So, it was very satisfying to have another good year [in 1993]. The only thing missing was the World Series. All the individual stuff was pretty much taken care of."

How do you follow winning consecutive Cy Young Awards? Well, Maddux produced two of the best seasons the game has seen. He posted a 1.56 ERA over 25 starts in the strike-shortened 1994 season and followed that with a 1.63 ERA over 28 starts during the 1995 strike-shortened season.

Maddux accounts for two of the three times a pitcher has produced a sub-1.65 ERA over 25 starts in a season since the mound was lowered in 1969. Dwight Gooden (1985) stands as the only other pitcher to do this.

"It was pretty special," Maddux said. "You know, it was a good time. And you know, I was fortunate enough to you know, learn a cutter so I was able to cut it and sink it. Not many guys were doing that at the time that it was just a big advantage because it was something that hitters didn't see much of."

Maddux made his MLB debut with the Cubs near the end of the 1986 season. After producing a 5.61 ERA in 1987, he started showing signs of his tremendous potential. His patented two-seam fastball danced like a Wiffle ball. But while playing at Wrigley Field, he became bothered by the frequency with which a left-handed hitter lifted an outside fastball into the wind and was awarded with an opposite-field homer.

Needing a pitch that would keep left-handed hitters mindful of his ability to attack the inner third, Maddux worked with Cubs pitching coach Billy Connors, who had him develop the slider grip Danny Darwin had used. What came out of Darwin's hand as a slider came out of Maddux's hand as an effective cutter.

Suddenly a good pitcher became a great pitcher and the Braves reaped most of the benefits.

Maddux remained with the Braves through the end of the 2003 season, compiling 194 wins and a 72.9 fWAR—second only to the 77.9 fWAR fellow Hall of Famer Randy Johnson compiled within this span (1993–2003).

"We were delighted to have him, and he fit right in," Schuerholz said. "He was competitive, the same kind of guy as Glavine and Smoltz were. He was a tough competitor and a master of pitching."

Maddux compiled a dazzling 2.22 ERA over the 191 starts he combined to make through his first six seasons with Atlanta.

His run of four straight Cy Young Awards was preceded by Glavine winning in 1991. His run was ended by Smoltz winning this honor in 1996. Glavine won again in 1998.

These three Hall of Famers, who accounted for six straight Cy Young Awards and seven within an eight-season span, spent 10 seasons as teammates. They filled the first three spots in Atlanta's rotation from 1993 to '99. This run was only interrupted when Smoltz underwent Tommy John surgery in 2000 and then returned as a closer.

As Smoltz was recovering from this elbow surgery, Glavine and Maddux were continuing to prove elite in their mid-thirties. They finished first and second, respectively, in balloting for the 2000 NL Cy Young Award.

Maddux and Glavine remained in the same rotation until Glavine left to join the Mets after the 2002 season. Smoltz celebrated the trio's last year together by setting an NL record with 55 saves.

"I think it's something we really appreciate more now that we're out of the game than when we were actually going through it," Maddux said. "When we were doing our thing, we were so locked into what we had to do to get ready for our next start. It was easy to sit there between starts and root for the other guys to do their thing.

"It's just a lot more special now that some time has gone by and there hasn't been a threesome or a staff like it since."

It was a special group that continues to draw great respect throughout the baseball world. They owned unique personalities and shared the ability to be highly competitive without ever showing one ounce of jealousy for the other.

"You had the stoic Glavine, non-emotional and not knowing what's going on," Smoltz said. "You had kind of the nerdy professor in Maddux and then I was goofy. I just kind of let it all hang out."

Had Smoltz opted to retire after the 2008 season, he likely would have been on the stage with Glavine, Maddux and their manager Bobby Cox when they were all inducted into Baseball's Hall of Fame in 2014.

Smoltz just had to wait one more year to enjoy his own special day. Now, he can travel to Cooperstown every year to reunite with the other members of the most accomplished rotation the game has ever seen.

It was a trio created by Maddux's desire to leave money on the table to become part of something he envisioned would be special.

16

Andruw Jones

ANDRUW JONES' PRE-TEENAGE ASPIRATIONS TO ONE DAY PLAY for the Oakland Athletics came in the midst of watching them reach the World Series three straight years, from 1988 to '90. But his hope to one day play in the Bay Area changed when the Braves showed interest in him during a tryout camp in his native Curaçao.

"The opportunity for me to realize my dream of playing professional baseball was right in front of my face," Jones said. "I chose the Braves right away because they are the ones who gave me the first chance. Right after that, other teams came asking about me, but I never tried out for any other teams.

When Jones began playing in the United States in 1994, he joined a Rookie Level Gulf Coast League team that included George Lombard, Wes Helms, Bruce Chen and Ron Wright, who was the only member of this quartet to never play in Atlanta. But remember that name.

Jones fared well when he rose to another Rookie Level team in Danville, Virginia, that same summer and cemented his place as one of baseball's top prospects when he hit 25 homers and stole 56 bases for Class A Rome in 1995.

Still, nobody, including Jones, envisioned what was going to happen in 1996.

Jones actually entered this memorable year feeling overlooked or slighted.

"I had just won minor league Player of the Year [in 1995] and they didn't invite me to big-league camp, but they invited Ron Wright, who I had played with the year before," Jones said. "All I wanted was to go to big-league camp so that I could get my own bats. I didn't care about anything else. Talking to Javy Lopez, Eddie Perez and some of the guys and they were like, 'Why aren't you in big-league camp?' It kind of motivated me."

This would never again be an issue. Seven months later, Jones would homer in the first two at-bats of his World Series career. But first, he had to get over the frustration of not getting a chance to win a Class A South Atlantic League title.

Let's just say Jones' recollection of 1996 is pretty funny.

With Jones, Wright and Helms all on the roster, Class A Durham qualified for the postseason by winning the first-half title. As Jones was participating in the SAL's All-Star Game, he learned he had been promoted to Double A Greenville (South Carolina).

"I was like, 'Oh man, come on,'" Jones said. "When I got to Double A, we didn't have that great of a team. I struggled the first couple weeks and our manager Jeff Cox called me in and told me to quit trying too hard. I got on a roll and had a nice hitting streak. Then, the day the hitting streak ended, the late José Martínez came to me and said, 'Are you ready?' I said, 'I'm always ready.' He was like, 'Are you ready to go to

Triple A?' I was like, 'Come on man, I was just starting to get going at this level.'

Jones played his first week with Triple A Richmond (Virginia) and then got a surprise when manager Bill Dancy asked him to play right field one night in Norfolk (Virginia).

"I said I'm not a right fielder," Jones said. "He said, 'Bobby Cox wants you to play right field.' So, I said, 'Ok.' You don't think about it when you're playing the game. It's getting toward the end of the season for Triple A. So, you think about going home and stuff like that."

So Jones didn't realize why he was in right field that night. He was just mad that the first ball hit to him sailed over his head and his throw attempting to retire the batter at second base wasn't handled by a middle infielder. All he was thinking at this time was that he wasn't a right fielder.

Jones ended the game in center field and then got some clarity the next afternoon, when he was told he would be joining the big-league team in Philadelphia the next day. Atlanta needed his bat and because Marquis Grissom was already situated in center field, the heralded prospect needed to play right field.

"I walked in to [the clubhouse] in Philadelphia wearing shorts and everybody was like, 'Who is this kid?'" Jones said. "I kind of rubbed everybody the wrong way a little bit there. But everybody knew who I was and the kind of player I was. They just wanted to make sure I knew the rules really well and what Bobby [Cox] expected from his players."

Braves general manager John Schuerholz knew this was an aggressive move, but he also knew this prospect wasn't like too many the game had seen.

"I was thinking we have a star on our hands," Schuerholz said. "I knew if he had the right temperament and attitude he would be fine. He didn't have that right away. But by talking to

Bobby Cox and teammates, he learned if he wanted to be the stud and star of the Atlanta Braves, this is what their principles are, and this is what you have to do to be a good Brave."

Still 19 years old and two years removed from his professional debut, Jones had realized the dream he developed in Curaçao. He homered in his second game, enjoyed a multi-homer game in his sixth game and ended up hitting .217 with five homers and a .709 OPS in 31 regular season games.

Again, nobody expected what was to come during the postseason.

Jones was primarily used as a late-inning defensive replacement during the first two rounds of the 2016 playoffs. He did start NL Championship Series Game 7 and responded by homering during a two-hit performance against the St. Louis Cardinals.

Back in the lineup for World Series Game 1 at Yankee Stadium, Jones became the youngest player to homer in a World Series game. One inning later, he joined the A's' Gene Tenace as the only players to homer in both of their first two career World Series at-bats.

"When you look back, it was like, 'Wow, am I dreaming or is this for real?' Jones said. "One thing that stuck with me when I left Curaçao as a teenager was that my dad told me, 'When you're given an opportunity, you have to take advantage, because if you don't you might never get it again.' That was my mindset every time I walked into a stadium."

But Jones was still young and learning. One of his most valuable lessons came when Cox removed him immediately after he had allowed a fly ball to drop in front of him during a July 21, 1998, game against the Cubs.

"You've got to respect the game," Cox told *The Atlanta Constitution* after the loss to the Cubs. "He did not try for the ball. He's only 21. But I didn't act that way when I was 21 and neither did Willie Mays or Hank Aaron."

It wasn't just about a lack of effort on that particular play. Jones had also run through third base coach Bobby Dews' stop sign, looked at a called third strike with two outs and the bases loaded, and remained stationary when Cubs catcher Scott Servais fumbled a third strike.

"I allowed one at-bat to screw my mind up and I lost focus," Jones said a quarter-century later. "We disagreed with each other, and we yelled at each other like an older kid does with a parent. We got everything off our chest, and we moved on. I didn't agree with him at that moment, but I learned a lot from it."

Chipper Jones and Andruw Jones spent more than a decade playing together and will forever be linked as two of the greatest players the Braves have ever had. They built a strong friendship as the years progressed, but it took some time for them to get used to each other.

"We weren't very close early in our careers," Chipper Jones said. "I think we were both pretty headstrong and cocky. I didn't like Andruw very much and he probably didn't like me very much, which is okay. We learned from watching each other. Through the years, we developed a respect for each other's game. We were in the lineup every single day. Upon gaining respect for each other's game, we became better friends and haven't looked back since."

Andruw Jones' finest season occurred in 2005, when he set a franchise record by hitting 51 home runs. He benefited from an adjusted stance and the new batting machine he had installed at his house the previous winter. But playing center field on nearly a daily basis for more than a decade took its toll.

After Jones hit .224 with 26 homers and a .724 OPS in 2007, the Braves immediately announced they wouldn't attempt to re-sign him. He entered free agency and spent the next six seasons with five different teams.

While the end of his career wasn't pretty, Andruw Jones spent a decade proving to be one of baseball's elite players. He won 10 Gold Glove Awards and is still considered by some to be the best defensive outfielder the game has seen.

Jones produced MLB's third-best WAR from 1998 to 2007. The two players who ranked ahead of him within this span were Barry Bonds and Alex Rodriguez. The man ranked immediately behind him was his longtime Braves teammate Chipper Jones, who received a first-ballot HOF induction in 2018.

How great was Andruw Jones defensively? He led all major leaguers with a 26.6 defensive bWAR during his 11 full seasons (1997–2007) with the Braves. Hall of Famer Ivan Rodriguez ranked second with 16.5.

"He established himself as one of the best players in the game," Chipper Jones said. "And I have no problem saying he's the best center fielder I've ever seen."

17

Eddie Mathews

CHIPPER JONES IS ONE OF THE GREATEST THIRD BASEMEN baseball has ever seen. But there are some who might argue he isn't even the greatest third baseman in Braves history.

Some think that distinction belongs to Eddie Mathews, who was the seventh player in baseball history to reach the 500-homer milestone. Mathews spent 15 seasons with the Braves and is the only person to have played for the franchise in Boston, Milwaukee and Atlanta.

"I've only known three or four perfect swings in my lifetime," Ty Cobb once said. "This lad has one of them."

There was no denying Mathews' incredible talent as he hit 25 homers as a 20-year-old rookie for the 1952 Boston Braves. His success would continue as the team moved to Milwaukee the following year. By 1954, he and Hank Aaron were forming one of the best power duos baseball has ever seen.

Aaron broke Babe Ruth's home run record. But Mathews was initially targeted as the guy who was going to do this.

Mathews hit 370 home runs through his first 10 major league seasons—all before the age of 30. The only players to hit more homers through their 29-year-old seasons are Alex Rodriguez (429), Ken Griffey Jr. (398), Jimmie Foxx (379) and Mickey Mantle (374).

Aaron tallied 342 homers before his 30-year-old season.

"We weren't jealous of each other," Aaron said. "That's one reason we were so successful."

The only three players to hit 400-plus homers for the Braves were Aaron (733), Mathews (493) and Chipper Jones (468).

Mathews' most influential home run was the walk-off homer he hit after the Yankees had taken a 4–3 lead in the 10th inning of Game 4 of the 1957 World Series. The Braves evened the series with that victory and then captured the franchise's second world championship with a Game 7 victory.

That was the only home run Mathews hit in 62 World Series plate appearances for the Braves.

"My feelings at that moment are hard to describe," Mathews said in his autobiography *Eddie Mathews and the National Pastime*. "I suppose it's like the feeling long-distance runners get, the high from endorphins being processed in the brain. I know I told the reporters when I rounded the bases, I felt 10 feet tall.

"I'm not the type of person who says, 'This was my biggest thrill in baseball' or my biggest moment, or any of that kind of baloney. Let's just say we had a hell of a good time at Ray Jackson's after the game."

Mathews also experienced the thrill of recording the final out of the World Series. He fielded a Moose Skowron grounder and stepped on third before running to hug catcher Del

Crandall and Lew Burdette, who notched three complete-game wins during the Series.

When the Braves returned to Milwaukee, they were welcomed home by fans who lined the downtown streets and the parking lots around County Stadium. Mathews' neighbors decorated his house and held a bonfire that he and his wife briefly attended before going to the team's private party downtown.

"It was a night to remember, although I don't remember most of it," Mathews wrote in his book.

Mathews helped the Braves return to the 1958 World Series and he finished second in NL MVP balloting after hitting 46 homers in 1959. He hit 30-plus homers over nine consecutive seasons before tearing ligaments in his left shoulder while swinging at a high pitch in 1962.

A declining Mathews was traded to the Houston Astros after the Braves played their inaugural season in Atlanta in 1966. He spent his final couple years playing for the Astros and Detroit Tigers.

After retiring, Mathews dipped his toe in the world of sales and then joined Atlanta's coaching staff in 1971. He became the Braves' manager in 1972, reuniting him with Aaron, who was happy to have his friend back around.

Going all the way back to his high school days, Mathews had a reputation of being both a good drinker and a good fighter. His fighting skills were seen on the field in 1960, when Frank Robinson received a flurry of punches after sliding into Mathews at third base.

"Eddie hit him with three punches that not even Muhammad Ali could have stopped," Spahn told Tom Haudricourt in a 2001 *Baseball Digest* article. "Eddie was a tough competitor and a tough guy. He didn't back down from anybody."

There were many stories of Mathews being involved in barroom brawls. Whenever he went to Pittsburgh, he supposedly sought one of the toughest guys in town and fought him.

That same no-nonsense demeanor he brought to the field as a player was seen during his years as the Braves' manager.

"He might have been the toughest baseball person I ever met," said John Holland, who spent 50 years as a Braves clubhouse employee. "He could be the scariest person in the world and sometimes he could be nice. But most of the time, he had a hard shell."

It was fitting for Mathews to be there as Aaron pursued Ruth's record. He had served as a teammate for so long and he now he was a protective manager.

Commissioner Bowie Kuhn made it clear he wanted Aaron to be in the starting lineup for each of the first three games of the 1974 season in Cincinnati. The Braves slugger entered the season with 713 homers and ended up hitting his record-tying 714th homer on Opening Day.

Braves owner Bill Bartholomay and Mathews didn't want Aaron breaking Ruth's record on the road. So they held him out of the lineup for the second game and played him for the first seven innings of the series finale, only after making it clear they had been threatened with fines.

Aaron hit his record-setting 715th homer during the Braves home opener on April 8, 1974. Mathews wrote an article that appeared in *The Atlanta Constitution* the following day. He praised his longtime teammate as a player and person.

"The best part is it couldn't have happened to a better guy," Mathews wrote. "As we like to say in the game, he's good people on and off the field. He's a pro on the field, not just because he has outstanding ability, which he does, but because he plays the game the way it's supposed to be played."

Like there was never any jealousy between Greg Maddux, Tom Glavine and John Smoltz during their long stretch as teammates, Aaron and Mathews had an incredible amount of respect for each other.

Mathews' tenure as the Braves' manager ended a few months after Aaron broke the record. Like with a few of his marriages, alcohol was to blame. He had allowed the traveling sports writers to drink on the team's tab at a bar in St. Louis. Then he also got into a drunken argument with traveling secretary Donald Davidson when the bus didn't arrive in time to pick up the team after a middle-of-the-night landing.

Still, long after his days with the Braves were over, his bond with Aaron remained strong.

"It was great to play ball with some one [sic] like Hank Aaron because he is a legend," Mathews wrote in his autobiography. "There's no question about that. My proudest accomplishment was the record he and I set, 863 home runs as teammates. Then, I was fortunate to be his manager when he broke Ruth's record. Most of all though, I'm proud to call Hank my friend."

18

Warren Spahn

WHEN ATTEMPTING TO RANK THE GREATEST PITCHING SEASONS in Braves history, it would be easy to start with each of Greg Maddux's first three within the organization. But during his incredible Hall of Fame career, Warren Spahn had one season that certainly rivaled some of those Maddux produced from 1993 to '95.

In fact, the greatest of Spahn's many great seasons was completed in 1953, the Braves' first season in Milwaukee. He went 23–7 with a 2.10 ERA, 24 complete games and five shutouts. He also produced a career-best 188 Adjusted ERA, which meant he performed 88 percent better than the average pitcher that season.

What made this season even more impressive? Spahn pitched the entire season with torn cartilage in his knee. But this is just another example of the toughness he showed throughout his career.

Spahn suffered a significant shoulder injury and broke his nose during one of his earlier minor league seasons. But he still showed a lot of promise within this span.

"He's only 20 years old and needs work," Casey Stengel said, per SABR's Jim Kaplan. "But mark my word, if nothing happens to the kid, he can be a great one. Someday he's going to be one of the best left-handers in the league."

Stengel was certainly correct. Military service during World War II prevented Spahn from experiencing his first full big-league season until he was 25. He received a Purple Heart after serving at The Battle of the Bulge.

Still, even though the war cost him three seasons, Spahn ended his career with 363 wins, which may forever stand as the fourth-highest total ever recorded. He notched 356 of those wins during the 20-season career he enjoyed with the Braves.

Spahn's win total hasn't even been approached by any other Braves pitcher during the modern era. The only other pitchers to collect even 200-plus wins as a Brave since 1900 are Phil Niekro (268), Tom Glavine (244) and John Smoltz (210).

It didn't take long for Spahn to establish himself among the game's elite. He led the National League in ERA (2.33), innings (298.2) and shutouts (7) during his first full big-league season in 1947.

Spahn helped the Braves reach the 1948 World Series. He lost Game 2 and then got the win in Game 5 with 5.2 solid innings of relief. Asked to pitch out of the bullpen again the next day, he allowed the Cleveland Indians to score an insurance run, which proved to be significant in the Boston Braves' one-run loss.

Spahn's success continued after the Braves exited Boston after the 1952 season. The 1957 season was a magical one in Milwaukee. Spahn won the Cy Young Award. Hank Aaron was named NL MVP and the Braves won their first World Series title since 1914.

Lew Burdette, one of Spahn's best friends, was named the 1957 World Series MVP after earning three wins in the series against the New York Yankees. He was forced to start Game 7 on just two days of rest because Spahn had contracted the flu.

This season wasn't a surprise to Spahn, who made a bold prediction after the Braves had collapsed during their pennant race against the Brooklyn Dodgers the previous year.

Before the 1957 season started, Spahn told *The Saturday Evening Post* contributor Furman Bisher, "This year, they can pick Milwaukee and not go wrong. The Braves will win the National League pennant. I'll go even further. The Braves will beat the New York Yankees in the World Series, four games to two."

So, the Series went seven games. Nobody is perfect.

When the Braves returned to the 1958 World Series to again face the Yankees, Spahn won Games 1 and 4. But when he was asked to pitch Game 6 with just two days of rest, he came up just short. Center fielder Billy Bruton misplayed one fly ball into a single and Andy Pafko was thrown out at the plate on a questionable send by the third base coach. This would be the last time Spahn pitched in the postseason.

Spahn pitched at least nine innings in four consecutive World Series starts. The lefty worked 10 innings in Game 4 of the 1957 World Series, and he matched this workload in Game 1 of the '58 Series. He returned to the mound four days later to complete nine innings, then worked another 9⅔ innings when Game 6 was played exactly one week after Game 1.

Spahn was 37 years old when he threw 28⅔ innings of World Series baseball within that seven-day span back in 1958. You certainly couldn't knock the durability of this lefty, who averaged 278 innings with a 2.96 ERA over a 17-season span from 1947 to '63. He threw fewer than 250 innings just once during that stretch.

Spahn won his only Cy Young Award during the Braves' 1957 World Series–winning season, but he finished in the top three in the voting five times within a span of six seasons (from '56 to '61).

The Braves welcomed Spahn to Atlanta in 2003 to see a newly constructed statue of him. The statue made the move from Turner Field and still sits outside Truist Park.

Spahn passed away a little more than three months later. Longtime sports journalist Gary Caruso knew and respected the southpaw as much as anybody.

"Warren Spahn was the Wyatt Earp of the National League," Caruso said during the funeral. "No one maintained law and order against the larger-than-life hitters of baseball's grandest era better and longer than the man we are here today to remember."

19

Phil Niekro

PHIL NIEKRO WAS ALWAYS TRYING TO HAVE FUN. SO MUCH so that even some of his closest friends never knew when he might be kidding.

"Phil came home one day and told his dad a scout had offered a chance to play for the Braves for $500," Niekro's childhood friend Gordie Longshaw said. "His dad said, 'Phil, we don't have that kind of money.'" Phil said, 'No, Dad, they are going to pay me.' Phil probably made that up, but that's just the way he was. He was funny."

Niekro was also one of the most determined pitchers baseball has ever seen.

Born on April 1, 1939, in Blaine, Ohio, Niekro learned the knuckleball with the help of his father, who taught both of his sons, Phil and Joe, the pitch between his shifts at the local coal mine. Joe, who was five years younger than Phil, enjoyed a 22-season career as a major league pitcher from '67 to '88.

Niekro was playing in a men's league when the Braves found him during a tryout camp. The future Hall of Famer bounced around the minors for a few years, made his MLB debut at 25 years old and didn't become a regular with Atlanta's rotation until he was 28.

Yet Niekro stands as one of 17 pitchers to record 300-plus wins during the modern era, which begins in 1900. His long, late-career success can be attributed to the knuckleball, which doesn't stress a pitcher's arm like other pitches do.

"Phil was a good athlete, but nobody ever looked at him as somebody who might pitch in the big leagues," Longshaw said. "It was the knuckleball."

Niekro was surrounded by Hall of Fame talent as he grew up in Lansing, Ohio, which is located across the Ohio River from Wheeling, West Virginia. One of his best friends at Bridgeport High School was John Havlicek, who would become a basketball Hall of Famer with the Boston Celtics. Up the river was Bill Mazeroski, another baseball Hall of Famer, who starred for the nearby Pittsburgh Pirates.

Legend has it that the only loss Phil took during his high school career came during his freshman season, when he lost a 1–0 game against Mazeroski and his Warren Consolidated High School teammates. The home run Mazeroski hit in that game was not quite as dramatic as the one that ended the 1960 World Series and helped him reserve his spot in Cooperstown.

Niekro finished second in NL Cy Young Award voting in 1969, which is the same year the Braves won their first division title in Atlanta. He also played a key role in the city's second division title. The knuckleballer was 43 years old when he went 17–4 with a 3.61 ERA for the 1982 NL West champion Braves.

Niekro made his big-league debut for the Braves on April 15, 1964. He enjoyed a breakout season in '67 when he posted a major league–low 1.87 ERA over 46 appearances (20 starts). But he didn't become a full-time starting pitcher until the following season.

Following a 23–13 season in 1969 that firmly established him as one of baseball's best, the durable Niekro consistently piled up innings and perplexed batters. The fluttering knuckler danced throughout the summers in the Atlanta heat, and by his late thirties Niekro became an absolute workhorse—averaging 336 innings a season from 1977 to '79 and becoming the last pitcher to post back-to-back seasons of at least 300 innings.

Niekro won 121 games after turning 40, threw a no-hitter against the Padres on August 5, 1973, and won his 300th career game on the final day of the '85 season by throwing just three knucklers—on his final pitches.

Niekro tallied far more wins (121) and innings (1,977) after turning 40 than any pitcher in baseball history. Jamie Moyer ranks second in both categories with 105 wins and 1,551⅓ innings.

After spending the first 20 seasons of his career with the Braves, Niekro signed a two-year deal with the Yankees.

Former owner Ted Turner's appreciation for Niekro led the Braves to retire Niekro's No. 35 during one of the Yankees' off-days in 1984. Three years later, at the age of 48, Niekro rejoined Atlanta to make one last start in the team's home finale. He then fulfilled his wish to retire as a Brave.

When Niekro debuted for the 1964 Braves, his teammate Hank Aaron had hit just 342 home runs. Aaron would hit another 400-plus homers and be retired for seven years before Niekro spent his last full season with the franchise.

Yeah, longevity highlighted the resume that earned Niekro a place in the Hall of Fame. But the 119 ERA+ the 300-game winner produced with the Braves proves that he managed to remain an above-average pitcher over the course of two decades.

When Niekro won his 200th game in 1979, Braves owner Ted Turner gave him a $20,000 bonus. Niekro gave all of the money to Tommie Aaron, Hank's brother who was battling leukemia.

Niekro remained in regular contact with Braves manager Brian Snitker, who last spoke to the Hall of Fame hurler about three weeks before his death. They had also talked in October, when Niekro called him to wish the Braves luck as they prepared to play the Dodgers in the 2020 NL Championship Series.

Niekro passed about two months later after a long battle with cancer.

"He was one of the nicest and most genuine guys you will ever know," Snitker said. "I don't know if you'll ever find someone who loved life as much as he did. He sucked the life out of every day that he lived. He was really a special, special guy."

20

Ernie, Skip and Pete

MANY LONGTIME BRAVES FANS ARE AS FAMILIAR WITH ERNIE, Skip and Pete as they are Maddux, Glavine and Smoltz.

The Dodgers had Vin Scully. The Tigers had Ernie Harwell. The Cardinals had Jack Buck. And the Braves had Ernie Johnson, Skip Caray and Pete Van Wieren. These broadcasters' voices provided the soundtrack of summer for countless baseball fans over the course of decades.

"Ted [Turner], Skip, Ernie and Pete should be in the Hall of Fame," Dale Murphy said. "They helped grow the game of baseball like no one ever had and no one ever has since. I recently talked to an Astros fan. He lives in Houston now. He said, 'I'm an Astros fan, but I'm a baseball fan because of TBS.'"

Turner's vision might not have been to grow the game of baseball. But to bring attention to *The Andy Griffith Show*,

Leave It to Beaver and other shows on WTBS, his new satellite network, he used the Braves to create ad revenue opportunities on a nightly basis.

As a result, he provided baseball fans their first opportunity to see an out-of-market baseball game whenever they wanted during the baseball season. This opportunity began in the late 1970s, as ESPN was forming and the Cubs were becoming a national option on WGN via cable systems throughout the United States.

Those WTBS voices heard on televisions ranging from Atlanta to Seattle and beyond belonged to Johnson, Caray and Van Wieren. They were the regular broadcasters for America's Team, the name Turner gave his baseball club after making them available nationwide on satellite TV.

Now, whether in San Francisco, Los Angeles or Chicago, baseball fans recognized these Braves announcers who had been showing up on their television screens throughout the baseball season.

"I wouldn't say we were rock stars," longtime TBS producer Glenn Diamond said. "But everywhere we went, people knew who we were."

Diamond joined the TBS team to oversee production of the three behind-the-scenes documentaries Turner wanted produced during the 1982, '83 and '84 seasons. Long before HBO's *Hard Knocks* was chronicling an NFL's preseason, Turner's network was chronicling his baseball team's entire season.

The documentaries were essentially bonus coverage. The games shown throughout the seasons were essentially reality television without scripts.

When the Braves parted ways with Bobby Cox as their manager after the 1981 season, Paul Snyder was lobbying for Eddie Haas to get the job. Haas was a slow-talking, old-school baseball man from Kentucky. He'd ultimately prove he wasn't fit for the job. He was fired after just 121 games when he became Atlanta's manager in 1985.

But concerns about Haas' baseball managerial skills may not have been the only reason he didn't get the job after the 1981 season. Some TBS executives were looking for somebody who might be a better TV fit. This certainly helped Joe Torre, who had the looks and communication skills Turner and his folks were seeking.

With Torre, Murphy, Bob Horner, Bruce Benedict, Phil Niekro, Glenn Hubbard and others, the Braves had a manager and players who were likeable. But the constant of the broadcasts were Ernie, Skip and Pete, who all had their own personalities.

"They were unique, and they blended so well together," Diamond said. "The chemistry blended so well, and they all respected each other. They all loved Ernie Sr. He was like a father figure. Skip was unpredictable. He would say things that would make you say, 'Did he just say that?' Pete was like the professor. He'd give you information that you never would have known about or never would have looked up."

Johnson was the godfather of the Braves' broadcast booth. He helped the Braves win the 1957 World Series with three valuable relief appearances. But his playing career ended a year later. He sold insurance and did some television work in Milwaukee before joining the Braves' front office in 1962. This led to him becoming a broadcaster and following the team to Atlanta in 1966.

Johnson was introduced to Caray and Van Wieren when they became his broadcast partners before the 1976 season.

Atlanta sports fans were very familiar with Johnson and Caray, who had spent the previous eight seasons calling games for the NBA's Atlanta Hawks. Caray had also used his sarcastic wit while doing baseball games for the minor league Atlanta Crackers in 1963 and '65.

Van Wieren was just 31 years old when he ended a two-season stint as the Tidewater Tides' broadcaster to realize his dream of becoming a big-league broadcaster. It didn't take long for him to fit in with the more experienced broadcasters.

"One of the early games we did together, Skip said, 'And now let's turn it over to the voice of the Braves, Ernie Johnson," Van Wieren said many times over the years. "Ernie immediately said, 'If you don't mind, we are all the voice of the Braves.'"

Johnson spent 10 seasons with Milo Hamilton as his broadcast partner before being teamed with Caray and Van Wieren. He ended his days as a full-time broadcaster after the 1999 season. So he had a chance to influence the careers of Joe Simpson and Don Sutton, a pair of broadcasters who sit alongside Caray and Van Wieren in the Braves Hall of Fame.

Sutton joined the Braves' broadcast team in 1989 and Simpson became a part of this group in 1992. They got to enjoy a significant portion of the 14 straight division titles that began in 1991.

When Simpson arrived, he had been forewarned that Caray had been rough on some of his previous broadcast partners. But he had already worked in Seattle with Hall of Fame broadcaster Dave Niehaus, who, like Caray, had a big personality.

Simpson often fired back at Caray, which drew the respect of the veteran broadcaster and helped start a strong friendship.

"The very first game I did was in Kissimmee, a spring training game between the Braves and Astros," Simpson said. "The stands came right up to our booth. So there is an aisleway that comes right up to our seats. There's a lady walking toward us with a crop top on, and she is well endowed. Skip didn't miss a beat. He said, 'Two out, here in the fifth.'"

As Caray reacted with his great belly laugh, Simpson gained a glimpse of how much fun it might be to come to the ballpark having no clue what to expect from Caray.

When the Braves would be getting blown out, which happened frequently before the 1990s, Caray would often say, "If you patronize our sponsors, you have my permission to walk the dogs." This was a man who didn't like change, as Diamond learned more frequently than anybody. Nor did he like promoting new products on the air without getting some direct compensation.

One such instance occurred during a television broadcast in 2002, when they were asked to help promote Vanilla Coke. Skip often objected to these kinds of on-air promotions. Knowing this, Simpson seized the opportunity to agitate his partner.

"I was all in, because he wasn't," Simpson said. "We were given these bottles of Coke. Skip took this one little mini swig and then you just heard him throw it in the trash can. Meanwhile, I'm guzzling mine. My eyes are burning. I was tearing up, but I was bound and determined to drink almost that whole bottle. I almost did. When I got done, I was like, 'Wow, that was great, did you like yours?'

"He's not even looking at me and he says, 'You know I'm a diabetic, right?' I said, 'Well, it didn't seem to bother you a while ago when you ate that whole bag of M&M's.' He was livid. He even went to our producer Glenn Diamond after the game and said, 'You better have a talk with that son-of-a-[gun].' He was so mad."

As for Van Wieren, he was the quieter and more professional member of the broadcasts. But his bond with Caray was strong. They shared many nights sipping a cocktail or two together on the road, especially during their early years. And they formed a brotherly bond as they spent more than three decades together.

Because owner Ted Turner thought some of his employees needed to earn their salary by filling two different roles, Van Wieren spent some of his earliest years in Atlanta serving as both broadcaster and traveling secretary. He was the man responsible for sneaking manager Dave Bristol out of the Pittsburgh hotel in 1977 when Turner told Bristol to take a 10-day break while he managed the club. That break lasted just one day, as MLB made it clear an owner couldn't concurrently be a manager.

"You never surprised Pete with something or made him feel uncomfortable because he was so knowledgeable," Simpson said. "He worked hard and loved it. If there was something funny about Pete, it was that he used a standard old Bic pen and he used them until they ran out. But he wrote so small that if anybody wanted to look at his score book to see what had happened in the third inning, there was no way to make out what it said. Sometimes, he couldn't make out what it said. And if Bobby ever made a late lineup change after Pete had put the lineup in his book, that would send him over the edge."

Caray and Van Wieren spent 33 seasons together as Braves broadcasters. They were together as folks across the country started to learn about the Braves on TBS during the late 1970s and early 1980s. And they were still together on September 30, 2007, when TBS ended its 32 seasons of serving as the Braves' primary television broadcast partner.

As Caray signed off that night, he said, "To all you people who have watched the Braves for these 30 years, thank you. We appreciate you more than you will ever know. Thank you folks and God bless you. And we're going to miss you every bit as much as you miss us."

Sadly, a little less than a year later, Caray passed away from complications of diabetes at 68 years old. Van Wieren decided to retire at the end of the 2008 season, partly because his good friend had died and he wanted to take advantage of the chance to get away from the grueling baseball schedule.

Van Wieren was dealt a cruel blow about a year later, when he was diagnosed with lymphoma. He took advantage of the chance to play in poker tournaments and enjoy his grandchildren whenever he could. But the cancer returned in 2010 and led to his death in 2014.

"Skip and Pete loved the team, and they loved the game," Braves president and CEO of Braves Development Co. Mike Plant said. "They did an incredible job to embrace Braves fans across the country. They were both really great guys that I know we all miss."

PART 3

THE CITIES

21

Boston

A FULL CENTURY BEFORE TED TURNER JOINED THE BASEBALL
world and Hank Aaron broke Babe Ruth's "unbreakable" home
run record, the club we now know as the Atlanta Braves was
formed in Boston by Harry Wright, a man Hall of Fame writer
Henry Chadwick referred to as "the father of professional baseball playing."

Born in England, Wright came to New York City as an
infant and was introduced to cricket at a young age. According
to the National Baseball Hall of Fame, his family moved to
Elysian Fields in Hoboken, New Jersey, because his father
wanted more space to build cricket fields. This was 1857. By
then, the New York Knickerbockers had already started playing
baseball in this area.

Wright quickly became more interested in this newer game
and became baseball's first paid player just a few years later. He
jumped from the Knickerbockers to the New York Gothams

during the Civil War and found himself playing in Cincinnati by 1866.

Wanting to create the best team in the country, Wright signed players from all over, including his younger brother George, who served as the team's star shortstop. The Cincinnati Red Stockings were stronger than anybody could have envisioned. They had no trouble against the clubs from New York or anywhere else. They went 57–0 in 1869.

But a few losses a couple years later led to decreased attendance and the decision to return the club to amateur status. This led the Wright brothers to Boston, where in 1871 they joined Massachusetts' version of the Red Stockings, who were set to compete in the new National Association. This marked the start of the current-day Braves, who lay claim to being the oldest continuously operating professional baseball team.

Ivery Whitney Adams founded the Boston Red Stockings in 1871 and immediately recruited the Wright brothers and Al Spalding, who would eventually found Spalding sporting goods. Adams made it clear he wouldn't found the club without the presence of both of the Wrights.

With Harry Wright continuing to be the game's premier manager, the Red Stockings won a fourth consecutive National Association pennant in 1875. This dominant run influenced the creation of the National League, a much more organized and structured governing body.

The Braves and Cubs (known then as the Chicago White Stockings) are the only franchises remaining from the original eight-team NL.

To differentiate from the Cincinnati club, sports writers began referring to the Red Stockings as the Red Caps. Wright guided this team to consecutive NL pennants in 1877 and '78.

But a couple losing seasons not long after led him to take his managerial career elsewhere.

The team didn't have another winning season until 1883, the year it became known as the Boston Beaneaters. Just as Boston is still referred to as Beantown, the name change was in reference to the city's love for baked beans.

With Hall of Famer Kid Nichols leading the way, the Beaneaters won the NL pennant five times from 1891 to '98. This club also won the last of the pre-modern World Series in 1892. This series pitted the NL's first- and second-half champions against each other. Boston and Cleveland played to a scoreless tie when darkness halted play in Game 1. The Beaneaters then won five straight games, including two against Cleveland ace Cy Young.

Unfortunately for the franchise, there wouldn't be much more success in Boston. Some of this could be blamed on the actions of team owner Arthur Soden, who refused to negotiate with officials from a union formed by the players. The formation of this labor group led many NL players to jump to the newly formed American League.

Many of the Beaneaters' stars went across town to join the new AL club, now known as the Boston Red Sox. The Boston NL club steadily faded. Soden sold the club to George and John Dovey after consecutive 100-loss seasons in 1905 and '06. This led the team's name to be changed to the Doves.

Another ownership change in 1911 led the team to be called the Rustlers, a nod to new owner William Russell. This was another 100-loss season. But there was a historic element, as Cy Young became the first of the many icons who have played within the Braves franchise.

Young joined the Rustlers near the end of August and threw a nine-hit shutout in Pittsburgh on September 22 to record the last of his 511 wins, a record that safely seems to rest within the "unbreakable" category.

It was common then for teams to be named after their owners. So when the team was sold to James Gaffney before the 1912 season, it became recognized as the Braves for the first time. Gaffney was an alderman for Tammany Hall, which used a Native American headdress for its emblem and referred to its members as Braves.

Any desire to alter the name was delayed in 1914, when the Miracle Braves battled back from last place in July to sweep the World Series.

The franchise continued to be known as the Braves until 1935, when owner Emil Fuchs' financial woes forced MLB to take control of the team and eventually sell the club to a group headed by Bob Quinn. The new ownership group polled its fan base and decided to change the team name to the Boston Bees, which stuck for five seasons.

Recognizing the name change had not halted the club's on-field woes, the franchise re-adopted the Braves name in 1941 and kept it when it relocated to Milwaukee and Atlanta.

One of the first great developments in the franchise's history evolved during what seemed to be a lost summer in 1914. The Miracle Braves became the first team to win a pennant after being in last place on the Fourth of July. They were 26–40 before winning 68 of their last 87 games to finish 10½ games ahead of the New York Giants. They then swept Connie Mack's heavily favored A's to capture the franchise's first World Series title.

The next two decades would be filled with futility, but Boston fans did get one last glance at Babe Ruth. The iconic slugger, who was famously traded from the Red Sox to the Yankees in 1920, returned to his roots to finish his career with the Braves in 1935. He hit just .181 with six homers in 28 games before retiring. But he enjoyed one last great moment, when he hit three homers in Pittsburgh on May 25.

The Braves had just five winning seasons from 1917 to '45. Their fortunes began to change in 1946, when Warren Spahn returned from World War II and began constructing one of the best pitching careers in baseball history.

As the Braves neared winning the NL pennant in 1948, *Boston Globe* columnist Gerald Hern penned a poem about Spahn and fellow starting pitcher Johnny Sain:

First, we'll use Spahn,
Then we'll use Sain,
Then an off day,
Followed by rain.
Back will come Spahn
Followed by Sain
And followed,
We Hope,
By two days of rain.

This marked the start of the popular "Spahn and Sain and pray for rain" phrase still recited by Braves fans. These two great pitchers carried the Braves to the 1948 World Series, where they would lose in six games to the Cleveland Indians.

The season created a lot of optimism. But it didn't take long for the team to begin falling apart, partly due to the decline of manager Billy Southworth, whose alcohol issues worsened when he lost a son after World War II.

Southworth constructed a strong career during his managerial days with the St. Louis Cardinals and he deserved credit for the success the Braves found after he arrived in 1946. But with Sain, Eddie Stankey and Alvin Dark among the players complaining about his drinking, he resigned with six weeks left in the 1949 season.

Though Southworth returned in 1950, the fans never really did. Declining attendance led owner Lou Perini to move the Braves from Boston to Milwaukee just before the start of the 1953 season.

For the first time since 1876, Boston wasn't going to have a NL team.

Bob Holbrook of the *Boston Globe* wrote, "It's the end of an era, but Perini isn't sad and neither are many of the other National League moguls, who love baseball, but have an even greater love for the financial stability of the league."

Boston's attendance dropped to 281,278 fans in 1952, around 800,000 fans fewer than the crosstown Red Sox.

Suddenly, there was room for the big-league Braves to move from Boston to the brand-new Milwaukee County Stadium, which was set to open at the start of the 1953 season. The stadium was built with the hopes of luring football's Green Bay Packers and an MLB team to Milwaukee. A big-league club hadn't existed in the city since 1901.

Fred Miller, who ran the Miller Brewing Company, was instrumental in the construction of this new stadium. He wanted to have it filled by the start of the 1953 season. When Perini indicated that would be too early, Miller threatened to have Bill Veeck's St. Louis Browns move to town.

Perini didn't want to miss this opportunity to move to this new stadium. So he expedited the process and helped expand MLB's landscape toward the west. The New York Giants and Brooklyn Dodgers would soon follow as they journeyed to California. As for Veeck's Browns, they became the Baltimore Orioles.

Perini announced his plans to move the team to Milwaukee on March 13, 1953. Five days later, as NL owners unanimously approved the move with an 8–0 vote, the Braves were playing a spring training game against the Yankees. They led 3–0 early before the approval was announced and then ended up losing 5–3.

This led the March 19 *Boston Globe* to include this headline: "Braves Win Last Game for Boston, Milwaukee Loses It."

But Boston's loss proved to be Milwaukee's gain.

22

Babe's Farewell

Most baseball fans likely know about the ill-fated decision Harry Frazee made to sell Ruth to the Yankees after the 1919 season. Some might even remember Ruth ending his career with the 1935 Boston Braves. But what prompted The Bambino's return to Beantown likely isn't as widely known.

As the 1934 season ended, Braves owner Emil Fuchs' financial woes had him searching for creative ways to increase revenue. His bid to place a greyhound track at Braves Field was denied. But he was successful with his attempt to increase interest in his club by landing Ruth.

Ruth hit .288 with 22 homers and a .985 OPS over 125 games in 1934. While he was understandably showing signs of decline at 39 years old, he still was one of the game's best offensive performers, as his 160 OPS+ would attest. But the decline led the Yankees to look for ways to cut ties with the aging and less-conditioned star, who had drawn a $35,000 salary in 1934.

With Hall of Fame manager Joe McCarthy already in place, the Yankees attempted to appease Ruth's managerial desires by offering him a chance to lead their top minor league club. Ruth balked at having to leave the big-league scene. But he accepted what he thought was a chance to become the Braves' manager, possibly as early as the 1936 season.

When Ruth signed with the Braves, he received a $25,000 base salary and the promise to receive a percentage of the club's profits. He was also named a vice president and assistant manager. But it didn't take long to realize those titles were essentially just a public relations spin. Fuchs had no intention to part ways with manager Bill McKechnie.

Fuchs simply wanted Ruth to spike interest in his club and possibly regain some of those Braves fans who had started to show greater favor to the crosstown Red Sox.

Initially, the plan worked. When Ruth's came to town to sign his contract, the *Boston Globe*'s James C. O'Leary wrote, "No king, potentate or conquering hero was ever given a more enthusiastic welcome than was accorded to welcome Babe Ruth home run king, extraordinary, upon his arrival at the Back Bay Station at 5:40 p.m. last night."

Countless fans and government officials, including Boston mayor Fredrick Mansfield, were in attendance to celebrate Ruth's return to the city.

Ruth's Braves tenure started auspiciously as he hit a home run off Hall of Fame pitcher Carl Hubbell in front of the estimated 35,000 fans who filled Braves Field on Opening Day. But over the next 21 games, he hit .127 with two homers and a .560 OPS. By May 12, he had told Fuchs it might be best for him to retire immediately.

Fuchs' ability to persuade Ruth to continue playing allowed the legendary figure to have at least one more great experience at the ballpark.

Ruth's last great career highlight was the three-homer game he produced against the Pirates on May 25, 1935. He homered in the first inning off Red Lucas and then damaged Guy Bush with homers in the third and seventh innings.

The significance of the seventh-inning homer extended beyond the fact it was the last of the 714 home runs Ruth totaled during his Hall of Fame career. The titanic shot was the first of the 18 balls that cleared the right-field roof at Forbes Field, which served as Pittsburgh's home park from 1909 to '70. Willie Stargell accounted for seven of those homers that left the stadium.

The *Pittsburgh Press'* Volney Walsh wrote, "No one before the Great Man ever had been able to hit a ball over that stand since it was erected in 1925. Some of them have done it in practice, but never in a championship game."

This wasn't a championship game, but it was a game savored by the 10,000-plus fans who came to see The Babe create three more legendary moments. His efforts unfortunately came in a losing cause.

The *Pittsburgh Press'* box score read:

RUTH 7, PIRATES 11

Ruth's final home run could also be considered retribution. Three years earlier in Game 3 of the 1932 World Series, he had hit a three-run homer in the first inning. To this day, fans and historians still debate whether he called his shot with that homer at Wrigley Field. Regardless, Bush might have been sending a message when he plunked Ruth in the first inning of Game 4.

Unfortunately for Ruth, what became the remainder of his career was forgettable. He went hitless over the 13 plate appearances tallied over the next five games, which were tarnished by a knee ailment he began to battle a few days after his three-homer game.

Knowing he would be unable to play, Ruth asked permission to travel to New York to attend a gala celebration for the arrival of the French ocean liner Normandie, which was being described as the world's fastest and most luxurious ship.

When Fuchs declined this request, Ruth announced his intention to be placed on the voluntary retired list. The Braves gave the slugger his unconditional release, ending what still stands as one of the greatest careers the sports world has ever seen.

The Sporting News responded by recapping this unfitting conclusion with these words: "If the Babe saw the hand writing on the wall, as he indicated that he did, it is too bad that he did not announce his retirement the day after he made three home runs in one game in Pittsburgh, so he could have gone out in a blaze of glory, instead of waiting to make his departure along a trail of unpleasantness."

23

Milwaukee

Long before he became MLB Commissioner, Bud Selig was among the throngs of Wisconsin residents who were overjoyed to learn the Braves were moving from Boston to Milwaukee for the start of the 1953 season.

"You had to see it to believe it," Selig said. "It was legendary."

Braves owner Lou Perini announced he planned to move the team on March 13, 1953. One year later, this would be the exact date Bobby Thomson broke his ankle in an exhibition game. Thomson's absence created a chance for Hank Aaron to begin his legendary career.

But that first March 13 marked the start of a new era and hectic stretch. The Braves had one month to get ready for Opening Day in their new city. Adding to the challenge was the fact their ticket manager didn't want to move. So, he stayed in Boston while the team borrowed one of the Cincinnati Reds' ticket managers to help navigate the hectic process.

This move also caused the Braves to relocate their Triple A team from Milwaukee to Toledo (Ohio). Fans who had already purchased tickets for those games were permitted to exchange them for the big-league games that would take place in the new stadium. But the team didn't have enough seats to accommodate the requests to make the exchanges for the April 14 home opener.

"Having been used to public apathy in Boston, we simply weren't prepared for such an enthusiastic response here," Braves PR director Charles Sands told United Press International.

An estimated 70,000 fans lined the downtown streets for a welcome parade that was staged ahead of a couple exhibition games. This was unlike anything Johnny Logan, Warren Spahn or Eddie Mathews had experienced over the previous few years in Boston.

The Braves had found a city within which they were no longer playing second fiddle, like they had for so long to the Boston Red Sox. They were greeted by thousands of fans when they returned to Milwaukee after an Opening Day win in Cincinnati.

Cincinnati had always hosted Opening Day games, going back to the 1800s. The Braves were the honored opponents in that event on April 13. The next day, they were in Milwaukee to host the St. Louis Cardinals.

More than 34,000 fans saw the Braves claim a thrilling 3–2, 10-inning win. Spahn went the distance and Bill Bruton took care of all the late scoring. After hitting a triple and scoring in the eighth, the center fielder hit a walk-off homer in the 10th. The ball hit off Enos Slaughter's glove and was initially ruled a double. But the umpires gathered together and reversed the ruling.

"I had my glove on it," Slaughter told reporters after the game. "But just as it hit, my elbow hit the top of the fence and jarred it loose. I might have caught it on the second stab, but some fan out there beyond the fence grabbed it before I could and took off."

The Braves won 92 games during that first year in Milwaukee, but still finished 13 games behind the Brooklyn Dodgers, who lost to the Yankees in the World Series.

Excitement increased as more than two million fans visited County Stadium in 1954. This proved to be a very special year, as Thompson's spring training injury opened the door for Aaron to make his MLB debut at 20 years old.

Suddenly, this team was loaded with star power. Spahn, Mathews and Aaron were all future Hall of Famers. This group would finish third during their first season together and in second place during both seasons that followed. The team was drawing more than 2,000,000 fans on an annual basis.

These fans were rewarded as the Braves developed into one of the game's best teams. Aaron won the National League MVP Award and Spahn earned the NL Cy Young Award in 1957. This was a celebratory year, as it concluded with the Braves beating the Yankees in a thrilling World Series.

After winning their first World Series since 1914, the Braves returned to the Fall Classic the following year. This time the Yankees prevailed.

Though the Braves never finished worse than second place during any of the three seasons following their repeat visits to the World Series, attendance started to decrease. They drew just over a million fans in 1961 and dropped down to a little more than 775,000 in 1962.

This was around the time Perini decided to sell the team to a group headed by Bill Bartholomay. It didn't take long for Braves fans to start hearing the team might relocate. Selig's fears were realized once he started checking with his friends with the Braves' front office.

"They weren't denying it," Selig said. "They just weren't saying. It was stunning."

Selig's budding friendship with Bartholomay soured upon realization that this Chicago businessman was set on taking the Braves away from Milwaukee just a little more than a decade after they arrived.

Court injunctions prevented the Braves from moving to Atlanta in 1965. But a year later, Aaron and Mathews were among the players who were migrating to the great unknown in Georgia.

"I really thought baseball was dead in Milwaukee," Selig said. "It stunned the community. It broke a lot of hearts. It made a lot of people very angry."

Who knows what would have happened to the city's baseball further had Selig not purchased the Seattle Pilots out of bankruptcy court in 1970 and brought them to Milwaukee to become the Brewers? His ownership of the club led him to become MLB's commissioner in 1998 and remain in that role until 2015.

"Billy [Bartholomay] used to kid me years later," Selig said. "He said, 'You owe me a big favor one day.' I said, 'Now, why is that, Bill?' He said, 'You became commissioner because of me.' I said, 'How do you figure that? He said, 'If I don't move the Braves, you don't buy the Brewers and then become Commissioner.'"

24
Atlanta

HOW CONTENTIOUS WAS THE BRAVES' MOVE FROM MILWAUKEE to Atlanta? As legal proceedings were taking place, Braves manager Bobby Bragan took a shot at Ernie Grobschmidt, the chairman of the Milwaukee County Board of Commissioners.

"I understand Grobschmidt went into a pizza house the other day," Bragan told the *Atlanta Journal*. "The guy behind the counter asked if he would like his slices cut into six or eight pieces. He said, 'Just slice it into six, I don't think I could eat eight.'"

Imagine baseball managers publicly shaming politicians.

Bragan's words certainly didn't bother Bill Bartholomay, who was the man responsible for bringing the Braves to Milwaukee.

Bartholomay was a devout baseball fan, whose connection to the Wrigley family allowed him to serve as a bat boy for the Cubs during his childhood. After following his father into the insurance world, he used some of his wealth to become a minority owner of the White Sox in 1962.

One year later, when Bartholomay heard Lou Perini was looking to sell the Braves, he headed a business group and spent $5.5 million to complete the purchase. This certainly seemed to be a sound investment for the Chicago businessman. The Braves were just five years removed from a second straight trip to the World Series and Hank Aaron was still in the prime of his career.

But attendance quickly dwindled. The Braves drew approximately two million fans during each of their first six seasons in Milwaukee (1953–58). The fans were treated to a World Series title in 1957 and another NL pennant in 1958.

Still, even with Aaron, Eddie Mathews and Warren Spahn on the roster, fans began losing interest at the start of the next decade. Attendance dropped to approximately 800,000 for the 1962 and '63 seasons. Bartholomay took a chance on reviving interest, but quickly turned his sights on moving the club to Atlanta.

The governor of Wisconsin and other politicians began attempting to block the move when they first heard about the possibility in 1963. But some civic leaders were more realistic regarding the situation.

After meeting with Braves officials, one Milwaukee politician estimated the Braves would need to sell 10,000 season tickets to stay afloat. They had sold 12,000 season tickets during their early years, but that number dipped below 4,000 in 1963.

The Braves were supposed to make the move to Atlanta in 1965, but legal issues led to them staying in Milwaukee and playing just a few regular season games that summer in Georgia.

Attendance dropped even further as politicians promoted the boycott of the Braves. Many more court proceedings occurred during this year, but ultimately, Wisconsin and Milwaukee officials were unsuccessful with their attempt to prevent the move.

Atlanta mayor Ivan Allen recognized how bringing sports teams to town would aid the city's economic development. Many of the city's first skyscrapers were built during his great tenure. So, too, was the $18 million Atlanta-Fulton County Stadium, which eventually lured the Braves to town.

Legendary Atlanta sportswriter Furman Bisher interviewed both Ty Cobb and Chipper Jones. There weren't too many sports figures he didn't come to know during a career that stretched over six decades. He brought famed Kansas City Athletics owner Charlie Finley to Atlanta to look for land for his team to build a stadium and relocate.

It was Finley who determined the land where I-20 and I-75/85 meet would be the perfect place for a stadium. He ended up moving his franchise to Oakland. But his confidence in the site led Allen to construct the stadium, which would attract both MLB (the Braves) and the National Football League (the Atlanta Falcons).

When litigation prevented the Braves from moving in 1965, the minor league Atlanta Crackers used the new stadium.

Bartholomay has vivid memories of what transpired as the Atlanta Braves played their first game on April 12, 1966. Six Hall of Famers—Roberto Clemente, Willie Stargell, Bill Mazeroski, Hank Aaron, Eddie Mathews and Joe Torre—played in that 13-inning Pirates victory, in which Braves starter Tony Cloninger went the distance.

"It was a fantastic evening for us and very exciting," Bartholomay said. "It was bittersweet because we lost the game. Joe Torre exaggerates a little bit, but on this one, he didn't. Our first two runs were scored on Joe Torre home runs."

Bartholomay took great pride in the fact that he was the first owner to bring a professional sports team to the Southeast during an era when this region still was influenced by racial tensions. At the same time, he has taken great joy in having the opportunity to watch the city of Atlanta celebrate the consistent success the Braves have experienced going back to 1991.

"It was the right choice for baseball and the right choice for America [to move the Braves to Atlanta]," Bartholomay said. "Americans needed some good news in 1966, with Vietnam and all the other things that were going on. Baseball being played in the Southeast 100 years after Reconstruction was a pretty good thing."

Bartholomay developed a friendship with Ted Turner after moving to town. Turner convinced his new friend to take games away from WSB-TV's strong signal and allow him to show approximately 60 games a year on his UHF station, which would eventually become TBS.

This led to Turner purchasing the team in 1976. Bartholomay stayed on as chairman of the board and spent the remainder of his life as a part of the Braves organization.

Inducted into the Braves Hall of Fame in 2002, Bartholomay will forever be regarded as one of the most influential and beloved figures in the club's history. He helped Hank Aaron's mother get on the field after her son hit his historic 715th home run and he welcomed Jimmy Carter back into the owner's box after the former President threw the ceremonial first pitch before Game 6 of the 1995 World Series.

Bartholomay died approximately one month after coming to the Braves' new spring training complex in North Port, Florida, to be with his longtime friend Hank Aaron as the team dedicated Hank Aaron Way on February 18, 2020.

He was an owner, a board member and a friend to countless individuals who were a part of the Braves organization that he so dearly loved.

PART 4

THE CHAMPIONS

25

1914

THE SECOND PARAGRAPH OF J.C. O'LEARY'S BOSTON GLOBE story about a July 4 doubleheader against Brooklyn began with "Stallings' men did poor work in both games." The next paragraph concluded with, "The work of the Braves on the bases was the poorest the Boston players have ever shown."

There really wasn't much to like when the Braves awoke on July 5, 1914, with a 26–40 record. They were 15 games behind the front-running New York Giants and at least five games behind every other National League team. A 12th consecutive losing season seemed inevitable.

"You boys don't think I have a ball team, but keep your eyes open, you'll see something," Braves manager George Stallings told reporters in July.

Stallings became known as "The Miracle Man" after the Braves made an incredible midseason turnaround. Beginning with a July 6 win, they went 68–19 the rest of the way and finished 10½ games ahead of the Giants to win the NL pennant for the first time in franchise history. They then swept the heavily favored Philadelphia A's to win the World Series.

This was the first four-game sweep in what was then just an 11-year history of the World Series. The Cubs had gone 4–0–1 during the 1907 Fall Classic.

The *Boston Globe*'s T.H. Murnane wrote, "It was by all odds, the cleanest cut victory ever attained on the ball field, for the Braves went against a wonderful combination, with nine-tenths of the best critics claiming the Boston team had very little show to carry off the honors."

But maybe this team shouldn't have been considered such heavy underdogs. Yes they may have sat in the cellar on July 5, but they were at least 20.5 games better than every NL club the rest of the way. Their .782 winning percentage during that span even trumped the .704 mark produced by the "heavily favored A's.

The Braves' turnaround was keyed by a pair of hurlers who combined to start 45 of the team's final 87 games. Dick Rudolph went 20–2 with a 1.82 ERA while totaling 201 innings over 24 appearances (21 starts) made after July 5. Bill James went 19–1 with a 1.55 ERA while totaling 214.1 innings over 27 appearances during this same span.

Another significant development occurred during the off-season, when Hall of Famer Johnny Evers left the Cubs and joined the Braves to form a double-play combo with a young, spunky shortstop, Rabbit Maranville, who also has been immortalized in Cooperstown.

Evers had served as the Cubs' player-manager the year before. He turned down a $100,000 offer to join the Federal League after the 1913 season. But even after electing to stay with the Cubs for far less money, the club removed him from his managerial duties, only after his presence in this role had led some players to sign with Chicago's NL club.

The Cubs then traded Evers to the Braves. Seven months later, the second baseman was a World Series champ and the winner of the Chalmers Award, which was the precursor to the current MVP award. Maranville finished second in the 1914 balloting.

With Evers, Maranville and skilled first baseman Butch Schmidt, the Braves had a double-play trio that rivaled the still-popular trio of Tinker-Evers-Chance.

Stallings was recognized as one of the first managers to ever successfully employ a platoon system. The team's most productive offensive player in 1914 was Joe Connolly, who hit .306 with nine homers and a .886 OPS over 120 games. The left-handed-hitting outfielder started against just three left-handed starters that year, but was often inserted into the game once the opposing team's starter was removed.

The Braves used 11 different outfielders during that championship season and platooned at each outfield position on essentially a daily basis. Stallings was given even more flexibility with a trio of midseason trades that gave him his desired mix of right-handed and left-handed hitters.

Maranville and Evers provided stability at the middle infield positions, but neither had a strong offensive showing during the miracle season. Maranville battled tonsilitis during the early months and Evers also battled illness as the team languished through the season's first few months.

Evers and first baseman Butch Schmidt were both left-handed hitters. Their daily presence combined with the outfield platoons often gave Stallings' team an advantage against right-handed pitchers. According to Bryan Soderholm-Difatte of the Society of American Baseball Research, the Braves had at least four left-handed position players in their lineup in 80 of the 102 games played against a right-handed starter. They had five left-handed position players in 14 of those games.

Making the Braves' run to this year's World Series even more interesting was the fact they ditched their home stadium with about six weeks left in the regular season. The South End Grounds served as the home of each of three ballparks the franchise used from 1871 to 1914.

A fire blamed on children playing beneath the right field seats had burned the second stadium in 1894, just six years after it had opened. The third stadium was built smaller because the previous one hadn't been properly insured.

As the Braves got on a roll during the second half of the 1914 season, they took advantage of the chance to draw larger crowds by playing their games at Fenway Park, which had opened for the Red Sox two years earlier. The decision proved masterful, as more than 20,000 fans packed the now-iconic stadium to see the Braves play their first home game there on August 1, 1914.

More than 35,000 fans filled Fenway for a September 7 doubleheader against the Giants. The South End Grounds welcomed 16,000 fans for one late-July game. But average attendance there was well below 10,000 during the 1914 season.

Just like the World Series titles the Braves would secure in 1957 and 1995, this championship run was highlighted by great pitching.

Rudolph provided a couple complete game victories as he allowed just two runs (one earned) over 18 innings. James pitched a two-hit shutout as the Braves claimed a 1–0 win in Game 2. The one run came after Charlie Deal was credited with a double on a fly ball lost in the sun. He later scored on a Les Mann single.

James and Mann took center stage again when the Braves claimed a 5–4, 12-inning win. Both teams scored a pair of runs in the 10th inning. This prompted the entry of James, who tossed two scoreless innings just two days after having gone the distance in Game 2. He earned another win when catcher Curt Gowdy, who had finished a homer shy of the cycle in Game 1, doubled to begin the bottom of the 12.

Mann entered as a pinch hitter and scored when A's second baseman Donie Bush threw wildly past third. This was just how it went for the Miracle Braves, who ended the World Series when Evers backed Rudolph's second complete game with a two-out, go-ahead single in the fifth.

Experts viewed this as one of sports' first monumental upsets. As baseball historian John Thorn pointed out, famed sportswriter Ring Lardner had written these words in September.

Y is for You, you brave Boston brigade!
You're made of the stuff of which champions are made!
If you win the title, you ought to feel great,
(Until the Athletics have trimmed you four straight.)
Z is for Zowie! and Zowie's the noise
That is made by the bats of the Connie Mack boys,
When the bats meet the ball, as they usually do,
(James, Rudolph, and Tyler, I'm sorry for you.)

This World Series also provided the first example of gamesmanship. Stallings insisted the A's refused to allow his team to work out at Shibe Park the day before Game 1 was played. Mack insisted the Braves had asked for a time during which his club was already scheduled to be on the field.

Stalllings made it clear he would punch Mack in the nose if given the opportunity. So, when the Series concluded, Mack was highly complimentary of the Braves, but he passed on the opportunity to shake hands with The Miracle Man.

"I desire to congratulate John Evers and all the Boston players on their great showing," Mack told reporters. "They played a masterly game every day we faced them and are well deserved in their victory. They are well named the Braves. The title suits them, for they are one of the nerviest and most courageous clubs I have ever seen. I have nothing but the kindliest feelings and greatest admiration for Evers and his men. They showed themselves to be great sportsmen in every respect. They are good winners and I think they would have been equally good losers if things had gone the other way.

"I shall not however congratulate Manager Stallings, whose actions before the Series in Philadelphia were not at all to my liking. I do not think he acted in a sportsmanlike character and I do not care to have anything to say to him."

So, Stallings and the Miracle Braves did have the last word.

26
1957

With the Braves just two games above .500 through the first 46 games of the 1956 season, general manager John Quinn replaced manager Charlie Grimm with Fred Haney. The team responded by producing a .624 (68 of 109) winning percentage the rest of the way.

But after leading the National League most of the summer and carrying a 3½-game lead into Labor Day, they finished second to the Brooklyn Dodgers.

Haney blamed a late-season slump. Quinn blamed some rainouts that led to some doubleheaders and a two-day layoff before the regular season's final series in St. Louis. But the Dodgers' Jackie Robinson gave *Sports Illustrated* a blunt assessment of the team's late-night habits.

"A couple of key men on the club...did not take care of themselves down the stretch," Robinson told the magazine.

It was no secret that Bob Buhl and Eddie Mathews were always among the league leaders in beers consumed. Warren Spahn and Lew Burdette were also never afraid to find some fun. This certainly wasn't a collection of saints. But the next years would prove this was indeed a special bunch.

When the 1956 season ended and he was retained, Haney told his players, "You're going to hate my guts next spring, but you'll love me when you see that World Series check in the fall."

In his autobiography, *I Had a Hammer*, Aaron remembered the following spring training as feeling like a boot camp.

"We ran sprints and did pushups and sit-ups, things athletes do when they're in training," Aaron wrote. "To us, it made Haney seem more like a drill sergeant than a field manager. We called him Little Napoleon."

Once boot camp concluded, Milwaukee fans were treated to an incredible 1957 season. The Braves entered the season as the favorites to win the NL pennant and didn't disappoint as they won 12 of their first 14 games. But they stumbled for a few weeks and found themselves 27–20 and in fourth place, 2½ games back on June 9.

Aaron was named the NL MVP and Warren Spahn was named the NL Cy Young Award winner at the end of this season. Their great seasons became even more valuable once the Braves satisfied their need to upgrade the second base position by acquiring Red Schoendienst from the Giants. The deal was completed a minute or two before the trade deadline on June 15.

Schoendienst was a 34-year-old 10-time All-Star, whose long tenure in St. Louis had ended when he was traded to the Giants in 1956. He strengthened the Braves lineup with a .310 batting average over his last 93 games.

"My first year in Cooperstown after I became commissioner, I was sitting with Eddie Mathews, who was really like family to my wife and I," Bud Selig said. "We were talking and in comes Red Schoendienst. He came over to congratulate me on becoming commissioner. As he walked away, Eddie said something I'll never forget. I told Henry [Aaron] and he said it's absolutely true. [Mathews] said as good as we were, if we don't get Red, we don't win."

The Braves really didn't get rolling again until the end of July, but they had built a seven-game lead by the time August ended. Aaron's production dipped slightly during the first couple weeks of September, but he certainly rose to the occasion just in time.

Milwaukee's lead over the St. Louis Cardinals fell to just 2½ games after a September 15 loss. But they proceeded to win each of their next six games and whittle their magic number down to one as they entered a September 23 game against the Cardinals.

Everyone wanted to be at Milwaukee County Stadium that night. Selig, a history major, was on his way to an accounting class he took only at his father's urging. But he reversed course en route and ended up among the tens of thousands who packed the park that night.

"I lived and died with the Braves," Selig said. "I mean every pitch and every out. I'm thinking to myself, 'They could win the pennant tonight, what am I doing?' So, I veered off the freeway, parked miles away, went to the [ticket] window. There were only a couple windows left. He said, 'Hey Buddy.' I was like, well, he knows my name.'

"He said, 'All I've got is one ticket and it's obstructed view behind a post.' I said, 'I don't care.' It was obstructed. Big post. He wasn't kidding."

Aaron scored the game's first run in the third inning and Mathews scored Schoendienst with a game-tying double in the seventh. Lew Burdette allowed just two runs, but was replaced by pinch hitter Frank Torre (Joe's brother) with the bases loaded and one out in the 10th. Torre grounded into a double play.

This prompted the entry of Braves reliever Gene Conley, who was one of six players on the 1957 team that had come with the Braves from Boston. He's also known for winning three NBA championships while playing with the Celtics.

But on this night, he was known for proving perfect in the top of the 11th. This set the stage for Aaron to create hysteria in the bottom half of the inning. He fittingly highlighted his MVP season by hitting a pennant-clinching walk-off homer against the first pitch he saw from Billy Muffett. Muffett was a rookie who hadn't allowed a homer in the previous 42⅔ innings he had completed that season.

This forever stood as Aaron's favorite home run. While he felt relief after breaking Babe Ruth's home run, this one allowed him to feel excited. He won the home run title when he pushed his season total to 44 the next night. But the thrill of winning an NL pennant certainly trumped an individual accomplishment.

"All I could think of as I rounded the bases was Bobby Thomson in 1951, the one that won the Giants the playoff series against the Dodgers," Aaron said. "I always dreamed to have a moment like that."

Despite losing Joe Adcock and Bill Bruton to season-ending injuries, the Braves avoided a second straight late-season collapse and further energized their appreciative fan base.

"It was unbelievable that night," Selig said. "People were crying, not wanting to go home. People were standing there thinking about how much it meant to themselves and how much it meant to Milwaukee. It's a night I've never forgotten."

There would be even better days for this Braves club as they prepped for a World Series matchup against the Yankees, who were led by Casey Stengel.

Nearly 70,000 fans filled Yankee Stadium to see Whitey Ford outduel Spahn in a 3–1 Yankees Game 1 win. Now it was Burdette's turn to exact some revenge.

Remember the "Spahn and Sain and pray for rain" phrase that was developed before those two pitchers helped the Braves reach the 1948 World Series?

Well, when the Yankees were battling for the AL pennant in 1951, they acquired that same Johnny Sain from the Braves in exchange for $50,000 and Burdette. Burdette had made one appearance for New York in 1950, but it looked like he was going to be stuck in the minors if he stayed in the Yankees organization.

Burdette initially struggled with the Braves, but found a spot in Milwaukee's rotation in 1953 and continued to thrive. By the end of the 1957 World Series, Stengel was wishing he hadn't given up on the young right-hander, who hadn't started pitching competitively before he arrived at the University of Richmond.

Wes Covington's two-run single in the sixth provided a 4–2 Game 2 win for the Braves and Burdette, who allowed two runs over nine innings. Get used to the complete game theme.

The Yankees chased Buhl in the first inning of their lopsided 12–3 win in Game 3. But in the process of claiming a 2–1 series lead, New York lost Mickey Mantle for a significant portion of the remainder of the series. The iconic slugger injured his left shoulder when Schoendienst fell on him while attempting to field an errant pickoff throw to second base in the first inning.

Mantle homered later in the game but totaled just nine plate appearances over the series' final four games. He was used as a pinch runner in Game 5 and missed Game 6.

With the bullpen stretched thin the day before, Warren Spahn allowed five runs and 11 hits over 10 innings in Game 4. He allowed a run in the top of the 10th and then watched Mathews cap a three-run rally with a walk-off, two-run homer in the bottom half of the inning.

Burdette came back to scatter seven hits over nine scoreless innings in the Braves' 1–0 Game 5 win. This was his second complete game in just four days. He'd take short rest to another level after Buhl struggled again in the Yankees' 3–2 Game 6 win. Ernie Johnson, who would become one of the Braves' most beloved broadcasters, tossed 4⅓ innings, but surrendered Hank Bauer's game-winning homer in the seventh.

The stage was set for Spahn to start Game 7. But he was sidelined by illness as a result of the 1957–58 influenza pandemic. So, Burdette took the ball on two days' rest and fired another seven-hit shutout. Mathews had a two-run double that positioned him to score on Aaron's RBI single in the decisive three-run third.

Five years after leaving an apathetic fan base in Boston, the Braves were World Series champions for the first time since 1914. They triumphed over the Yankees, who had won 15 of the past 30 World Series, including seven of the past 10.

Some New Yorkers questioned why the Braves would move from Boston to a minor league town they considered to be Bushville. The incredible support the team received during its earliest years in Milwaukee was anything but bush league.

A major league celebration greeted the Braves when they landed in Milwaukee around 7:30 PM CT. An estimated 20,000 fans were in or around the airport to celebrate the title the team had secured that afternoon.

Milwaukee's population was around one million at the time. But multiple reports estimated nearly 300,000 fans lined the downtown streets to cheer their heroes during a parade and to party into the wee hours of the Friday morning that followed.

There were just a handful of arrests for public intoxication and disorderly conduct. When these individuals came before District Judge Robert Hansen, they were all given suspended sentences.

"Any Milwaukeean ought to be forgiven, because last night was a night to celebrate," Hansen said in the *Milwaukee Journal*.

The Braves would blow a 3–1 series lead to the Yankees in the 1958 Fall Classic. But Milwaukee fans continued to hold great memories of what Burdette did while constructing one of the greatest World Series performances ever seen.

Burdette ended the 1957 World Series with 24 consecutive scoreless innings. The only pitchers to claim three wins in one World Series since he did were Bob Gibson (1967), Mickey Lolich (1968) and Randy Johnson (2001). He remains the most recent pitcher to tally three wins and two shutouts in the same Fall Classic. The only other two to do this have been Bill Dinneen (1903) and Christy Mathewson (1905).

The Braves would move to Atlanta in 1966 and then wait an additional three decades before winning another World Series. So, memories of what Aaron, Burdette and the others did during that special 1957 season remained strong long after the club left Milwaukee.

27
1995

Those who lived through it all have said to truly appreciate the Braves winning the 1995 World Series, you must remember the heartache felt at the start of the decade.

"You know, 1995 was so magical," Braves Chairman Terry McGuirk said. "We had been good for so long at that point, I think the city was getting a little callous to who we were at that point. The 1991 worst-to-first season was such a cultural revolution."

The Braves were cellar dwellers during most of the 1980s and they made five trips to the World Series in the 1990s. It was incredible decade marred by the reality the Braves were victorious in just one of those World Series. In fact, they won just one Fall Classic while winning 14 straight division titles from 1991 to 2005.

"I'd rather lose in the postseason than not go, obviously," Greg Maddux said. "I'd rather lose than not pitch at all. I know that's not a winning-type attitude, but it was what it was."

It was a streak that came from out of nowhere. Bobby Cox transitioned from general manager to manager during the 1990 season and John Schuerholz came to Atlanta to begin his legendary GM tenure after that same season. Schuerholz added outfielder Otis Nixon, shortstop Rafael Belliard, third baseman Terry Pendleton and first baseman Sid Bream to significantly upgrade the defense.

Still, nobody entered this season thinking this team was going to finish one win away from a World Series title. Right?

"We finished in last place in 1990, but we shouldn't have," then Braves president Stan Kasten said. "Our top free agent Nick Esasky played just nine games. Pete Smith, who was one of our Young Guns, went down. And our closer, Mike Stanton, went down. So, we lost a starting pitcher, a closer and our cleanup hitter. We thought we saw it coming in 1990, but by 1991, we had all of the pieces in place."

Tom Glavine posted a 1.98 ERA during the first half of the 1991 season, but the Braves still entered the All-Star break at 39–40, 9½ games behind the first-place Dodgers and 4½ games behind the second-place Reds in the National League West.

The Dodgers had gained that comfortable lead by winning the final two games before the break against the Braves. Pendleton responded after the second loss by going up and down the bench at Dodger Stadium telling his discouraged teammates that the race wasn't over.

This was part of what made him the 1991 NL MVP.

John Smoltz was on the brink of falling out of the rotation during the first few months of the 1991 season. But he and Steve Avery were two of the NL's best starters during the second half. Their efforts were backed by Ron Gant and Pendleton, who led the offense during the season's final months.

The Braves erased seven games off their division deficit as they won nine of their first 11 games after the All-Star break. Not a single game was played against the Dodgers during this span. The race remained tight over the next couple months. But the first of David Justice's most memorable home runs pushed Atlanta toward its first division crown since 1969.

With five games remaining, the Braves trailed the Dodgers by one game. Neither team could afford to squander any opportunities, or allow six runs in the first inning. Or so it seemed.

Charlie Leibrandt allowed the Reds to jump out to a 6–0 lead in Cincinnati on October 1. But the Braves kept chipping away and set the stage for Justice to hit a go-ahead, two-run homer off Rob Dibble in the ninth inning. Atlanta celebrated a 7–6 comeback win, moved into a first-place tie the next day and kept rolling.

The Braves claimed a 5–2 win over the Houston Astros on October 6 and then stayed on the field to watch the Dodgers lose to the Giants. Los Angeles' loss gave the city of Atlanta the division title it had been seeking throughout what had become a raucous season at Atlanta-Fulton County Stadium.

"It was a historic pennant race," Kasten told the *Atlanta Journal* during the celebration. "Every night, each team's games being wild and crazy. And this tomahawk phenomenon, you can't explain it. This is a race that will be talked about for years."

Braves fans reveled in the opportunity to continue doing "the chop" during the victorious NL Championship Series against the Pirates and during the World Series against the Twins.

The Braves lost the first two games of the 1991 World Series, but then claimed three straight home wins against the Twins. They returned to Minnesota needing just one more win to put an incredible end to a sensational season. But Kirby Puckett hit a game-ending homer in the 11th inning of Game 6 and Smoltz's 7⅓ scoreless innings in Game 7 weren't enough to best Jack Morris, who gave the Twins a title with 10 scoreless innings.

Even with the disappointing conclusion, thousands of fans lined the streets of Atlanta for an incredibly enthusiastic parade. Any passerby who didn't know the result of the World Series might have assumed the Braves won.

"To see where we were in 1989 and 1990 and the beginning of 1991, to where we were near the end of 1991, was incredible," Glavine said. "I'd be driving down [Interstate] 75 and people would recognize me and start doing the chop while driving 80 miles an hour. The wave of excitement that took over that city was unbelievable."

Fortunately for Braves fans, that excitement extended throughout the decade.

The Braves lost the 1992 World Series to the Toronto Blue Jays, who were managed by Cito Gaston. Coincidentally, it was Bobby Cox who had brought Gaston to Toronto to be part of his coaching staff in 1982.

Brian Snitker was living with Gaston during Braves instructional league when Cox called to offer Gaston the job.

Gaston's response? "I didn't even know Bobby liked me."

Gaston and the Blue Jays won a second straight World Series in 1993, after an incredible pennant race may have exhausted the Braves. A mid-July acquisition of Fred McGriff helped Atlanta end the season on a 51–17 run. Their 103 wins were one more than the Giants in the NL West race. But they looked like a fatigued squad while losing to the Philadelphia Phillies in the 1993 NLCS.

After the 1994 World Series was cancelled because of labor strife that ended play in August, the Braves entered the 1995 season with a roster bolstered by young talent. Chipper Jones began his tenure as an everyday player. As for Javy Lopez and Ryan Klesko, they became more integral portions of a lineup that included veterans David Justice and Marquis Grissom, who had come over from the Expos as a free agent during the offseason.

Maddux made his way toward a fourth straight Cy Young Award and Jones enjoyed a strong rookie season. There really was never any suspense as the Braves won the National League East (they changed divisions after 1993) by 21 games.

"It's my favorite season," then Braves GM John Schuerholz said. "We had good young players and we had great leaders in the clubhouse. The young guys listened to the older guys and learned what the expectations of the Atlanta Braves were."

Having already visited the World Series twice in the decade, anything short of a title would now be a disappointment.

Jones homered twice in his first postseason game, including a go-ahead shot in the ninth inning. This helped the Braves eliminate the Colorado Rockies from the NL Division Series. Mike Devereaux, who had been acquired from the Chicago White Sox on August 25, was named NLCS MVP after Atlanta swept Cincinnati in the NLCS.

The World Series matchups against the Twins and Blue Jays had seemed to be a coin flip. But the Cleveland Indians entered the 1995 World Series looking like the stronger team. They won 100 games in a 144-game season and had an incredible lineup that included Kenny Lofton's speed and Albert Belle's power.

"It was a very solid lineup," Maddux said. "It's just a good thing we grew up believing good pitching beats good hitting any day of the week and twice on Sunday."

Maddux threw a complete game gem during the Saturday-night Game 1 win and Glavine again supported the belief as he beat the Indians with a strong six-inning effort in Sunday night's Game 2. Ryan Klesko homered in each of the next three games in Cleveland. But Atlanta's only road win in this series came when Steve Avery silenced the Indians' offense in Game 4.

When the series shifted back to Atlanta, the focus was placed on Justice.

The *Atlanta Journal-Constitution*'s headline on the morning of Game 6 read: "Justice takes a rip at Braves fans."

Four years after getting a hero's welcome after returning from the heartbreaking Game 7 loss in the 1991 World Series, Justice decided to tell reporters, "If we don't win, they'll probably burn our houses down."

Needless to say, Justice heard a chorus of boos from Braves fans every time he came to bat during the early innings of Game 6. But the booing stopped when he drilled a solo homer off Jim Poole in the sixth inning.

Indians manager Mike Hargrove allowed Poole to hit with one on and nobody out in the top of the sixth inning. The American League relief pitcher's rare plate appearance resulted in him popping out on a sacrifice bunt attempt.

Hargrove wanted Poole for the lefty-versus-lefty matchup against Justice to begin the bottom half of the inning. Justice saw Poole use a pair of curveballs to strike out fellow left-handed slugger Fred McGriff to end the fifth. So, he went to the plate intent on jumping on an early fastball.

Justice hammered Poole's 1–1 fastball and watched it sail over the right field wall. His solo homer backed Tom Glavine's eight scoreless innings and provided Grissom a chance to catch Carlos Baerga's game-ending flyout against Mark Wohlers.

"Talk about elation," Schuerholz said. "That is when the burden was lifted."

Yeah, the burden was lifted. There was no longer reason to be concerned about coming up short in 1991 and '92. But elation isn't eternal in the sports world.

Wohlers can certainly attest to this. He produced the final out in the 1995 World Series and delivered the most costly pitch during the next year's Fall Classic.

Andruw Jones homered in his first two World Series at-bats at age 19 and the Braves took the first two games of the 1996 World Series. It seemed like Atlanta was going to celebrate for a second straight year. But they lost Game 3 and then blew the 6–0 lead they carried into the sixth inning of Game 4.

Wohlers hung a slider that Jim Leyritz belted for a game-tying homer in the eighth inning of New York's Game 4 win. Smoltz lost a 1–0 battle against Andy Pettitte the next night and the Yankees secured a World Series title by winning Game 6 at Yankee Stadium.

Smoltz and many others have wondered how different the remainder of the decade would have looked had the Braves won that Series. Would longtime Yankees owner George Steinbrenner have blown up his roster? Who knows. But Atlanta certainly wouldn't have been viewed as the team that squandered too many opportunities.

"You can only shock people once," Smoltz said. "In '95, we got it done. What happened in '96, unequivocally, is the biggest gut punch. I still believe the destiny of the Atlanta Braves changed that year. We were going to win two in a row and then three out of four and maybe four out of five like the Yankees did. As great as '95 was, that's how devastating '96 was."

The Braves claimed 101 wins during the 1997 regular season and seemed primed to make another run toward the World Series. But their bid was stopped by the Marlins in the 1997 NLCS. Plate umpire Eric Gregg's ridiculous strike zone in Game 5 benefited Livan Hernandez and irked Atlanta fans for decades to come.

Before the 2023 Braves began showing their incredible potential, the 1998 Braves were viewed as possibly the strongest club in franchise history. The team won 106 games with the strength of a lineup that included Andres Galarraga, Javy Lopez, Chipper Jones and Andruw Jones, all of whom hit 30-plus homers. Glavine won his second Cy Young Award. Maddux and Smoltz also posted a sub-3.00 ERA.

But that great Braves offense was silenced twice by the Padres' Sterling Hitchcock in the 1998 NL Championship.

The Braves ended up being swept by the Yankees in the 1999 World Series. But given that Smoltz was heading toward Tommy John surgery and Javy Lopez missed half of that season recovering from knee surgery, there was a greater sense of disappointment at the end of the 1998 season.

Yeah, the Braves captured just one title while making five trips to the World Series during the 1990s. But the organization made incredible strides during what was the only decade of excellence within the franchise's history.

"It was disappointing that we only won one, but I'll tell you what, it was unbelievable coming to spring training every single year knowing we had a chance," Glavine said. "As a fan of other teams, I would rather have a team that has a chance to win every single year. I think that's the same from a player standpoint and for our fans in Atlanta. They'll tell you, it was disappointing to win just one, but it was a whole lot of fun to be a part of something like that."

28

When Sid Slid

AFTER HELPING THE PITTSBURGH PIRATES WIN THE 1990 National League East, Sid Bream was told he was the team's top offseason priority. This was good news for the first baseman, who had been raised a few hours east of Pittsburgh. He purchased a new house in the city around this same time.

Pittsburgh was where he would finish his playing career and raise his family. The second part proved to be true. His desire to fulfill that first wish was erased, as the Pirates wouldn't give him the salary or the no-trade clause he desired.

Little did anybody know what this decision would lead to just a couple years later.

Bream signed a three-year deal with the Braves in early December. Three decades later, he is still celebrated in Atlanta for the dash that crushed Pittsburgh's World Series dreams.

"I still have a gentleman I work with who, every time he sees me, he says, 'You were out,'" Bream said. "Still when I speak places there around Pittsburgh, folks will say, 'How could you do that to our city?' It was a very difficult day. It was like Zombieville up there after they lost that game, and it hasn't gotten any better. They continue to say it was the Bream curse."

That game that significantly influenced baseball history in two cities was the 1992 National League Championship Game 7 matchup between the Braves and Pirates. This was the second straight year these two teams met in Game 7 of the NLCS.

Bream and the Pirates lost to the Reds in six games during the 1990 NLCS. Pittsburgh lost the 1991 battle against the Braves when John Smoltz provided a glimpse of what he could do in Game 7 starts. Now, with Bobby Bonilla having already left via free agency and Barry Bonds about to do the same, this was the Pirates' last chance.

The Pirates evened this best-of-seven series after losing three of the first four games. Now they had their ace, Doug Drabek, matching up against Smoltz in the win-or-go-home game at Atlanta-Fulton County Stadium.

Smoltz exited with a 2–0 deficit after six innings. Around this same time, television and MLB officials began heading to the visitors' clubhouse, where longtime clubhouse manager John Holland begrudgingly watched them begin preparing for a celebration.

"The most nervous I've been is that night that Sid slid," Holland said. "I was in the visitors' clubhouse. All of the Pirates' team was on the bench. It was the ninth inning. The CBS crew and all the people from the League office were getting the champagne, the trophy, the podium, the plastic and the lights up. I was kneeling in front of a 20-inch television because that's all we had in the clubhouse those days."

Drabek entered the ninth seeking a shutout. But Terry Pendleton doubled to begin the bottom half of the frame and sure-handed second baseman Joe Lind then botched a David Justice grounder. Bream then drew a four-pitch walk to load the bases and prompt the entry of Stan Belinda.

After Pendleton scored on Ron Gant's sacrifice fly to left field, Damon Berryhill drew a key walk that moved Bream to second base.

"The at-bat before, I had hit a double off Doug Drabek and they literally tried to pick me off second base twice," Bream said. "But being on second base with Stan Belinda, I knew they weren't going to try to pick me off second. He was in there for one thing and that was to get that out. So, I did get a much better lead. If they'd have thrown back there, I'd have probably been out by a mile."

Once Brian Hunter popped out for the inning's second out, Bream could take off at the crack of the bat. This was important, given the fact that the only reason he wasn't the slowest player in this game was the fact that Pirates catcher Mike LaValliere was present.

So, the Pirates still seemed to be in a great spot, especially when the Braves sent Francisco Cabrera to the plate to pinch hit with two outs. Cabrera had totaled just 11 plate appearances at the major league level during the 1992 regular season. But two of his three hits were home runs.

Cabrera got ahead with a 2–0 count, fouled Belinda's next pitch and then sent his game-winning hit toward Bonds in left field.

"Swung, line drive, left field, one run is in and here comes Bream," longtime Braves broadcaster Skip Caray bellowed into his microphone. "Here's the throw to the plate. He is…safe. Braves win. Braves win. Braves win. Braves win Braves win."

Bream had a good lead and was able to run at the crack of the bat. He was rounding third as Bonds fielded the ball in left field. The throw forced LaValliere to lean toward the first base line before lunging back to make the tag.

Umpire Randy Marsh signaled safe, and Bream suddenly found himself at the bottom of a dogpile. With a three-run ninth, the Braves had produced one of Atlanta's greatest sports moments and earned a second straight trip to the World Series.

"I had a lot of things in my favor, and I still only beat [the tag] by four inches," Bream said.

More than 30 years later, Braves Hall of Fame executive John Schuerholz still grows excited when asked about this moment.

"Everybody remembers him making that turn and coming in and sliding on his knee brace," Schuerholz said. "It was remarkable that he had the gumption and determination to get to the plate before the ball got there."

As the players celebrated on the field, CBS and MLB staffers had to feverishly rush to move the trophy and celebration stage through the stadium's tunnel to the home clubhouse, which was located on the first base side.

"When Sid slid, I jumped up and said, 'Everybody get the [expletive] out of here,'" Holland said. "I went down one row of lockers and down the other ripping the protective plastic down. I told my assistant to roll the champagne cart down to the Braves' clubhouse. He was going so fast and pushing so hard, he couldn't stop when he got there."

There was an incredible sense of excitement swirling around Atlanta-Fulton County Stadium that night. Drabek had been in total control for eight innings. But just when it looked like the Pirates would be going back to the World Series for the first time since 1979, a barely used backup catcher hit a ball to a seven-time MVP, whose throw to the plate wasn't good enough to retire an aging veteran with shoddy knees.

And the ultimate ruling was made by Marsh, who started the game as the first base umpire and moved behind the plate when John McSherry fell ill in the first inning.

"I really and truly believe if Bobby [Cox] could have done it all over again he'd have had somebody run for me," Bream said. "But I also say God had me out there for a purpose, to be able to do what I've been able to do all these years."

More than 30 years later, Bream is using his platform to serve as a Christian motivational speaker. He still spends time with LaValliere, who always greets his former teammate with "you were out."

Bream also stays in contact with Andy Van Slyke, the Pirates outfielder who sat in the outfield grass looking dumbfounded after the Braves completed their rally.

"We've always heard about Andy telling Barry to move in before the pitch was thrown and Barry giving him the Hawaiian peace sign," Bream said. "But Andy has since said if he would have moved in, with the angle he would have had to go to get that ball, he might not have been able to right himself as quickly to throw the ball."

The Braves had tried to acquire Bonds before the start of this 1992 season and the Pirates opted to let Bream walk after the 1990 season. As fate would have it, their paths would cross on October 14, 1992, the date you will find inscribed on anything Bream autographs.

"Most players become obsolete within a couple years after they get done playing," Bream said. "It's just their friends and family who recognized that they played. If it wasn't for that play, I would have been one of those players."

29

McGriff's Arrival

FRED MCGRIFF'S BRAVES DEBUT WILL ALWAYS BE LINKED TO the press box fire that delayed the start of a July 20, 1993, game against the Cardinals at Atlanta-Fulton County Stadium.

"[Former Braves owner] Ted Turner came down on the field and watched the fire with us," Braves Hall of Fame executive John Schuerholz said. "He was as calm as a cucumber. He said, 'John, the stadium caught fire tonight and so too will our Braves.'"

Turner's words proved prophetic, as the Braves would go 51–17 the rest of the way and finish one game ahead of the Giants, who had a nine-game lead in the National League West before McGriff arrived and provided an immediate spark, both literally and figuratively.

"It's remarkable that sort of thing happened," Braves Hall of Fame executive John Schuerholz said. "I'm glad I was on the remarkable side of it and not the disappointing side."

Everything about McGriff's arrival was crazy, including the trade that brought him to Atlanta.

It was no secret the Braves were pursuing McGriff. The assumption was they would have to part ways with one of their top prospects to get the future Hall of Famer. So Chipper Jones, Ryan Klesko and Javy Lopez were among those who spent the first couple weeks of July worried they might be included in the deal. They were all with Triple A Richmond at this time.

"To say we were a little on the edge is an understatement," Jones said. "But lo and behold, we get Freddie McGriff for cheap, especially with what the Braves had to offer from their Triple A roster. That was a steal and maybe one of the greatest trades of all time."

Schuerholz acquired McGriff for Vince Moore, Donnie Elliott and Melvin Nieves. Not only did the Braves get a Hall of Famer without having to trade any of their top prospects. They gained one of the game's top sluggers without losing anybody Braves fans would care about a couple years, or maybe even months, later.

Moore never reached the majors and Elliot's big-league career consisted of 35 innings. Nieves produced a .685 OPS while totaling just 127 games over three seasons with Detroit. As for McGriff, he helped the Braves win the 1995 World Series and two of the four NL pennants awarded during his five-season tenure with Atlanta.

"[The Padres] were on another pathway," Schuerholz said. "They were trying to get young players and they liked the quality of our young players."

McGriff's successful tenure in Atlanta included one more game than he had anticipated.

Remember that press box fire? Well, it occurred on this night when he was expecting to rest the sore ribs he had suffered while the Padres and Giants brawled a week earlier.

McGriff began his six-plus-hour drive from Tampa, Florida, around noon on July 20, 1993, because he knew he would arrive too late to be put in the lineup. Or so he thought. Not knowing the game had been delayed because of the fire, he entered Atlanta-Fulton County Stadium around 6:30 PM and found his name in the starting lineup.

"I was like, 'Oh boy,'" McGriff said. "I headed to the trainer's room because my ribs were still sore from the issues we had with the Giants. And then, the stadium catches on fire. The Man Upstairs was down on me and saying, 'You need to be ready to play.'"

The Braves faced a five-run deficit entering the sixth inning of that game against the Cardinals. Jeff Blauser hit a three-run homer and two batters later, McGriff hit a game-tying two-run homer that propelled Atlanta to a comeback win.

"The proof is in the pudding," Chipper Jones said. "From the second he got there, everything and everyone caught on fire."

Barry Bonds lost to the Braves in the 1991 and '92 NLCS. Now in his first year with the Giants, he was positioned to be on the right side of his latest battle against Atlanta.

The Braves entered the All-Star break 11 games above .500 and nine games behind San Francisco. Atlanta won 75 percent (51 of 68) of its remaining games in 1993 and won the NL West with 103 wins, one more than the Giants.

McGriff hit .284, averaged 32 homers per year and constructed an .886 OPS during his 19-season career. With the Braves, he batted .293, bashed 130 homers and had an .885 OPS.

Among Braves with at least 2,500 plate appearances for the team, McGriff ranks fourth in career slugging percentage

(.516), fifth in on-base percentage (.369) and seventh in batting average (.293).

"He was the prototypical cleanup hitter of that time," Jones said. "I know this. I was [darn] glad to have him as my protection in the lineup. This is long overdue. When you sit down and look at the numbers, that guy was some kind of consistent."

McGriff helped the Braves add to their excellence during the 1990s. He helped the Braves win the 1995 World Series and return to the Fall Classic the following year. Atlanta advanced to the National League Championship Series again in 1997, the first baseman's final season with the team.

"He was a great teammate, and he always had a smile on his face," Braves Hall of Fame pitcher John Smoltz said. "He's a gentle giant, and those guys don't come around too often. You enjoyed being around Fred McGriff."

McGriff played more games for the Braves than he did with any of the other five major league clubs that employed him. He again became linked to Jones, Smoltz, Schuerholz, Tom Glavine, Greg Maddux and Bobby Cox when he was inducted into Baseball's Hall of Fame in 2023.

"Bobby Cox is a great man, and he was a great leader," McGriff said. "He kept everybody together, and he was the boss man and so forth. It was just a great bunch of guys. [Greg Maddux], Mark Lemke. You go down the list with David Justice. It was just good people. It's a great honor to be in the Hall of Fame with those guys."

30
2021

Maybe it was fitting that the 2021 season began on April Fools' Day. The Braves spent the season's first four months fooling everybody. There was no reason to think they were journeying toward a World Series title. In fact, it looked like they were heading toward an idle October, especially after Ronald Acuña Jr. tore his right anterior cruciate ligament two days before the All-Star break.

Max Fried missed a few weeks with a hamstring strain and fellow front-line starting pitcher Charlie Morton didn't really find a groove until June. Starting catcher Travis d'Arnaud missed three months with a thumb injury suffered on May 1. Michael Soroka's hopeful return was nixed when he tore his right Achilles tendon for a second time. And Marcell Ozuna missed the season's final four months after being arrested for domestic violence while on the injured list.

As for 2020 National League MVP Freddie Freeman, he started the year very slowly. He struggled being away from his wife and the two new sons they gained during the previous offseason. But he was also upset about the fact the team hadn't approached him about a new contract. He wasn't his usual jovial self during the season's first few months.

Still, with adversity and mediocre results surrounding them, the Braves entered the All-Star break just 4½ games back. Their record was one game below .500 (44–45). But Anthopoulos looked at the situation and essentially deduced, *So you're telling me there's a chance?*

Knowing he needed to provide an immediate spark to lessen the sting of Acuña's season-ending injury, Anthopoulos acquired the energetic Joc Pederson from the Cubs on the final day of the All-Star break. Pederson had made deep postseason runs with the Dodgers over the previous few years. He came with an attitude and swagger to his new team.

"It was a piece to replace Ronald, but it also told the clubhouse, 'We're still buyers and we can win a lot more games and we can keep going,'" Braves reliever Tyler Matzek said. "It just pumped some energy into the clubhouse."

But to really understand how Braves president of baseball operations Alex Anthopoulos reconstructed his roster, it's best to look at all he accomplished over the final hours leading up to the trade deadline. His haul was arguably the most impactful ever gained at the trade deadline.

Anthopoulos' haul included Pederson; Adam Duvall; Eddie Rosario, who would be named National League Championship Series MVP a couple months later; and Jorge Soler, who was named World Series MVP a couple months later.

Like most professional sports organizations, the Braves entered 2021 with financial uncertainty. The COVID pandemic had slashed revenues in 2020 and it remained to be seen how soon stadiums would fill again with fans.

There might have actually been some previous indications business would quickly pick up in Atlanta. Players and coaches who lived in The Battery during the 2020 season were always astonished to see the restaurants and bars crowded as they walked home after playing in front of an empty stadium filled with cardboard cutouts.

So maybe it wasn't incredibly surprising to see the Braves draw great attendance numbers even as they dealt with some health-stipulated capacity restrictions during the early weeks of 2021. The big crowds led team chairman Terry McGuirk to give Anthopoulos some additional financial flexibility leading up to the trade deadline.

Safe to say, he spent the extra money wisely.

Sometime after midnight, a little less than 16 hours before the 4 PM ET trade deadline on July 30, Anthopoulos called Marlins general manager Kim Ng one more time. Ng had been reluctant to move Adam Duvall over the previous couple weeks.

Having seen Kyle Schwarber, Starling Marte, Joey Gallo and a few other outfielders already moved, Anthopoulos knew he was running out of options. Thus, he wanted to take one more chance at reacquiring Duvall, who had signed with the Marlins after helping the Braves reach the 2020 National League Championship Series.

"We had been talking to them about Duvall for at least 10 days and it just wasn't going anywhere," Anthopoulos said. "That [late-night] call was a breakthrough conversation, but there would still have to be discussions the next day. Then finally around 12:30 or 1 o'clock, we got that deal done. We had been talking to the Indians [about Eddie Rosario] that morning, because we didn't know what would happen to Duvall—and the [Jorge] Soler talks had stalled."

Not knowing he would land Duvall and eventually Soler, Anthopoulos was also still in communication with the Indians about Rosario. The Braves knew Rosario was hurt and may not play until closer to September. But without the ability to make August waiver trades this year, this was one last opportunity to add much-needed outfield depth to the organization.

While finalizing the Duvall deal around 12:30 PM ET, Anthopoulos and his group were also completing the trade that sent Pablo Sandoval to the Indians for Rosario. This was just a cost-savings move for Cleveland, which immediately released Sandoval.

The Braves were willing to take a gamble on Rosario, knowing he'd likely be out until September with the strained abdominal muscle he'd sustained in early July.

As the final minutes before the trade deadline elapsed, the Braves acquired right-handed reliever Richard Rodríguez from the Pirates and surprisingly completed the last-second deal for Soler.

The Royals had made it known they weren't going to move Soler if they had to eat any of the approximate $2.8 million he was still owed. But at around 3:30 PM ET, assistant general manager Jason Paré suggested the Braves call Kansas City one more time.

Soler produced an .882 OPS and showed his plus power during the regular season for Atlanta. But it should be remembered: He was hitting .192 with a .658 OPS when the deal was done. He was also essentially a designated hitter who hadn't played much outfield recently. Still, the Braves took a chance and immediately threw him in right field when he arrived on July 31.

The initial plan was to do some defensive work with Soler and then put him in the lineup on Aug. 1. But manager Brian Snitker altered that plan with an early call to Anthopoulos on July 31.

"Snit said, '[Soler] is swinging the bat great, maybe we should put him in there today,'" Anthopoulos said. "My thought had been to get him acclimated, but I said I thought it was a great idea. That's why this is a collaborative thing."

Everything seemed to work like magic.

Austin Riley began the season battling Johan Camargo for the everyday role at third base. He ended the season with 33 homers and a seventh-place finish in NL MVP balloting. Freeman got rolling during the second half and the pitching staff benefited from d'Arnaud's return in August.

The Braves were five games back in the NL East on August 1. After winning 16 of their next 18 games, they had a 4½-game division lead. But they certainly didn't look like World Series hopefuls as they lost 11 of 17 from August 30 to September 17.

Fried stopped the bleeding by tossing seven scoreless innings during a September 18 win in San Francisco. This marked the start of an 11–1 stretch that culminated with a September 30 division-clinching win over the Phillies at Truist Park.

"I feel like I've never been part of a season that never had as much adversity as this one," Braves shortstop Dansby Swanson said when the division was won. "But I think that's a good characteristic for this team, to be able to battle and fight for everything. I feel like we've earned every bit of what we have this year."

Fittingly, this resilient bunch began the postseason with a Game 1 loss in Milwaukee. An Ozzie Albies double and Riley homer backed Fried's strong start in the Braves' Game 2 win. The NL Division Series then shifted to Atlanta, where Braves fans were introduced to Joctober.

As the regular season came to a close, Pederson began wearing a set of pearls while playing. By the time he hit a pinch-hit homer to lead the Braves to a Game 3 win over the Brewers, it seemed like everyone in Atlanta was wearing pearls.

It was Freeman's turn to steal the spotlight the next night.

Freeman's tiebreaking solo homer with two outs in the eighth inning off Josh Hader gave the Braves a 5–4 win over the Brewers in Game 4. He became the first Braves player to ever hit a go-ahead homer in the eighth inning or later of a postseason game.

With free agency looming, Freeman entered the lefty-versus-lefty matchup against the dominant Hader knowing this could have been the final home plate appearance of his celebrated career with the Braves.

"I had a lot of cool moments in my career, but I think that's going to top them all right there," Freeman said. "Hopefully, that's not the last cool one."

It certainly wasn't. The Braves had halted their NLDS woes the previous year when they eliminated the Marlins to face the Dodgers in the NLCS. Before beating the Reds in the opening round of the 2020 postseason, Atlanta had lost 10 consecutive playoff series going back to 2001.

But the 2020 postseason was different because of COVID restrictions. There weren't any fans present during the series against the Reds and the next two rounds were played at neutral sites in Texas (Houston and Arlington).

So, this was the first time in 21 years that Braves fans got to experience an NLCS unfolding within their team's stadium. And the matchup against the Dodgers provided an opportunity to exact revenge against the club that had eliminated Atlanta from the postseason in 2013, 2018 and 2020.

Having home-field advantage would prove significant as the Braves claimed walk-off victories in both Games 1 and 2. Riley homered and delivered a game-ending single in Game 1. Pederson homered off Max Scherzer and Riley hit a game-tying double off Julio Urias in the eighth inning of Game 2. This set the stage for Rosario's two-out, walk-off single in the ninth.

After teaming with Luke Jackson to blow a late lead in Game 3, Jesse Chavez cruised through an inning as an opener and Drew Smyly contributed 10 big outs as a reliever in Atlanta's 9–2 win in Game 4. Just six weeks earlier, the Dodgers had pounded Smyly and essentially knocked him out of Atlanta's rotation.

The Braves' bid to end this series before heading back to Atlanta evaporated as Fried struggled with his command during an 11–2 loss in Game 5. Chris Taylor hit three homers and AJ Pollock hit two more for the Dodgers in their lopsided victory.

It didn't take the Braves long to get rolling in their decisive 4–2 victory in Game 6 at Truist Park. Riley produced an RBI double in the first and Rosario hit a three-run homer off Buehler in the fourth. All of this set the stage for Tyler Matzek to produce maybe the best relief appearances in Braves postseason history. He entered with runners on second and third with no outs and Atlanta leading 4–2 in the seventh.

Three strikeouts later, he electrified a fan base that was six outs from celebrating the Braves' first NL pennant since 1999. Matzek delivered one more perfect inning and Will Smith sealed the deal in the ninth.

Rosario was named the NLCS MVP after hitting .560 with three homers and a 1.647 OPS. Sometimes things work out much better than expected. Rosario might not have received as many plate appearances as he ended up getting had Soler not tested positive for COVID near the end of the NLDS.

By the time the World Series arrived, Soler was ready for the Snitker-versus-Snitker matchup.

This was Braves manager Brian Snitker's first trip to the World Series as a participant. But he had attended the 2019 Fall Classic to support his son Troy, who was in his first year as the Astros' hitting coach.

Now it was father versus son, as the Braves were facing the Astros in the World Series.

"I don't know how I'll feel about the whole thing," Ronnie Snitker said before her husband competed against her son in the Fall Classic. "It will be different because this time I'll be going in with the Braves group. It's different than when I went in there the last time as Troy's mom."

A little more than a week after saying this, Ronnie Snitker was on the field celebrating with her husband and feeling for her son.

A plethora of storylines surrounded the Braves' first trip to the World Series in more than two decades. One of those was the memory of the great Hank Aaron, who had passed away in January. Aaron spent nearly his entire career with the Braves and within that span he mentored a young teammate, Dusty Baker, who was now the Astros' manager.

Morton became a postseason hero when he helped the Astros win the 2017 World Series. He became recognized as a warrior, as he actually recorded an out with a broken leg while starting for the Braves in this 2021 Series.

Quite honestly, everything seemed normal after Morton took a Yuli Gurriel comebacker off his shin to begin the bottom of the second inning. The play resulted in an out and there wasn't any sign of a limp as the veteran pitcher made his way back to the mound. He recorded two more outs, went to the dugout and, unknowingly to those away from the visitors' clubhouse, had his leg X-rayed.

With no sign of a fracture, Morton returned to the mound and struck out Jose Altuve to begin the third inning. As he threw his final pitch, he felt the pain that proved to be caused by a fracture.

"I'm sure my leg was broken after I got hit by the ball," Morton said. "But who knows? If I don't turn on my leg like I do when I throw, maybe it doesn't displace."

So less than a third of the way through Game 1, the Braves had already lost one of their top starters for the remainder of the Series. But again, this was a fitting development for a team that had defied expectations all year.

By the time Morton exited, the Braves had already gained a lead courtesy of Soler's leadoff homer. He became the first player to ever homer in the first plate appearance of any World Series. This still might not have been his most memorable blast of the series.

Fried struggled as the Braves lost Game 2, but Kyle Wright made an under-the-radar mop-up relief appearance that altered the trajectory of his career. It also indirectly influenced how this series would end.

With the series split, the Braves returned home and used five scoreless and hitless innings from Ian Anderson to claim a 2–0 win in Game 3. Snitker pulled Anderson because the rookie had struggled with command and was set to face the top of Houston's lineup for a third time. The bullpen responded with four scoreless innings. This marked the first time the Braves had won a World Series game in Atlanta since securing the 1995 Fall Classic with a Game 6 victory.

Swanson and Soler created a lasting memory when they hit back-to-back home runs in the seventh inning to give the

Braves a lead they wouldn't relinquish in a 3–2 Game 4 victory. Dylan Lee was used as an opener, despite the fact his career consisted of two innings completed during the regular season's final weekend and a two-inning mop-up stint in NLCS Game 5.

Lee retired just one of the four batters he faced and left a bases-loaded mess for Wright, who proceeded to let just one of the three inherited runners score. The right-hander had battled inconsistencies since being taken with the fifth overall selection in the 2017 MLB Draft. But he allowed just one more run over 4⅔ innings and used the confidence gained from this game to become MLB's only 20-game winner in 2022.

Wright's effort set the stage for the decisive back-to-back homers hit by Swanson and Soler. Suddenly, the Braves were one win away from the fourth World Series title in franchise history.

Before the World Series started, Snitker's grandsons Luke and Jude told their Uncle Troy that he had to let Grandpa win. But knowing they would be able to board the charter flight back to Houston if Atlanta lost Game 5, they let their grandfather know they wouldn't be cheering for him that night.

A return to Houston didn't seem likely when Adam Duvall hit a grand slam in the first inning of Game 5. Though the night ended with a loss, some Braves still consider the slam to be one of their favorite moments of the Series.

"I was on base, and I've never heard the stadium like that," Braves third baseman Austin Riley said. "It was like a blurry loud feeling. Everything was shaking, even in real life."

It was an incredible start to a wet, cold night. But attempting to navigate their way through a second straight bullpen game proved to be too much for the Braves, who blew the lead and hit the road in search of one more victory.

Coming off two rough starts, Fried was masterful and courageous. Despite having his ankle trampled as he covered first base in the first inning, the lefty tossed six scoreless innings and benefited from a power barrage. Freeman homered in what proved to be the last game of his Braves career and Swanson had the privilege of homering and fielding the game-ending grounder.

But what most Braves will vividly remember from this game was losing sight of Soler's three-run, third-inning blast. The monstrous homer sailed out of the stadium far beyond the left field wall and ended up across the street.

Soler was hitting .192 with a .658 OPS when he was acquired at the end of July. He also missed the NLCS atter testing positive with COVID. So, given the unpredictability of the season, it was only fitting for him to be named World Series MVP.

Nobody was expecting this. Nor were they expecting the Braves to come out of nowhere to win what might have been the most satisfying World Series title in franchise history.

31
Matzek's Inning

TYLER MATZEK SPENT A PORTION OF THE 2019 PITCHING FOR the Texas Air Hogs, an independent-league team that drew less than 60,000 fans that entire season.

Two years later, he energized a sold-out Truist Park with what is arguably the greatest relief appearance in Braves history. His ability to clean a bases-loaded mess and then throw an additional scoreless inning in Game 6 of the 2021 National League Championship Series stands as one of the most significant contributions Atlanta received on the way to winning the World Series a little more than a week later.

"That had to be one of the coolest pitcher moments I've ever seen, like ever," veteran Braves pitcher Charlie Morton said.

To truly appreciate what Matzek did that night against the Dodgers, it's best to understand how he fought to give himself a shot to be in this situation.

"A few years back, I just said I don't want to be out of base-ball," Matzek said. "I'm going to keep going until I get back. I want to look back when I'm 70 or 80 years old and say I gave it everything I had. That's really the only thing that is pushing me. I don't want to look in the mirror and be upset with any decision that I made."

Matzek made these comments on March 8, 2020. He wasn't even a non-roster invitee. He was an extra, which basically meant he appeared in spring training games only if needed. Fortunately, he was needed twice that year and both times he made a strong impression.

This wasn't necessarily a surprise to Braves bench coach Walt Weiss, who was the Colorado Rockies' manager when Matzek made his MLB debut for the club in 2014. That debut, either coincidentally or fittingly, came against the Braves.

Weiss was also there with the Rockies when Matzek developed the yips and fell into a downward spiral that kept him away from the MLB scene for almost five full seasons. Depression and anxiety worsened over the years, but the lefty continued to fight and was fortunate the Braves found him pitching for the Air Hogs.

Matzek made a good impression with the late-season appearances he made for Triple A Gwinnett in 2019. Still, nobody was anticipating he'd become a part of Atlanta's bullpen in 2020.

Unfortunately for Matzek, just as he was turning heads during spring training, the world was shut down by the COVID-19 virus. Once the Braves were cleared to have a short minicamp in Atlanta in July, president of baseball operations Alex Anthopoulos and manager Brian Snitker put together a list of players to invite.

Matzek wasn't part of the plan until Snitker said, "What about that left-hander from spring training?"

That was a wise addition. Matzek became one of Atlanta's top relievers in 2020 and he was even better while making 69 appearances in 2021.

All of this sets the stage for the appearance that made him a hero to all Braves fans.

"Those are moments that can reveal who you really are, and he didn't crack," Morton said. "It was awesome."

The Braves entered Game 6 of the NLCS with a chance to punch their ticket to the World Series for the first time since 1999. Their bid was threatened in the seventh inning, when Luke Jackson issued a walk in between two doubles. The Dodgers closed within 4–2 and had runners at second and third with none out.

"I was in the dugout because I had pitched the innings before," Braves reliever A.J. Minter said. "Luke was disappointed in himself, but we knew we had Matzek coming in and it just felt like he was going to do something crazy."

Crazy might have ended up being an understatement.

Matzek's assignment was to at least limit damage while facing three dangerous right-handed hitters in this order: Albert Pujols, Steven Souza Jr. and Mookie Betts.

"There was something about the situation or the way the balls were coming out of his hands that made me think this wasn't going to be good for the Dodgers," Morton said. "I knew he was going to get out of it."

A guy who had been out of the majors for four years and in an independent league just two years earlier walked on baseball's biggest stage and asked them to brighten the lights.

"I just remember he came in with a weirdly calm demeanor about him and he just blew fastballs by them," Braves third baseman Austin Riley said. "I remember it went from a gut-wrenching feeling to a very impressive feeling."

Braves catcher Travis d'Arnaud just wanted to limit the damage to one run and prevent the Dodgers from erasing the Braves' 3–1 series lead in the NLCS for a second straight year.

"Pujols was getting to mostly away [pitches] with the heater and then any slider he was getting to away as well," d'Arnaud said. "So, when Matzek came in, I knew he could throw the four-seamer and the slider on the inner lane. I was trying to limit damage, so I was almost pitching to contact with the pitches I was calling. Then he got strike one and strike two and I was thinking, 'Let's get the punchy now.' The down-and-in-slider he threw was pretty devastating."

After Pujols chased a two-strike slider below the zone, Souza came to the plate with some of the same strengths as Pujols. So, the attack was similar, but the sequencing was altered. Souza looked at a first-pitch slider for a strike, benefited from a missed call on a fastball, swung through another fastball and then stared at a 99.2 mph heater at the knees, on the outer third.

With A.J. Pollock at second base throughout this appearance, d'Arnaud had to change the signs again for Betts.

"That year, [Betts] was struggling against lefty sliders," d'Arnaud said. "So, I thought he would sit on a slider, so I wanted to surprise him with a heater. His heat map was basically anything down the middle. The first pitch we threw was right in his hot zone and he took it. So, my first thought was, 'That was weird, normally, he's all over that. Why did he just look at that down the middle?' The way his take was, it looked like he was taking all the way. So, we threw another one down the middle and same thing, he didn't pull the trigger. So, in my mind, he was looking for something soft. Matzek throws 98 [mph]. So, I knew I had a lot of room for error, especially with [Betts] looking for something soft. So, we threw another heater and struck out the side."

This incredible escape created one of the loudest eruptions in Atlanta sports history.

"That was just pure dominance and probably one of the most clutch moments in Braves history," Minter said.

As the stadium shook, Matzek pumped his first, jumped and screamed in jubilation. The southpaw became the first pitcher in postseason history to strike out three consecutive batters in the seventh inning or later with multiple men in scoring position.

"I had to calm myself down and get refocused to pitch that next inning," Matzek said. "But as I was coming off the mound after that first inning, I was thinking, 'I can't believe I just did that.' It was like, 'We're doing something special right now."

Matzek retired Corey Seager, Trea Turner and Will Smith in a perfect eighth inning to set the stage for Will Smith to clinch a World Series berth with a perfect ninth.

"Having a lot of friends and family members who were Dodgers fans, it was pretty sweet to just put that in their face. I want to be competitive, even with friends and family. So, to be able to do that and silence some of the people they cheer for was a huge thing."

Longtime Braves fans will remember Hank Aaron clinching the 1957 NL pennant with a home run. They'll remember where they were when Sid slid and when David Justice's homer preserved Tom Glavine's Game 6 gem. Matzek's game sits right there with those legendary performances.

Whenever Braves fans reminisce about how their team won the 2021 World Series, they'll fondly remember Matzek's heroics in NLCS Game 6. They'll also fondly remember his association with the Night Shift, the name given to what was a rock-solid bullpen throughout that postseason.

"I'm newer to the team and I'm newer to Atlanta, but you could feel, like, the need and want for a championship team or championship," Matzek said. "To be part of the team that gave the city a championship is amazing."

PART 5

THE ARCHITECTS

32

Ted Turner

IF WANTING TO KNOW WHAT IT WAS LIKE TO HAVE TED Turner as an owner, one might want to go back and read what *Atlanta Journal-Constitution* columnist Ron Hudspeth wrote after the Braves experienced their first home opener with Turner as their owner in 1976.

"The 37-year-old man is the wildest item to hit the Atlanta sports scene since Friday night wrestling at the City Auditorium staged a 26-man battle royale," Hudspeth wrote.

These words were penned shortly after Turner reacted to the loss to Cincinnati's Big Red Machine in that first home opener. He walked through the clubhouse telling his players to keep their heads up and then approached a table that included crackers, lunch meats, cheese and onions.

Turner grabbed the onion and said, "You feed my players onions?" as he hurled the onion against a steel door. While exiting a few minutes later, he kicked this same steel door and broke his toe.

When Turner returned to the stadium the following day, he was wearing a straw hat and walking with a cane.

You never knew what Turner was going to say or do. But you knew he was always looking for a way to have fun and make money, even if it meant venturing into something he didn't really understand, like the baseball world.

One of the greatest media moguls the world has known, Ted Turner was the most influential owner in Braves history. He purchased the team for $12 million in 1976, primarily because he needed content for his satellite television venture.

Over the years that followed, Turner transformed the way the world consumed television programming, created a daily national viewing audience for a baseball team and eventually saw the Braves become the envy of the baseball world.

"Ted was awesome because you knew he owned the team, but he wasn't there day in and day out, say like a George Steinbrenner," Glavine said. "But you knew if there was anything you needed as a team, you got it."

Turner bought the Braves in 1976 to place content on WTCG, a television station that would become WTBS Superstation, known now as TBS. He'd shown a small percentage of Braves games on his UHF channel going back to 1972.

"UHF television was a good way to lose a lot of money because nobody could see it," McGuirk said. "You bought programming and you had little rabbit ears on a TV. That's hardly any cable television."

But over the next five years, the Braves went from being picked up by rabbit ears to being beamed nationwide via the satellites that transmitted WTCG's signal. Suddenly, approximately

130 games per year were available in homes in Atlanta, Honolulu and every cable television market in between.

"Our expectation was it was going to be all Southeast dominated," McGuirk said. "When we went on the satellite, we were thinking Charleston, Tallahassee, Mobile, Knoxville, that kind of an orbit. "The rest is history. It all exploded. Of course, all of the sports leagues and the movie companies and programming companies, all rebelled. They didn't want it to happen."

Generating revenue and product visibility by beaming Braves games into enemy markets was just one of the things that led Turner did to draw the ire of other owners, MLB Commissioner Bowie Kuhn and National League president Chub Feeney.

McGuirk began working with Turner in 1972 and became one of his top lieutenants within a couple years. Kasten joined Turner's company as legal counsel in 1976 and quickly learned how much fun this challenge might be.

"My first full season working for the Braves, I went home one night to my bachelor apartment and turned on the television to watch the Braves game," Kasten said. "There's a new person running around the dugout and I'm like, 'Oh, my God, it's Ted Turner.'"

This was the night Turner made himself the team's manager. After the Braves lost a 16th straight game on May 10, 1977, their 38-year-old owner told manager Dave Bristol to take a 10-day break and made himself the interim manager.

This was ridiculous on many levels. But this was life with Ted, the businessman who really didn't know much about sports before he became one of the sports world's most influential figures.

"Ted had never been a sports guy growing up," McGuirk said. "He sailed boats, which was what sportsmen did on that front. But anything with a ball and a bat, he had no idea. He'd never played Little League. I don't think he'd ever thrown a football."

Kuhn and National League president Chub Feeney certainly weren't amused. The ploy lasted just one day, as Feeney pointed out a rule was in place that said owners could not manage their teams.

"They must have put that rule in yesterday," Turner told reporters the next day. "If I'm smart enough to save $11 million to buy the team, I ought to be smart enough to manage it."

Turner also irked fellow owners when he gave Andy Messersmith one of the first huge deals provided during the early days of free agency. Messersmith fought baseball's reserve clause and became one of the game's first free agents. He had been one of the game's top pitchers during the first half of the 1970s, but most owners decided not to pursue him, fearing how a bidding war might influence the cost of future salaries.

The Angels made a pitch, and the Padres did too. But when Messersmith remained unsigned two days into the 1976 season, Turner traveled to California and gave the hurler a three-year, $1 million deal that included a no-trade clause.

Turner further agitated owners when he attempted to advertise his television station by giving Messersmith a jersey that had "Channel" above No. 17.

Then, there was the time during the 1976 World Series when Turner told Giants owner Bob Lurie he was going to steal Gary Matthews away from him. Matthews ended up signing with the Braves and Turner was levied a one-year suspension for tampering and a $10,000 fine. This also cost the Braves a first-round draft pick.

With an appeal leading to the Braves regaining the draft pick, there are some who believe Turner wasn't bothered by the punishment. First of all, as he waited for a decision, he continued to do crazy things, like impersonate a manager that night in Pittsburgh. Once the suspension was upheld, he kept his plan to spend the summer on his yacht. It was during that summer of 1977 when the talented skipper won his first America's Cup title.

But it was during the appeal hearings that the world got a better feel for Turner's eccentric personality. According to the *Washington Post*, he said, "Keep this up and when this is over, you'll get a knuckle sandwich" to an attorney who was cross-examining him.

"Baseball was like running a carnival for him," McGuirk said. "It was the means to an end. He came to love the game, but it was the ball bearings of this media empire. He understood showmanship so well and he was able to use it for all the needs this growing media empire needed. If you had to base the growth of this gigantic media empire on something, it was based on the Atlanta Braves."

Long before James Earl Jones was saying, "This is CNN," baseball fans across the U.S. and beyond were hearing Ernie Johnson Sr., Skip Caray and Pete Van Wieren speak to them about that day's Braves game. These three iconic announcers were among those who had no clue what kind of impact the Braves on TBS was having on widespread fans who appreciated the chance to see baseball on their living room televisions on a nightly basis.

"It was amazing as I'm listening and understanding, we have fans in Hawaii?" Kasten said. "We have fans in Idaho? We have fans in California? Terry and I were the first sacrificial lambs who had to go in and explain to these National League owners who were now having Braves games shown in their territories, why this wonderful new idea of a superstation was good for everyone.

"It was the only time in my life that I have ever spoken to [longtime Dodgers owner] Walter O'Malley. I'm only 24 years old and he had a way of referring to me as counsellor as if the word had six syllables. This wasn't a popular idea across the league. Yeah, the early times at the Superstation were interesting."

McGuirk remembers those days when he and Kasten had to lobby about this new concept of bringing out-of-market games to televisions on a regular basis. Postseason games or a major network's Game of the Week for so long had served as the only way for fans to see out-of-market players.

Now, Phil Niekro, Bob Horner and a young Dale Murphy were as easy to find as *Wheel of Fortune*'s Pat Sajak on a daily basis.

"Baseball never really understood what was going on there," McGuirk said. "They didn't understand the economics. Baseball still gets substantial compulsory license revenue all these years later, every year, as a result of out-of-market baseball games."

Turner was a visionary, whose success as a satellite television pioneer changed the way the world could consume baseball, a sport he really knew nothing about before using the sport to expand his media empire. His need to learn the sport led him to disguise McGuirk as a non-roster invitee during the early weeks of spring training in 1976.

"I helped him figure out the rules of baseball," McGuirk said. "He was such a quick study. He came out of that first spring training with a pretty solid knowledge of how a baseball team works."

Donald Davidson might not have shared this same opinion. Davidson was a little person who began his 37-year tenure within the organization as a batboy for the 1939 Boston Bees. He handled public relations, but spent a majority of these years as the traveling secretary. He essentially ran the club when it moved to Atlanta and owner Bill Bartholomay spent most of his time in Chicago.

But Donaldson's days of control ended as he found himself regularly telling the new owner, "You can't do that."

There was the time when Turner had a girlfriend from France staying with him during spring training. Donaldson got a call at the stadium, which prompted him to rush to the team hotel to tell this woman she couldn't sunbathe topless at the hotel pool.

Turner also had a problem with Donaldson getting a suite at each hotel on the road. This was customary for all managers and traveling secretaries. But the Braves' new owner didn't approve, telling him, "You don't need a suite, you can sleep in a drawer."

Again, you never knew exactly what might come out of Turner's mouth.

Bill Lucas was Hank Aaron's brother-in-law and he remained one of his best friends even after his sister divorced Aaron. Lucas also became one of the organization's most respected figures as he joined the front office after playing in the Braves' farm system.

Lucas was recognized as the highest-ranking black executive during the late 1970s. He should be remembered as baseball's first black general manager. Turner's desire to have all of the power prevented him from giving Lucas this title, despite asking him to perform all the responsibilities of a GM.

One of Lucas' greatest challenges was Bob Horner, who went straight from Arizona State to the big leagues after the Braves selected him with the top overall pick in the 1978 MLB Draft. He won the National League's Rookie of the Year award that summer and then threatened to sit out the 1979 season if his contract demands weren't met.

Lucas continued to battle with Horner's agent, Bucky Woy, into the next summer. Braves front office employees heard Lucas sharing a heated telephone conversation with Woy on May 1, 1979. The two sides were preparing for an arbitration hearing.

Some Braves fans might remember this as the same day Phil Niekro won his 200th game in Pittsburgh. Lucas watched the game from his Atlanta residence, called Niekro to congratulate him and then suffered a massive brain hemorrhage a short time later. He died four days later.

Horner's relationship with the Braves remained contentious, especially after Turner blamed Lucas' death on Woy.

"I don't want Bucky coming around my organization and killing anybody else," Turner told the AJC. "In my opinion, Bucky Woy is guilty of manslaughter."

Turner was a mastermind, whose visions created the fortunes from which the Braves benefited throughout the 1990s. Some of that same financial advantage also existed throughout the 1980s, but it wasn't until he got out of the way that the team truly began to flourish.

Cox became the GM a few weeks after the 1985 season and Kasten was named the team's president before the 1986 season began. Slowly but surely, the team began heading toward sanity and success.

"I was always pretty critical of Ted, in his management of the team, because I knew he didn't know what he was doing from a winning standpoint," McGuirk said. "The '70s and '80s were a pretty miserable experience from the winning perspective. The clubhouse was always a mess. General managers always came and went. They were seen almost like an unnecessary evil."

But with Cox and Kasten in place, Turner finally began turning his attention toward things he actually understood. As a result, the Braves began winning and he had a chance to deliver this fitting line before the epic Game 7 of the 1992 National League Championship Series.

"He came in and said, 'Fellas, it's essentially Game 7 tonight,'" Tom Glavine said. "Then something along the lines of 'nobody is going to die out there tonight. We're going to go out there and play hard and I'm going to make a million bucks either way.'"

33

Terry McGuirk

TERRY MCGUIRK DIDN'T KNOW EXACTLY WHAT HE WAS JOINING when he graduated from Middlebury College in 1972 and headed to Atlanta to become an account executive for WTCG, which stood for Turner Communications Group but was widely recognized by the slogan Watch This Channel Grow.

When Turner acquired the channel a couple years earlier, it was one of those UHF channels that McGuirk described as "a good way to lose money."

McGuirk was one of approximately 30 employees when he joined what would become Turner's empire. He helped grow the company in Charlotte for a couple years and then returned to Atlanta in 1975 to become the director of cable relations, or more precisely, Turner's right-hand man.

"He had this television station full of people and nobody really believed in what he was thinking," McGuirk said. "He was going to put this station on the satellite, and they were like,

'You're going to do what?' Everybody went about their business and didn't pay much attention to it. I think the reason I got recruited to be Ted's assistant is because I was dumb enough to believe it could work."

McGuirk spent much of the 1980s building CNN, TBS, TNT and many of Turner's other ventures. His focus on the Braves has been strong going back to the 1990s and he has been the chief decision maker throughout most of this century. But his impact on this organization goes back to the late 1970s, when his efforts to spread TBS' reach helped create America's Team.

Initially, the thought was to spread TBS' feed via the microwave hops that existed approximately every 19 miles throughout the Southeast. As McGuirk was doing this in Mobile, Alabama, and other cities, he began to wonder if the product would be worth the expense. But this was about the time HBO began sending its signal via satellite.

Turner decided his station would also be beamed nationwide.

"I remember the guys in the television station were saying, 'You'll ruin your career,'" McGuirk said. "'You've just gone off the deep edge, you know there's no chance of succeeding.' I was getting laughed at it for my career choice."

Turner's attempt to distribute Andy Griffith, the Braves and other shows required some adjustments. He formed a common carrier because there was a need to have one between the television station and the cable system.

But...

"This was illegal to do because if you can't find the programming, and a copyright for Atlanta, and then you're responsible for distributing it somewhere else, that that breaks the copyright that you bought," McGuirk said. "If a third party is doing it on behalf of the cable system and the distant place, that fulfills all of the legal requirements. But we didn't initially have that.

"Ted and I were the only officers. We immediately got rid of it. We had a lot of lawyers saying, 'Oh my God, you idiots. Do you know what have you done?' That's where Southern Satellite Systems popped up."

Turner formed SSS and sold it to former Western Union executive Edward L. Taylor for $1. This allowed him to get around the FCC rule that prohibited a common carrier from being involved in the program's origination.

Taylor uplinked the WTCG signal to the Satcom 1 satellite and not long after, Ernie Johnson Sr., Skip Caray and Pete Van Wieren became familiar voices to the countless folks, far and wide, who took advantage of the chance to watch the Braves on a nightly basis. This was long before teams were shown within their own local markets every night.

This was exactly what Turner had envisioned when he decided sports could bring daily value to his new venture.

"Ted wanted to win, but winning was sort of a byproduct," McGuirk said. "To him, baseball was a soap opera. Literally every day, it was a fresh new chapter of a soap opera. Every old folks' home in the United States had televisions tuned in to say, 'What's Dale Murphy doing today?'"

McGuirk helped create the medium that added to the Braves' popularity and has spent more than two decades serving as the team's top decision maker. He was involved in day-to-day affairs when he had an office at Atlanta-Fulton County Stadium during Turner's first few years of ownership. This allowed him to extend the intermediary responsibilities he held when he was placed in uniform during spring training in 1976.

Braves manager Dave Bristol certainly didn't appreciate having a plant going through the workouts with his players.

"He did what they called a shin burning," McGuirk said. "We're out in the outfield, and outfielders are shagging flies, and they're getting hops, you know, get the ball throw home, and the ones that are coming at me are bouncing at 100 miles an hour, four feet in front of me, you know, and I mean, I was bloody and, and that was his way of disagreeing with my presence.

But Turner loved every minute of his first experience around professional baseball.

"During the workouts, Ted was on a golf cart going around everywhere," McGuirk said. "He'd ask a thousand questions about what was going on and it didn't take him long to at least get a feel for what was happening. This man was one of the great learning sponges. He got his answers and then he was done with me. I had fulfilled my role."

Far from it.

McGuirk spent much of the 1980s helping build CNN, CNN International, TNT. He even got a glimpse of Hollywood when Turner bought MGM Studios. When he returned home near the end of 1987, he and his wife determined he had spent 180 days that year in Asia or Europe.

Quite honestly, this was a good time to be away from the Braves, who went back downhill after halting their losing ways during the memorable 1982 season.

McGuirk did return to the scene in time to help Kasten prompt Bobby Cox to return to the dugout during the 1990 season. This was around the same time McGuirk began his role as executive vice president of TBS. He had spent the latter portion of the 1980s serving as president of Turner Sports.

When TBS Inc. merged with Time Warner Inc. in 1996, McGuirk succeeded Turner as chairman, president and CEO.

Quite honestly, this was a great time to be with the Braves, who won the first of 14 straight crowns with their worst-to-first club in 1991. A second straight trip to the World Series would follow. But it wasn't until 1995 that Atlanta had its first opportunity to celebrate a world championship.

"[Winning the World Series] was a little anticlimactic for me," McGuirk said. "We had been up to bat enough times; it was our time. It was great, but it sort of came and went. That '95 experience for me wasn't nearly as big as what I experienced when we won again in 2021."

McGuirk oversaw plenty of change between these two World Series titles. His responsibilities also grew as he served as the CEO of the Braves, the National Basketball Association's Atlanta Hawks and the National Hockey League's Atlanta Thrashers from 2001 to '03.

Turner's power began to fade as Time Warner, which had merged with TBS in 2006, was purchased by AOL in 2001. This lessened the tycoon's autonomy and bankroll. He lost an estimated $7 billion when the stock plunged soon after the merger.

These changes, which led to the sale of the Hawks and Thrashers, also led Kasten to resign as president of the Hawks, Braves and Thrashers in 2003. Cox retired from his managerial role in 2010 and Schuerholz's reign began to fade during this century's second decade.

The one constant through all this change was McGuirk, who oversaw a couple decisions that guided the Braves from disaster to the promised land.

As the Braves made their way toward winning the 2013 National League East title, McGuirk and his top business executives, Derek Schiller and Mike Plant, were setting their sights on possibly building a new stadium.

"I went to see [Atlanta mayor] Kasim Reed and told him the stadium that he got from the Olympics was breaking down," McGuirk said. "We needed $100 million immediately to fix it. The elevators and escalators were breaking down. The concrete was breaking, and the stadium leaked. It was a mess."

McGuirk had to clean more than a couple messes over the past decade. But the organization is now as strong as it has ever been, both in terms of on-field talent and financial strength.

Along with overseeing the construction of the cash cows that are Truist Park and The Battery Atlanta, McGuirk took charge and was responsible for hiring Anthopoulos after international market infractions brought embarrassing attention to the Braves at the end of the 2017 season.

"There were a lot of very smart people that came through this organization," Schuerholz said. "Some were here before I was here, and some came after me and added to the strength of the organization. Terry was here the entire time, and he wasn't just some Johnny-come-lately to the organization or being a cheerleader. He was smart. He knew how organizations should be."

34

Bobby Cox

BILL ACREE AND JOHN HOLLAND HAD THE PLEASURE TO SPEND more time with Bobby Cox around a baseball field than anybody else. The longtime clubhouse workers were there the day Cox reported to the team's West Palm Beach spring training facility in 1978 to begin his Hall of Fame managerial career.

Cox and his best friend Pete Ward drove cross country from California and opted to take a short jog soon after getting familiar with their new surroundings. Ward served as a minor league manager with Cox in the Yankees' system and came to Atlanta to be part of the Braves' 1978 coaching staff.

"Bobby came in as gregarious as ever, like he had known you for 100 years," Holland said. "It was great. I said, 'Alright, this is going to be good working for him.' From the day he got there, he was the same person that we all had the pleasure to be around for so long. He was one of the best people you'll ever know in your life. I was so blessed to work for him."

Holland's sentiments are echoed by the thousands of folks who crossed paths with Cox during his legendary career. He served as the Braves' manager from 1978 to '81 and then held that same role with the Blue Jays from 1982 to '85. After leading Toronto to its first postseason appearance, he returned to Atlanta to serve as the general manager who forever changed the course of what had been a middling organization.

Cox ended his GM duties midway through the 1990 season, returned to the dugout and spent the next 20 years constructing one of the greatest managerial careers in baseball history. He played with Mickey Mantle, managed Chipper Jones and continued to enrich the Braves organization long after he ended his days as a manager.

It was Cox who decided to move Dale Murphy to the outfield before the 1980 season. It was Cox who chose to take Jones with the first overall pick in the 1990 MLB Draft. It was Cox who guided the Braves to 14 straight division titles, five National League pennants and the 1995 World Series title. It was Cox who unknowingly helped create the Night Shift, the group of relievers who helped the Braves win the 2021 World Series.

When Alex Anthopoulos was put in charge of the baseball operations department a month into the 2017 offseason, he found himself playing catch-up with an organization he didn't really know. As it came time to decide who to non-tender, he called Cox and asked him if he would mind going over some players with him.

Cox, who began serving as a special assistant immediately after ending his managerial career in 2010, jumped in his truck and was at Truist Park less than an hour later.

"I said, 'Is there anybody on this list you wouldn't non-tender?' and he said, 'Luke Jackson,'" Anthopoulos said. "I was like, 'Wow.'

I was shocked. I told Luke that later and he was shocked. Bobby just said that was not a guy he would get rid of that point."

Jackson had a 4.62 ERA, a 14.7 percent strikeout rate and an 8.5 percent walk rate in 2017. There was nothing appealing about these results. But Cox saw potential in the hard-throwing hurler.

Consequently, the Braves kept the reliever, who would spend part of 2019 as their closer. Jackson then posted a 1.98 ERA while producing a 26.8 percent strikeout rate during the 2021 season. He joined with Will Smith, A.J. Minter and Tyler Matzek to form the Night Shift.

Cox's fingerprints on the Braves can be seen over a span of five decades going back to 1978, when Ted Turner gave him his first big-league managerial job. He was fired after the 1981 season, returned at the end of the 1985 and, minus a few hours during spring training in 2008, he never left the club again.

Cox never enjoyed being around Frank Wren, who became the Braves' GM after the 2007 season. So, it wasn't necessarily surprising to hear he snapped after believing Wren had disrespected the coaching staff during a meeting that was staged as spring training began in 2008.

A furious Cox packed his car and headed back toward Atlanta. He was a couple hours north of Orlando, near Ocala, Florida, when Acree called and convinced him to return.

To truly understand this fiercely loyal and competitive man, it's best to go back to his hometown of Selma, California, which is located within the Fresno area.

Fortunately, famed Dodgers scout Red Adams was also from this neck of the woods.

Cox was an all-around athlete who garnered attention from Notre Dame to play football. His hopes to play at another level were lessened when he suffered a significant elbow injury that prevented him from playing baseball his senior year of high school.

But Adams had heard enough about the kid, who lived about four miles from him. So, he paid Cox a visit and asked him to accompany him to Los Angeles for a workout with the Dodgers at old Wrigley Field in June 1959.

Cox earned a $40,000 signing bonus and began a 12-year playing career that included a short stint with the Braves' Triple A Richmond, Virginia, team in 1967. He reached the majors as he served as the New York Yankees' third baseman most of the next year. Mantle was still around to play first base during the final season of his career. But he and the club were beyond the previous glory years.

One of Cox's highlights was teaming to turn a triple play with Mantle during a June 3, 1968, game against the Minnesota Twins. He was seldom used the following season, but he benefited from another season around Yankees manager Ralph Houk, who had a great influence on Cox's managerial career.

When Cox's aching knees prevented him from making the Yankees' big-league roster out of spring training in 1970, he was thinking about becoming a high school football coach. But he opted not to do so when Lee MacPhail offered him a $2,000 raise to play one more year as a backup for Triple A Syracuse.

At the end of the 1970 season, Cox met with MacPhail and accepted an offer to manage the Yankees' Class A club in Fort Lauderdale, Florida.

"If it wasn't for Mr. MacPhail flying down there and having lunch, I probably would have become a high school football coach," Cox said.

Cox became the manager of the Yankees' Triple A affiliate in Syracuse, New York, in 1973 and enjoyed four straight winning seasons there. He was a candidate to become the

Pittsburgh Pirates' manager after the 1976 season, but the job was given to Chuck Tanner. Baseball is a small world. These two men would be linked yet again nearly a decade later.

Viewing Cox as a possible replacement for manager Billy Martin, the Yankees brought Cox to New York to serve as their first base coach for the 1977 season. He had to keep Martin out of fights in the bars and he was tasked with keeping Reggie Jackson happy in his new clubhouse.

As for the other big personality in the room, Cox also had good memories of the summer spent working for Yankees owner George Steinbrenner.

There was a phone in the middle of the home clubhouse at old Yankee Stadium. Cox got a call from a friend who wanted tickets. As he responded, "I'll see what I can do, but Steinbrenner is tight with that stuff," he felt a tap on his shoulder and realized it was Steinbrenner.

A few months later, Ted Turner came calling and Braves history was changed forever.

Hank Aaron didn't want to become the Braves' manager. Phil Niekro did, but he wasn't considered a serious candidate, primarily because he was still in the midst of a pitching career that would last another decade.

Really, the only guy Bill Lucas wanted was Cox. Lucas was now handling the Braves' general manager duties. But in 1967, when Cox spent time with the Braves' Double A and Triple A affiliates, Lucas was a young member of the Braves' baseball operations department.

Turner was never willing to give Lucas the GM title. But he certainly listened and respected wishes like this to hire Cox, who was the youngest manager in baseball when the Braves made him their skipper after the 1977 season.

During his introductory press conference, Cox described himself as easy-going and a manager with his own ideas. His good friend and fellow Hall of Famer Pat Gillick traveled to Atlanta for the occasion and chuckled at the first description.

"He's his own man all right, I can tell you that," Gillick told the *Atlanta Constitution*. "But easy going? He is until somebody backs him into a corner. Then, he's a tough sonovagun. He's easy going if you put out and hustle for him. Don't put out and he's meaner than hell."

McPhail, the man responsible for bringing Cox into the managerial world, also provided a prophetic endorsement to an *Atlanta Constitution* writer.

"Bobby Cox is the kind of man you can grow a club with," McPhail said. "He'll grow with the job there. Wait and see."

A decade later, when Cox returned to serve as the Braves' GM, he grew the Braves unlike anybody else ever had. But he really didn't have much to work with when he began his first stint as the Braves' manager in 1978.

Cox's first team included Niekro, who was three years older than his new skipper, and closer Gene Garber. The lineup had a couple productive veterans in Jeff Burroughs and Gary Matthews. But the most talented players were a 22-year-old first baseman named Dale Murphy, who was experiencing his first full major league season, and Bob Horner, who came straight to the big leagues after being selected with the No. 1 overall pick that summer.

"Bobby was very intense," Murphy said. "You knew you better bring it every night because Bobby was into it, like really into every game. The obvious manifestation in that is the arguing with the umpire. Obviously, from our first get-go, Bobby wasn't shy about getting out there and protecting his guys, even if we were losing a lot."

It's hard to imagine anyone ever breaking Cox's MLB record of 162 career ejections. The first one seemed to be quite comical in that it involved the scoreboard.

Four balks were called during a May 1, 1978, win over the New York Mets. Second base umpire Joe West made three of these calls and three of the four went against the Braves. Still, even New York manager Joe Torre was upset at the end of the night. (Just like with Tanner, the Torre–Cox connection would continue in this small baseball world.)

"It's not the umpire's fault," Torre told the *Atlanta Journal*. "It's [secretary of the rules committee] Fred Fleig. He doesn't have anything to do over the winter but sit around and think of ways to screw up the game."

But while the balks might have stoked the flames, the ejection came after first base umpire Satch Davidson called Burroughs out on a bang-bang play. Cox came on the field, argued and returned to the bench without any incident.

But after the crowd booed when Davidson was shown on the matrix board, plate umpire Nick Colosi told Cox if the board showed the umpires again, they were walking off the field.

"I went over and tried to tell him like a nice guy, and he came out yelling that it wasn't in the rule book, and they could put anything they wanted up there," Colosi told the *Atlanta Journal*.

This was enough for Cox to earn his first ejection.

Colosi also said, "Someday, somebody is going to get killed here because of that thing and then maybe the commissioner will do something about it."

Oddly enough, the most dangerous incident in Atlanta occurred during the 2012 Wild Card game, when fans littered Turner Field with cups, bottles and other items in protest of an infield fly call. The MLB representative on site that day was Torre, who was then serving as baseball's chief baseball officer.

Intersecting storylines like this are what makes baseball history so interesting.

The Braves struggled again in 1979, but went 81–80 in 1980. Three years into his first tenure, Cox had led Atlanta to its first winning record since 1974 and just its fifth since relocating from Milwaukee in 1966. But a 50–56–1 record during the strike-shortened 1981 season led Turner to replace Cox with Torre, who had just been fired by the Mets.

"It's just about the hardest [decision] of my life," Turner told the *Atlanta Journal*. "I know Bobby is going through hell and I'm so sorry for that. I feel awful about it. But what he's going through can't be much worse than what I'm going through. I hate these things. I love everybody on that team. I'd like to keep them all, but I'd like to win too."

Cox knew the Braves were close to winning and he cheered them from afar in 1982, when they won the National League West as he was helping build the Blue Jays into postseason contenders. This move reunited him with Pat Gillick, who was Toronto's GM.

Toronto had experienced five straight last-place finishes before Cox arrived and helped the Blue Jays tally a winning record in just his second season as their skipper. He guided the club to its first American League East title in 1985.

As the Blue Jays were getting beat by John Schuerholz's Royals in the AL Championship Series, the Braves hired Tanner to be their new manager. But Cox's desire to return home to his family led to him becoming Atlanta's GM, the role Schuerholz would grab just a few years later.

Cox never really felt comfortable in an executive role, but his eye for talent was unmatched. This was exactly what the

Braves needed as they attempted to make a significant transformation by placing the focus on pitching.

"My whole career turned around when Bobby Cox became the general manager in 1986 and we started working closely together," legendary Braves pitching coach Leo Mazzone said. "He said he was going to turn an offensive-oriented organization into a pitching one. They always said you could not have pitching in Fulton County Stadium. We dispelled that myth."

Tom Glavine was already a part of the organization, having been drafted in 1984. But it was Cox who traded Doyle Alexander for a struggling minor league hurler named John Smoltz in 1987. He also oversaw drafts that brought Chipper Jones, Steve Avery, Kent Mercker and Ryan Klesko to the organization.

Two of his most valuable generals during this span were scouting guru Paul Snyder and Bobby Dews, who helped develop decades' worth of Braves players. Snyder had been in more of an administrative role when Cox first served as Atlanta's manager.

But Cox and Stan Kasten, who became the Braves' president before the start of the 1986 season, knew it was best to allow Snyder to ignore paperwork and just let his scouting eyes bring value to the organization.

As for Dews, his connection to Cox grew even stronger via some tough love. Dews battled alcoholism throughout the 1970s and '80s. But after more than a couple battles with his friend, Cox finally helped his good friend and valuable coach get sober.

When Dews passed away in 2015, he had proudly been clean for nearly three full decades.

It was during those years he had a chance to enjoy the value of the reconstruction process he had teamed with Cox and Snyder to engineer.

"There was a sense that we had some really good players in the minor league system," Glavine said. "Once we started to get to the big leagues, you knew Avery and Justice weren't far behind. So, we knew we had a chance to have a good team. Those teams built with players Bobby Cox was drafting were winning at the minor league level. That helped create that expectation to win once we all got to the big leagues."

At the urging of Kasten and McGuirk, Cox returned to the dugout midway through the 1990 season and reassumed his managerial duties. Schuerholz arrived a few months later and began cultivating the fruitful farm system Cox had built during his years as the GM.

Cox had the pitchers in place. Schuerholz altered the defensive landscape by acquiring third baseman Terry Pendleton, shortstop Rafael Belliard, first baseman Sid Bream and center fielder Otis Nixon during his first offseason.

Suddenly, everything changed. Cox had a team capable of winning and a group of guys who respected that he treated them like men. There wasn't any micromanaging. He just wanted his players to show up on time, dress properly and play hard.

At the same time, when the games started Cox brought that same intensity that Murphy and the members of that 1978 Braves team felt. The difference was he was now influencing thoroughbreds capable of winning the race.

"I didn't want to go out there and have a bad game, more so for him than for me, because I didn't want to let him down," Glavine said. "I hated letting him down and I think most everybody who ever played for him felt the same way. I think that's why you heard so many guys, they would run through a wall for him. It's because we knew how hard he was fighting for us. So, we wanted to fight for him."

All of this helped the Braves construct their great worst-to-first season in 1991. A team that had lived at the bottom of the standings for the past six seasons ended up one win away from winning the World Series.

But this was just the start of one of the greatest managerial stints in history. The Braves won 14 consecutive division titles. If you throw in the division title the Blue Jays won during Cox's final year as their skipper, he tallied 15 consecutive division titles.

The Braves won five National League pennants during the 1990s but won just one World Series. Some have used this as a knock against Cox and the organization. But there was just one of those Fall Classics that just got away.

Coming out of nowhere to even reach the 1991 World Series was an accomplishment. It's hard to be critical about losing Game 7 to the Twins in extra innings. Getting to the 1992 Fall Classic was also an accomplishment, given the Braves entered the ninth inning of Game 7 of the 1992 NL Championship Series trailing the Pirates 2–0.

After beating a favored Indians team in the 1995 World Series, the Braves blew a 2–0 series lead to the Yankees in the 1996 Fall Classic. Cox's team was up 6–0 through the first five innings of Game 4. But New York struck for three runs during a sixth inning that rookie outfielder Jermaine Dye didn't enjoy. First base umpire Tim Welke blocked him from catching a foul ball ahead of Derek Jeter's leadoff single. Then he misplayed another ball during the three-run frame. Mark Wohlers later hung a slider to Jim Leyritz, who hit the game-tying homer that propelled the Yankees to a 10-inning win.

Thoughts of gaining revenge in the 1999 World Series matchup against the Yankees were more than optimistic. Catcher Javy Lopez had suffered a season-ending knee injury in June and Andres Galarraga missed the season to undergo cancer treatments. Smoltz was also dealing with arm issues that would lead to Tommy John surgery the next year.

Yeah, it was disappointing to win just one World Series, but Cox also deserved credit for helping the Braves get there five times during the decade.

To put in perspective how long the Braves' division streak was, the last of the 14 straight crowns was won with the assistance of the Baby Braves, a group of 2005 rookies led by Brian McCann and Jeff Francoeur. These two Atlanta-area products were in the first grade when the streak began in 1991.

Speaking of Francoeur, he had an opportunity to benefit from Cox's belief that players should be free to have some fun during spring training. There wasn't a need for workouts that lasted into the late afternoon. Nor was too much focus placed on the early part of the Grapefruit League schedule.

John Smoltz would play golf with Tiger Woods at least once during every spring training. Annika Sörenstam, who was at the top of her iconic career, would often join them. Francoeur and Chipper Jones rounded out the foursome most of the time.

So, Francoeur was somewhat disappointed to see his name in the lineup on a day he was supposed to join Smoltz, Woods and the rest of the gang on the links. He never said anything to Cox. But when the beloved skipper caught wind of the plans, he called Francoeur over for a brief conversation.

"He said, 'Why didn't tell me you had a chance to play with Tiger?'" Francoeur said. "He said, 'Here's what we'll do: take your first at-bat and then we'll take you out and say your hamstring was sore.' So, I grounded out, grabbed at my hamstring as I was going through the base and then headed to the golf course."

Free agents would arrive in Braves camp and be amazed as the starting pitchers would be heading out around 11 AM for a tee time. What they didn't initially know was many of these pitchers had arrived before dawn to get some of their work done.

"Playing for Bobby was great," Maddux said. "The best job in baseball is being a starting pitcher and the best starting pitching job in baseball is playing for Bobby. We had the best of both worlds."

Knowing Cox always had their back, Maddux had some fun with the skipper at the expense of an undeserving umpire.

When Cox went to the clubhouse to grab a coffee, he came across Maddux, Glavine and Smoltz, who were all watching the game on television. Not sure about the strike zone that day, he asked his top starters what they had seen. Maddux said something like, "He's been all over the place."

Glavine and Smoltz laughed and said, "Why did you do that? You know what he's going to do." It wasn't long before Cox had been ejected and sent to the clubhouse to also watch the game on TV.

When Cox was inducted into Baseball's Hall of Fame with Maddux and Glavine in 2014, he told this funny story.

"Glavine's pitching this game. As usual, it's tight and late," said Cox. "I'm not looking at the situation. Runners on second and third, two outs. At least that's what I'm seeing. I go out to the mound and [third baseman] Chipper [Jones] comes in with the other infielders. I say, 'Hey, Tommy, what do you think? Why don't we just walk this guy instead of pitching around him?' He said, 'Skip, that's one of the better ideas you've had in the last month, but where are we going to put him?' So I looked at third, looked at second. There's runners there. I glance over at first, and there happens to be a runner there, too. So I said,

'Look, if this gets out to the press tomorrow, each one of you is going to be fined $1,000.'"

Cox had the pleasure of returning to Cooperstown to see Smoltz inducted in 2015 and Schuerholz inducted in 2017. Chipper Jones was enshrined in 2018.

These were proud moments for the beloved skipper, who was an integral contributor to the organization until he had a stroke the day after the 2019 home opener. He lost some motor and communication skills, but he still keeps up with the Braves on television and via visits from Snitker and other organization members.

Cox's presence at the stadium ended with the stroke. But his impact will be felt for generations to come.

"He is the Atlanta Braves," former Braves catcher Brian McCann said.

35
Derek Schiller and Mike Plant

PHIL KENT WAS THREE MONTHS INTO HIS TENURE AS CEO of Turner Broadcasting when he called Mike Plant to his office and offered him the chance to run the business side for the Braves. A few weeks later, Kent asked Plant if he knew anything about Derek Schiller, the man Kent wanted to put in charge of the team's revenue streams.

"I was like, 'Yeah, I've known him since he was 14,'" Plant said. "His dad was the best man in my wedding."

Two decades later, Plant and Schiller remain a strong team. They distanced the team from the revenue concerns that existed at the beginning of this century and eventually created the blueprint for financial success across all sports.

Hundreds of sports executives from around the world have come to visit Truist Park and The Battery Atlanta, which is the mixed-use development adjacent to the stadium. The shops, restaurants, bars and residential areas within this development have created an incredible revenue stream that should benefit the Braves for decades to come.

"The brand is stronger than it was 20 years ago, and it was an extremely strong brand then," said Schiller, who now serves as the Braves' president and CEO.

When Schiller and Plant arrived, the Braves were still basking in the glory of having made five trips to the World Series during the 1990s. The team had won 12 consecutive division titles and it was just seven seasons into a new stadium, Turner Field.

But the team's revenues were becoming a concern, especially as the Braves continued to have one of the game's top payrolls. So Plant and Schiller were tabbed to take the team into the new age.

Opportunities to grow around Turner Field were limited. The stadium was located a little too far for most to walk from their downtown hotels and the closest MARTA (Atlanta's subway system) station was nearly three-quarters of a mile away from the ballpark's gates.

So, there was a need for the parking lots that surrounded the stadium. But the Braves still made many attempts to find ways to add stores, restaurants and residential options to these lots.

"All we were was 81 home games a year," said Plant, who is now president and CEO of the Braves Development Company. "There was nothing else around that area to draw people during the remainder of the year. We wanted to be a year-round destination."

Plant was a member of the 1980 United States Olympic Speed Skating team, and he was part of a contingent of athletes who lobbied with President Jimmy Carter before the United States boycotted the 1980 Summer Games in Moscow. He was also on the board of directors for the Atlanta Committee for the 1996 Olympic Games.

So, he understood the historical significance of Turner Field, which was transformed into a baseball stadium after serving as the Olympic Stadium for the '96 Games. But at the same time, there was a desire to create additional revenue opportunities around the stadium.

Plant spent eight years attempting to convince the Atlanta Fulton County recreation authority to allow him to pursue opportunities to build upon the 46 acres of asphalt parking lots. The deal was the Braves would be the control agent. But the recreation authority never showed any interest in providing consent.

The Braves went to Atlanta mayor Kasim Reed in November 2012 to discuss what they viewed as their options, which included signing a five-year extension to the lease, gaining permission to be the control agent for a mixed-use property or pursuing opportunities outside of Atlanta.

There was some initial hope for progress, but it never materialized. The Braves estimated they needed more than $130 million to make repairs at Turner Field. But the recreation authority wasn't even willing to provide the $50 million it was contractually obligated to provide.

McGuirk remembers Reed telling him, "You guys don't have enough money to go build a new stadium. You're going to be back in this stadium. You'll have to go fix it up."

Remember when Fay Vincent told McGuirk John Schuerholz would never come to Atlanta? Well, Reed provided similar motivation.

The Braves explored the option of building a new stadium where an old GM factory had sat in Doraville. But thoughts of this materializing quickly died when it was realized the city and DeKalb County couldn't provide necessary funding.

Plant then found a willing partner in Cobb County Commissioner Tim Lee. The two introduced themselves to each other over lunch at the Marietta Country Club on July 3, 2013. Within the next five weeks, the Braves had purchased $49 million worth of land from B.F. Saul, a longtime real estate investor from Bethesda, Maryland.

Located adjacent to where I-75 and I-285 meet on the north side of Atlanta, this was prime real estate. Most prospective buyers weren't interested because of the need to move pipeline. But the Braves had already found a company capable of doing this work.

So, the big surprise came on November 11, 2013, when the Braves announced they would be leaving Turner Field and downtown Atlanta after the 2016 season. The team was able to keep the purchase and negotiations from city and public officials, who may have been preoccupied while helping the NFL's Atlanta Falcons complete plans to build their new stadium.

As more than 10.2 million visitors now visit Truist Park and The Battery Atlanta on annual basis, the Braves know they found the perfect spot. They drew more than three million fans to the stadium during the 2023 season. More than double that total spent money at hotels, shops, restaurants and bars all located on the adjacent land, which is all owned by the Braves.

"I thank God every day," Plant said. "It's beyond our expectations."

As the Braves held pregame parties before their 2021 World Series games, McGuirk, Schiller and Plant could stand above The Battery and proudly see a sea of people. The vision to provide fans more than just a ballpark to visit 81 times a year has created a cash cow and the opportunity for the Braves to again have one of the game's top payrolls.

The Braves have tripled their revenues since Schiller and Plant arrived at the end of the 2003 season. The Battery Atlanta accounts for just 10 percent of that revenue, but it's a reliable revenue stream and, most importantly, one every professional sports team would like to have.

At one point, the Braves had the advantage provided by TBS' national exposure. Now, their advantage comes via the countless entertainment options that sit just beyond their outfield gates.

"It's part of the reason we have fans who come here and want to come back night in and night out, year in and year out," Schiller said. "They come here and have a good time, partly because of what they can do before and after those games."

Along with improving the business model, Schiller has served as a strong leader of an organization that has more than doubled its workforce since he arrived. He kept morale high while the team dealt with significant MLB sanctions after the 2017 season and again when the 2020 season was affected by the COVID pandemic.

Schiller's efforts to fill Truist Park as quickly as possible after the 2020 COVID shutdown led to the profits that prompted McGuirk to tell president of baseball operations Alex Anthopoulos he had some financial flexibility heading into the 2021 trade deadline.

When the Braves won the 2021 World Series, there was further reason to praise what Anthopoulos had acquired before the deadline. One of his acquisitions was World Series MVP Jorge Soler and another was National League Championship Series MVP Eddie Rosario. Adam Duvall and Joc Pederson also made an impact after being added for the final months.

So, while Snitker and Anthopoulos received all the leadership praise, there's reason to argue Joctober wouldn't have even become a thing in Atlanta without the leadership Schiller and Plant provided.

"When people look at a baseball team, they see what that culture is on the field," Schiller said. "Many times it's an extension of the culture happening off the field. Our culture is very important to us."

36

Stan Kasten

TED TURNER'S WILLINGNESS TO STAY OUT OF THE WAY ON the baseball side began to be seen as his focus turned to CNN and other ventures during the late 1970s and early '80s. But this was truly visible before the 1986 season, the first during which the Braves had Stan Kasten as their president and Bobby Cox as the general manager.

Kasten had already spent many years as the president of the NBA's Atlanta Hawks. Now, he was running two major professional sports teams for the same guy.

"Ted didn't give you a lot of his time, because he was busy saving the world on a hundred other fronts. The United Nations, Africa, he was all over the place. So, when I told him some of the things we wanted to do, he said, 'Stan, I don't need a lecture, just do it.' People will say that. But when Ted said, 'Just do it, Stan,' he literally meant it. That allowed us to set the course."

When evaluating what Cox and Schuerholz did as the general managers during the Braves' finest era, Kasten factors into a significant portion of the success. In fact, he stands as one of the most influential figures in Atlanta sports history.

An avid baseball fan, Kasten began a tour of various ballparks shortly after graduating from Columbia University in 1976. He ran into Turner during a game in St. Louis, asked for a job and then spent the next two and a half decades working for all of Turner's sports teams.

Kasten handled legal matters for the Braves and sat in on the team's board meetings during his earliest years in Atlanta. But he didn't truly gain a leadership title in the baseball world until 1986, when he became team president for both the Braves and the NBA's Atlanta Hawks.

"When Ted approached me with this, the Braves were a last-place team with the game's highest payroll," Kasten said. "That's very hard to do. I was reluctant, to say the least. But he managed to convince me it would be good to run both teams."

With Kasten in place, Cox found somebody who had a better feel for the organization needed in the corporate environment. At the same time, he gained somebody who could serve as an effective intermediary between the team and Turner's bank account.

"Bobby's philosophy was the same as mine, which was to build the farm system," Kasten said. "I was able to turn the dial all the way to the right with Ted's support. Bobby only felt comfortable with what was his limited authority at the time. But with what Ted asked me to do, Bobby had a lot more horsepower to get done what we needed. In retrospect, we built a heck of a farm system."

"Someone very close to the organization said, 'You need to get rid of Paul Snyder because that is where the breakdown is,'"

Kasten said. "I said, 'Okay, thanks. I'll make my own decision, but I appreciate that.' He was in an administrative role and that's not where he should have been. Bobby and I felt strongly about this. So, we let him return to being a scout, supervisor and crosschecker. Let me tell you, that decision made a big difference for the next decade or more. He's an unsung hero."

Kasten had a good feel for the baseball operations department. This seemed to help build the strong union he shared with both Cox and Schuerholz.

"The three of us, me and Bobby and John, had different jobs and we respected the job the others did and let them do their job," Kasten said. "We disagreed lots of times on lots of things, but eventually one of us would have to make a decision and the other two respected that decision."

Schuerholz has always credited Kasten for helping him make a smooth transition from Kansas City to Atlanta.

"Stan and Bobby Cox were the two guys who really made me feel comfortable," Schuerholz said. "Stan kept telling me, don't do anything different than you've been doing your whole career. Every once in a while Ted would come around. But Stan and Bobby were really the ones who made it easy."

Kasten immediately earned Turner's trust and thus was able to gain the funds necessary to help turn the Braves around. But it's not just about gaining the money, as Atlanta fans saw throughout the 1970s and 1980s when high payrolls often netted last-place finishes.

With Cox providing direction, the Braves began to spend their money much more efficiently. The ability to sign Terry Pendleton, Sid Bream, Rafael Belliard and Otis Nixon before the 1991 season helped create a winning culture, recognized by the likes of Greg Maddux.

When it came time for Maddux to find a new employer two years later, the Braves had both the money and the product he was seeking. This was a rare instance when a Scott Boras client didn't take the top offer. The four-time Cy Young Award winner passed on the Yankees' offer to become a part of what Cox, Kasten and Schuerholz were building in Atlanta.

Kasten also played a significant part in the transformation of Olympic Stadium into Turner Field after the 1996 Olympics ended in Atlanta. A couple years later, he found himself overseeing the transformation of The Omni to Phillips Arena, which is now named State Farm Arena.

Kasten left the Braves after the 2003 season and has since enjoyed stints as president of both the Nationals and the Dodgers. He has been away from the Atlanta sports scene for nearly two decades, but his fingerprints remain. He served as the Braves' president during what remains the best era in franchise history.

"I grew to appreciate Stan's role and as time went on, I grew to appreciate what he did even more," John Smoltz said. "He played a big part in our success."

37

John Schuerholz

THE MOST SUCCESSFUL GENERAL MANAGER IN BRAVES HISTORY was a schoolteacher who got his start in baseball after writing a letter in a teachers' lounge within a school in Baltimore.

That letter led to a job within the Orioles' baseball operations department, which led to a long, successful stint with the Kansas City Royals, which led to a legendary stint with the Atlanta Braves, which led to an unprecedented and unmatched 14 consecutive division titles.

"I don't know if anybody will ever do that again," Schuerholz said in reference to the Braves' division dominance that ran throughout the 1990s and into the 2000s.

Schuerholz grew up in Baltimore and planned to stay there his entire life. That is until Lou Gorman finally persuaded him to journey with him to Kansas City, where he could help build the expansion Royals from the ground up.

A little more than a decade later, Schuerholz became the team's GM in 1981 and provided the city its first World Series title in 1985. There was no reason or plan to leave Kansas City until the Braves came calling after the 1990 season. Atlanta provided the chance to work with Bobby Cox and a stacked farm system.

Schuerholz again reluctantly relocated and found success. His first season with the Braves is still celebrated in Atlanta. A team that had sat at the bottom of the National League West standings most of the past two decades won the division on the regular season's final day and finished one win shy of a World Series title.

This incredible 1991 season marked the start of the run of 14 straight division crowns. Bobby Cox had spent the past five seasons serving as the general manager. He rebuilt the farm system and then headed to the dugout, where he constructed his Hall of Fame managerial career.

Cox had built a pitching staff that included Tom Glavine, John Smoltz and Steve Avery. Schuerholz aided these pitchers by significantly improving the team's defense. He did this by adding shortstop Rafael Belliard, first baseman Sid Bream, center fielder Otis Nixon and third baseman Terry Pendleton, who was named 1991 NL MVP.

After the Braves won the 1992 NL West, Schuerholz completed one of the greatest free agent signings by landing reigning NL Cy Young Award winner Greg Maddux, who would win three more Cy Youngs within his first three years in Atlanta. Then, he strengthened his club halfway through the 1993 season by acquiring Fred McGriff.

Thirty-plus years later, the Braves' acquisitions of Maddux and McGriff are two of the best in baseball history. Both Hall of Famers helped Atlanta win the 1995 World Series.

Glavine and Maddux were around for each of the Braves' five trips to the World Series. But they were surrounded by a different supporting cast throughout the great decade. Schuerholz was responsible for all of those decisions that gave Atlanta a World Series hopeful on an annual basis for a decade and a half.

By signing Maddux after missing out on his attempt to acquire Barry Bonds, Schuerholz enhanced the strength of his rotation for a decade. McGriff's arrival stirred an incredible second half and one of the greatest pennant races in baseball history. But along with helping the Braves win 104 games and overcome the 103-win Giants in 1993, McGriff served as a strong middle-of-the-lineup presence for a few more years to come.

When McGriff's tenure was done, Schuerholz signed Andrés Galarraga, who came to Atlanta in 1998 as one of the game's premier power hitters. The savvy GM also made valuable trades to acquire some quality starting pitchers like Denny Neagle, who contributed value for a few years and then was sent to the Cincinnati Reds in a trade that brought Bret Boone's power to Atlanta in 1999.

While Schuerholz can also be lauded for bringing Gary Sheffield to Atlanta for two seasons (2002–03), his critics will point out the long-term effects of trading top prospect Adam Wainwright for one year of J.D. Drew in '04. The club also needed some time to recover from the decision to use a group of top prospects for what amounted to one calendar year of Mark Teixeira ('07–'08).

But there's no denying the long-standing success of Schuerholz, who saw the Braves produce an MLB-best .593 winning percentage during his 17-season reign as GM. Yes, those 14 trips to the postseason yielded just one World Series title—but that's one more than any other GM has netted since the club relocated to Atlanta in 1966.

Schuerholz established himself as a leader via his willingness to listen to his employees and delegate responsibilities.

Schuerholz's longtime assistant general manager in both Kansas City and Atlanta, Dean Taylor, was a first-year, entry-level employee in the Royals' baseball operations department in 1981. Still, his opinion was requested when Schuerholz asked staff members whether to take Mark Gubicza or C.L. Penigar with the team's second-round draft pick. Gubicza is now a member of the Royals Hall of Fame. Penigar never advanced past Triple A.

"That was the first example I ever saw of his complete inclusionary management style," Taylor said. "He wanted to get everyone's opinion before the final decision was made. As I went through [my career] with him, I came to find that was John Schuerholz."

Schuerholz credits his listening skills to going deaf in his right ear after acquiring German measles when he was five years old.

"I had to learn to be a more attentive and intentional listener, which I believe worked quite well throughout my life," Schuerholz said.

One of Schuerholz's most successful pupils was Dayton Moore, who spent 11 seasons within the Braves' front office before leaving during the 2006 season to become Kansas City's general manager. He helped the Royals win the World Series in 2015.

Moore and Schuerholz are the only GMs to lead the Royals to a World Series title.

"John had an amazing way of transferring responsibility and giving power to his people," Moore said. "Because of that, we all felt extremely loyal to him and wanted to make him proud. He taught me to use whatever platform or position I had to do good, and that's what we've all tried to do."

Schuerholz transitioned from GM to team president after the 2007 season. He quelled the situation both internally and externally when Glavine didn't get the respect he deserved when he was released during his 2009 comeback attempt. But for the most part his day-to-day interactions weren't as frequent. Still, he remained heavily involved, expanding his interests to the business side.

Unfortunately, the end of Schuerholz's long, successful tenure was tarnished by the fact he had brought John Hart into the organization, and he determined John Coppolella was ready to serve as the GM at the end of the 2014 season. Both were removed from the organization after the 2017 season, when MLB levied major sanctions for illegal practices on the international market.

Still, the incredible value Schuerholz brought to the organization will never be forgotten. Cox planted the seeds during his time as the GM and Schuerholz spent decades cultivating what continues to be a very fruitful garden.

"It seemed like he always got the right players, especially toward the end of the year," Maddux said. The trades always seemed to be good for us. He found the right guys and it always seemed like we had the right fits at the positions we needed."

38

Alex Anthopoulos

ALEX ANTHOPOULOS' JOURNEY TOWARD BECOMING ONE OF baseball's top executives actually began with his desire to purchase a snowboard.

Instead of making his annual summer trip from Canada to Greece, Anthopoulos opted to work at his father's heating and ventilation company. He gained the money needed for the snowboard, but he also started to learn this might not be the life for him.

"It was like, you had to use a blow torch, so you'd be dirty and grimy and sweaty," Anthopoulos said. "I remember sitting there messy with a blowtorch in my hand, when my father walked by with a shirt and tie and said, 'Do you really want to do this for the rest of your life?'"

Still, there was a desire to do whatever he could to help the company his father, John Anthopoulos, started. This business had provided him ski trips during the winter, summer trips to

Greece and top-notch private education. His plan was to take economics in college and help his dad on the business side once he graduated.

During the summer after his sophomore year in college, Anthopoulos was at lunch with his father when his father told him about some chest pains. Alex returned to the office and John visited his cardiologist, who informed the elder Anthopoulos that he may have had a heart attack two days earlier.

John Anthopoulos was admitted to the hospital on Wednesday and was visited by family members again on Thursday. But after doctors took him off blood thinners on Friday, he suffered a fatal heart attack.

So, a little more than a week shy of his 21st birthday, Alex became even more determined to sustain the company his father had built from scratch. He handled his university studies during the afternoon hours and took heating and ventilation classes at night.

"I was doing everything I could, and I hated it," Anthopoulos said. "I did it for two years. I remember thinking, 'Wow, I'm 23 and I could end up doing this for another 40 to 45 years. This is awful.' I was working hard, but I did not have any passion or joy for any of it. But I still loved baseball."

Anthopoulos' passion for baseball began around the time he was 14, when the early-1990s Montreal Expos started to become one of baseball's most talent-rich teams. He attended games with a friend who had season tickets and quickly found himself immersed in the sport. He read Bill James' books and soaked in any statistical analysis he could find.

So, if he wanted to do something he loved, it only made sense for him to pursue a job in baseball. He sent letters to many clubs and the Marlins offered an internship in the community relations department. They rescinded the offer when they realized it would be difficult to obtain a work visa.

With the focus now squarely on MLB's two Canadian teams, Anthopoulos called the Expos and was fortunate enough to be given general manager Jim Beattie's office number at the team's spring training complex in Florida.

"He answers the phone and says, 'Jim Beattie,' and I hang up and go, 'Holy smokes,'" Anthopoulos said with a laugh. "I was a little nervous. I took a minute, called him back and he told me to send him my information."

The Expos began an internship that year just to have somebody sort and deliver fan mail to the players. Anthopoulos didn't care what the responsibility was. He just wanted an opportunity. After making approximately five calls to check on the status of the job opening, he was told, "You want this worse than anybody else, so we're going to give you the job.'"

As fate would have it, Fidelity Investments called the same day to offer Anthopoulos a lucrative job opportunity with benefits and growth in Toronto. But he decided that job could still be available down the road. He wanted to spend at least two years in baseball, even if it required him to just deliver fan mail on the weekends for free.

Anthopoulos took care of his expenses by working at the Royal Bank of Canada in Montreal during the week. Once his fan mail chores were completed on the weekends, he would sit alongside the scouts behind the plate and get a feel for the scouting world.

Veteran scout Mike Toomey took a liking to Anthopoulos and introduced him to an old video of former Braves scout Bill White talking about the art of evaluating players. Other scouts like Russ Bove also took time to talk to Anthopoulos about the finer points of their craft.

The Expos eventually sent Anthopoulos to Florida and the Dominican Republic to do some scouting for free. When it came time to go to scouting school, the club agreed to sponsor Anthopoulos, but he had to pay for the schooling.

Two years into this opportunity, Anthopoulos was beginning to run out of money. Fortunately, this was around the same time the Miami Marlins and Expos switched ownership. Omar Minaya was brought in to run Montreal's baseball operations department and one of his first hires was Dana Brown, who became the team's scouting director.

Nearly two decades later, Anthopoulos and Brown would team to create draft classes that strengthened the Braves throughout the 2020s.

But this was 2002 and Anthopoulos was weeks or months away from poverty forcing him to walk away from his dream job. Brown convinced Minaya to give this eager kid a scouting coordinator role for $25,000 a year, a salary the CFO argued was too high.

"Alex was a young, energetic intern who spoke four languages," Brown said. "He had a deep love for the game and was a sponge with a teachable spirit. His passion for the game was unmatched. He lived in Montreal and already filled the office presence on baseball ops that we needed. He was relentless. One of my top selections."

With his promotion, Anthopoulos was reintroduced to some of the players, who had previously only met him while he was handling their fan mail.

"So I got to fly home with the team from spring training," Anthopoulos said. "I had known Michael Barrett since I had done the fan mail thing. He said, 'Hey, you made the team.'"

Anthopoulos was named the Expos' assistant scouting director after two years. This was around the same time the Blue

Jays came calling with a scouting coordinator position. The title was inferior to what he had already gained. But with the Expos planning to move to Washington, D.C., to become the Nationals, there was concern about the visa issue.

"I remember Tony Tavares, who was the Expos' president at the time, pulling me aside and saying I was on the fast track and how they had big plans for me," Anthopoulos said. "I politely said, 'I appreciate it, but you can't guarantee me the immigration thing won't be an issue and if you guys are wrong, my career is over.'"

Anthopoulos took a pay cut and headed to Toronto, where the Blue Jays also had big plans for him. He was named assistant general manager two years later and became the team's GM at the end of the 2009 season, when he was just 32 years old.

"I've never chased the money," Anthopoulos said. "I've done it for all the right reasons, and it's always worked out in the end."

Anthopoulos was talking about the decision to join the Blue Jays. But he could have also been referring to his decision to leave Toronto after the 2015 season.

Everything seemed to be going great as the Blue Jays progressed toward an American League East title in 2015. Offseason acquisition Josh Donaldson produced an MVP season. His success, combined with the trade deadline acquisitions of David Price and Troy Tulowitzki, had Toronto prepping for the postseason for the first time since Joe Carter ended the 1993 World Series with a walk-off home run.

But just as Anthopoulos was preparing to get rewarded with a nice contract extension, the Blue Jays hired Mark Shapiro to become the team's new president. Shapiro had run the baseball operations department for the Cleveland Indians. Though he would be responsible for business ventures in Toronto, it seemed apparent he would also oversee baseball operations.

Anthopoulos has never said the lack of autonomy led him to decline the Blue Jays' very lucrative five-year offer. But it was easy to understand if he viewed Shapiro's arrival to be a slap in the face. He had built Toronto's first division winner in more than two decades and now he was being given a new boss.

"If I didn't feel comfortable with who I was going to work for and with, there wasn't going to be anything that moved me," Anthopoulos said. "It wasn't going to be money. It wasn't going to be anything."

While the Blue Jays advanced to the 2015 American League Championship Series, Anthopoulos lost the opportunity to pursue GM vacancies with the Phillies and Angels. Nobody knew he was even planning to leave because he didn't want to distract from what his team was doing on the field.

But once the season concluded with a loss to the Royals in the ALCS, Anthopoulos rejected the Blue Jays' lucrative offer and eventually accepted the reduced salary he received as the Dodgers' vice president of player development.

Anthopoulos had to move his family from Toronto to Los Angeles and accept a lesser title. But he was happy and that's what he valued most.

Anthopoulos joined a Dodgers front office that included Andrew Friedman and Farhan Zaidi, who were also highly regarded baseball executives. He essentially got his master's degree in roster building and maintenance while spending two years in Los Angeles.

But just as he and his family were settling down in California, the Braves called with what he deemed to be the perfect opportunity. He was getting another opportunity to run a baseball operations department and he would report directly to the control person (team chairman and CEO Terry McGuirk).

But most importantly, the dinner he shared with McGuirk and Cox during his interview gave him reason to believe he was also surrounding himself with the people who would provide him the best chance to succeed.

"When John [Schuerholz] called to make the offer, I said I already know I'm taking this job because it's for the right reasons," Anthopoulos said. "Before you mention a dollar amount or years, I can tell you I'm taking this job because it's the right opportunity and right job."

It certainly has seemed to be the right fit. The Braves have won the National League East every year since Anthopoulos came to Atlanta.

Anthopoulos has made plenty of valuable roster decisions since being tasked with distancing the Braves from the despair the organization faced when MLB's sanctions overhauled the front office at the end of the 2017 season.

In fact, one of his most valuable moves was the first big one he made.

Around the same time Anthopoulos was acquiring Tulowitzki and Price ahead of the 2015 trade deadline, Coppolella was acquiring Hector Olivera in a three-team trade with the Dodgers and Marlins. The Braves made a strong push to sign Olivera on the international market and lost out to the Dodgers.

Given a chance to acquire him again, Coppolella made this trade, which also brought a competitive balance draft pick to the Braves. The selection was used to get Joey Wentz, who was used to acquire veteran reliever Shane Greene from the Tigers before the 2019 trade deadline.

Greene gave the Braves two solid months at the end of 2019 and a couple more good months during the COVID-shortened 2020 season. That's far more than Atlanta gained from Olivera, who seemed destined to be a bust long before a domestic violence incident at the start of 2016 essentially ended his career.

Wanting to get rid of Olivera, the Braves agreed to take a chance on Kemp and pay him approximately $8 million per year during the final three full years (2017–19) of his contract.

Kemp produced an .855 OPS over 56 games for the Braves in 2016 and came to spring training in good shape the next year. He got off to a good start. But as his weight began to rise during the summer months, his production drastically dropped. Team employees became tired of his act, but it didn't seem likely he and his bulky contract could be moved.

Remember when Coppolella infuriated Snitker by questioning his decision to let Kemp face a right-handed reliever in the ninth inning of a meaningless final-weekend game in 2017? Snitker understood keeping Kemp happy was important, especially with the possibility he'd be back the following year.

So, Coppolella was definitely wrong to be angry at the moment. But the fact he wanted Matt Adams to pinch hit in that situation provides a clear picture of where Kemp stood at the end of 2017.

Anthopoulos wasn't around for all of this. But he did see the value of moving Kemp, especially with heralded prospect Ronald Acuña Jr. set to debut early in the 2018 season.

So, Kemp was traded to the Dodgers in exchange for right-handed pitcher Brandon McCarthy, left-handed pitcher Scott Kazmir, utility man Charlie Culberson, first baseman Adrian Gonzalez and $4.5 million in cash.

McCarthy went 4–0 with a 2.08 ERA against the Phillies, who stood as the Braves' chief threat to a division title for nearly three-quarters of the season. Culberson became a fan favorite as he delivered a few big home runs during his first couple months with his hometown team.

By getting Kemp off the books for 2019, the Braves were able to sign Josh Donaldson, who played a key role in Atlanta winning a second straight division title.

This move gave McGuirk even more confidence he had made the right choice and put the organization in the right hands. He was impressed with the maturity and strength Anthopoulos showed after Shapiro arrived in Toronto. But now, he was getting a chance to see how his team's new leader could make impact moves to clean the mess he inherited.

"Having your compass right was very important too, because we had just come out of this very traumatic period where Coppy [Coppolella] had disappointed us," McGuirk said. It was a very easy decision to hire Alex, and what a breath of fresh air it has been."

McGuirk changed the management structure once MLB levied the international market sanctions that led the team to part ways with Coppolella and John Hart, who had served as president of baseball operations.

Coppolella had reported to Hart, who reported to Schuerholz, who reported to McGuirk. Schuerholz is still part of the organization, but his legacy was tarnished, and his power was diminished because he had approved the hires of Coppolella and Hart.

Now, Anthopoulos reports directly to McGuirk without any intermediaries.

39

Brian Snitker

ONE OF BRIAN SNITKER'S FAVORITE RESPONSES TO QUESTIONS about an inevitable tough stretch for his team or one of his players goes something like, "If you weather the storm and get yourself through it, there's usually something good waiting for you on the other side."

Unbeknownst to him, he has essentially been describing what he has experienced during his nearly 50 years within the Braves organization.

"I've never really thought about it that way," Snitker said. "I've always thought about it with teams, over six months, you're going to have rough times. Vary rarely can anybody say everything went smooth and as planned."

Snitker certainly couldn't have predicted what the next five decades would look like after he hit .254 with 23 homers and a .706 OPS while spending four seasons as a catcher in the Braves' minor league system.

Nor could he have predicted he'd currently stand as one of the most influential figures in Braves history after being demoted or, using his term, "recycled," a few times during his long tenure with the organization. But he weathered the storm and ultimately found something great on the other side.

"He means so much to this organization," Freddie Freeman said. "He's put on every hat in this organization."

Long before he guided the Braves to the 2021 World Series title and long before he became the third-winningest manager in franchise history, Snitker was a 26-year-old pondering his post–baseball playing career. He didn't wait long.

Shortly after releasing Snitker, then-minor league director Hank Aaron had his personal assistant, Susan Bailey, call Snitker to offer him his first coaching job.

"Hank said he wanted me to go down to Bradenton because they didn't really have a pitching coach down there," Snitker said. "Then they called and said they had a bunch of catchers get hurt in Durham. So, I went back there and lived with Dirty Al at his apartment."

Dirty Al? This was in reference to Al Gallagher, who served as Class A Durham's manager in 1980 and '81.

How did he get his nickname? Well, he was known to arrive at and leave the ballpark wearing the same pair of underwear that he wore under his uniform during batting practice and that day's game.

Snitker remembers sleeping on the couch and hearing Dirty Al's wife tell her husband, "Do not get in his bed before you shower."

Fortunately, Snitker's roommate during instructional league in Bradenton that fall was much cleaner. He still has great memories of spending those weeks rooming with Cito

Gaston. Snitker actually met his wife, Ronnie, thanks to one of Gaston's friends.

"I learned a lot from Cito," Snitker said. "We'd go to the park and then come home, drink beer and talk baseball every night."

Nobody had a clue both men would one day have the distinction of being a World Series–winning manager.

Snitker was just 26 years old when he got his first minor league managerial job with Low A Anderson (South Carolina). One year later, he began the first of two stints with High A Durham (North Carolina). It was at the end of that second stint in 1987 that Kevin Costner, Susan Sarandon and Tim Robbins came to town to begin filming *Bull Durham*. The catcher's mitt Costner used in the classic film was an old one Snitker found in his office.

"It's really cool now when I watch it and see all the guys I managed that are in it [as extras]," Snitker said. "Our bus driver, Sam, was the bus driver in the movie. All of it was just awesome. I love that movie."

Snitker spent 1985 as Atlanta's bullpen coach, but returned to the minors when Chuck Tanner became the Braves' manager before the 1986 season. He'd wait almost 20 more years before returning to the major league level to become Bobby Cox's third base coach in 2007.

But he influenced countless careers while filling a variety of roles over the years that followed. He was Class A Macon's hitting coach when a young switch hitter named Chipper Jones arrived in 1991. He managed Macon the next year and was begrudgingly reassigned to be a roving instructor the next year.

Snitker was furious. But he quickly realized it was the best thing for him.

While serving as an instructor in 1993, Snitker experienced a series of life-altering events within approximately two weeks. He spent a portion of the summer in Arizona caring for an aunt after she developed a brain tumor. Then, upon returning from a road trip with Rookie League Danville, he learned his father had died from a massive heart attack.

After they went back to his hometown of Decatur, Illinois, for the funeral, his wife, Ronnie, rolled over in bed, felt a lump and later learned she had breast cancer. The following months were spent in Atlanta waging what proved to be a successful battle against the disease.

"Going through that whole thing and getting that perspective was the best thing that ever happened to me," Snitker said. "It's all horrible stuff, but in retrospect, it was good I could get out of the mix and detox and tell other people good things. It gave me a really good feel for what everybody goes through. It made me realize you can't take this stuff too serious, because life is too short to be banging on these guys."

When John Smoltz crossed paths with Snitker, he viewed him as an intimidating drill sergeant. By the time Jeff Francoeur and Brian McCann crossed paths with the longtime baseball manager, they found a somewhat softer version of Snitker, whose venom was now usually reserved for protecting his players.

One of Francoeur's favorite stories occurred after he homered a few times for Double A Mississippi and then got drilled in the ribs against Montgomery. Snitker instructed a reliever to retaliate. When the pitcher simply buzzed a batter, Snitker blasted the pitcher in the dugout and told him to get out of his sight.

When one of Mississippi's pitchers retaliated the next inning, the benches cleared, and the umpires halted the game.

"After we got back in the clubhouse, [Snitker] grabbed a beer and told us he had never been more proud of the way we came together as a team that day," Francoeur said. "If you play for him, you know he's always going to protect you and have your back."

Snitker became Atlanta's third base coach in 2007 and remained in that role until former general manager Frank Wren reassigned him to be Triple A Gwinnett's manager after the 2013 postseason.

Stunned and angry, Snitker waited a few days before accepting the assignment. He felt like he was being made a scapegoat. Others felt Wren simply wanted to bring Doug Dascenzo in to serve as both the third base coach and clubhouse mole.

"I was like, 'I'm too old to go somewhere else,'" Snitker said. "I'm a Brave. Why would I want to go somewhere else and start over?"

This decision still angers many of the Braves' longtime employees.

"Brian was done wrong by Frank Wren," Braves broadcaster Joe Simpson said. "That was so unjust. I appreciated that Fredi Gonzalez, who was the manager at the time, said if he's going to go to Triple A, you can't cut his pay."

As furious as he was during those years, he now realizes there was some benefit to this move. Just as he ended up being there for his wife in 1993, the role as Gwinnett's manager allowed him to spend time with his mother during some of her final years.

Snitker was able to regularly visit his mother, as she lived in an assisted living residence located near Gwinnett's home stadium.

"So, that ended up being a really good thing, too," Snitker said. "If she needed me for anything, I could be there. I couldn't have done that if I was coaching third in the big leagues. You can't just step away from that job. Things happen for a reason."

By this point, Snitker had given up hope of ever becoming a big-league manager. So it's safe to say he was shocked on May 20, 2016, when he received a call telling him he needed to get to Pittsburgh the next day to begin his tenure as Atlanta's interim manager.

The Braves' plan was to tell Gonzalez he was being replaced the next day. But Gonzalez learned his fate prematurely when he received an email from Delta Airlines with details about a return flight to Atlanta he never knew had been booked.

This was how Gonzalez learned he had been fired. Instead of using that plane ticket, he rented a car and drove to Philadelphia, where he spent time with his girlfriend, Tricia, who is now his wife.

Snitker didn't love that his dream was coming true at the expense of one of his best friends. He had been the third base coach during the first three seasons (2011–13) of Gonzalez's tenure as the Braves' manager.

But it was great to finally be a big-league manager, even if this first job didn't come until he was 60 and even if it came with a team that had lost 28 of its first 37 games.

The circumstances could have been better. He was tasked with guiding a club through the most painful portion of a massive rebuilding process. But all that he had experienced over the previous four decades prepared to him to be exactly who the Braves needed.

"When he came and gave a speech before his first game [in 2016], I felt like we were 28–9 instead of 9–28," Braves first baseman Freddie Freeman said. "We all gave him a standing ovation. He was just awesome from day one."

Snitker was a motivator in front of the players, but he was a realist. He nearly had to pull his starting pitcher in the first inning of his first game as a big-league manager. After the Braves ended up losing 12–9 to the Pirates that night, he came in his office and showed his wit by telling bench coach Terry Pendleton, "I'm surprised you guys have won nine games."

A little humor is needed throughout a long baseball season. But, as he had been since first becoming a coach, Snitker was totally committed to his players and doing whatever he could do to help them succeed. It helped that his first team included Francoeur and Kelly Johnson, whom he had crossed paths with at both the minor league and major league levels.

After that 2016 season, the Braves interviewed both Bud Black and Ron Washington as managerial candidates. Black and Washington were impressive. But the experience they had as big-league managers didn't trump the tremendous support Snitker received from his veteran leaders Freeman and Nick Markakis.

Snitker's interim tag was removed, and he was given a chance to again serve as Atlanta's manager in 2017.

Freeman and Markakis continued providing unwavering support, especially when president of baseball operations John Hart and GM John Coppolella made it clear they had no interest in keeping Snitker beyond the 2017 season.

Hart and Coppolella stormed into the clubhouse after Jim Johnson blew a lead during an August 23 loss to the Mariners and berated Snitker about using the declining veteran in a high-leverage situation. The exchange was loud enough for Markakis to hear. He responded by making it clear he would "kick Hart's ass" if he came in the players' portion of the clubhouse.

A little more than a month later, after the Braves lost a meaningless game to the Marlins on September 30, Coppolella berated Snitker for not using lefty slugger Matt Adams to replace right-handed hitter Matt Kemp when the Marlins brought Brad Ziegler in during the ninth inning.

Coppolella was focused on one final-weekend game that had no bearing on the postseason picture. Snitker knew there was a chance Kemp would be back with the club the following season. So he didn't want to send the moody veteran into the offseason with a sour taste in his mouth.

Kemp was traded two months later. But Coppolella wasn't around to make that move.

MLB called the following morning to inform Coppolella he needed to return to Atlanta immediately to meet with the investigators.

Coppolella resigned two days later, leading the Braves to extend Snitker, who would be named the NL Manager of the Year approximately 12 months later.

Snitker has guided the Braves to six consecutive division titles and one World Series title since the international market transgressions committed by the previous regime opened the door for him and Anthopoulos to form a GM-manager combo that conjures memories of the success Cox and Schuerholz had together.

"It took some time for he and Snit to figure out that working relationship," McGuirk said. "But that has turned out to be a great relationship. It's a bunch of mature people doing mature things. There's no foolishness."

Just three years separated the Braves from the start of a massive rebuilding project and the division title captured in 2018. They were overmatched against the Dodgers during the NL Division Series that year. A questionable decision to give Mike Soroka just one start influenced the loss to the Cardinals in the 2019 NLDS.

Once the Braves pushed the eventual world champion Dodgers to Game 7 of the 2020 NL Championship Series, it was obvious they were ready to be a factor for many years to come. Snitker guided the club to the 2021 World Series title, despite losing Ronald Acuña Jr. to a season-ending knee injury in July. A second straight world championship might have been realized had Max Fried and Spencer Strider not entered the 2022 postseason ailing.

With Snitker serving as their manager, the Braves have experienced the second-best era in franchise history. It seems like Aaron knew what he was doing when he transformed the catcher into a coach.

"He's the reason I'm here," Snitker said. "I'm forever thankful for all he did for me and my career."

Snitker could have allowed his anger to get the best of him by going elsewhere after a couple of those demotions. But he stayed the course and found something rewarding on the other side. He now will forever be remembered for the countless contributions he has made to the Braves.

During those first few spring trainings, he was tasked with trying to catch Phil Niekro's knuckleball. He was on Atlanta's coaching staff during Dale Murphy's heyday. He was introduced to young versions of Glavine, Smoltz and Chipper Jones. He told both Francoeur and Brian McCann they were coming to the big leagues. And now, he has had the pleasure of managing Ronald Acuña Jr., Austin Riley, Ozzie Albies, Spencer Strider and a wave of young superstars who could make the Braves a World Series contender for many years to come.

"It's a special organization because it's always been about the people," Snitker said. "Cito and I still text all the time. He said, "Once a Brave, always a Brave. That place is different.""

PART 6

THE FUTURE

40

Ronald Acuña Jr.

Hank Aaron is one of baseball's greatest icons. Warren Spahn may forever have the distinction of being the winningest left-handed pitcher in baseball history. Chipper Jones, John Smoltz and Tom Glavine were no-doubt first-ballot Hall of Famers.

But the greatest Braves player of all time is still in the early stages of his career.

"[Ronald] Acuña [Jr.] is the most talented player to ever wear a Braves uniform," Jones said.

Despite the fact that so many greats once donned the uniform, it's hard to dispute this tremendous compliment, especially after Acuña became the first player to ever hit 40-plus homers and tally 70-plus stolen bases in the same season. The dynamic superstar did this in 2023, his first full season after recovering from a right ACL tear he suffered two days before the 2021 All-Star break.

"I'm just glad I had a front-row seat to watch it," Braves manager Brian Snitker said. "You never know when he's going to find a new way to amaze you. You definitely don't want to look away when he's on the field because there's always a chance he's going to do something special."

Adding to the splendor of Acuña's journey is the understanding of his beginnings. He grew up in a baseball-rich family that included a handful of major leaguers, including Alcides Escobar and Kelvim Escobar. They were all from La Sabana, a small fishing town in western Venezuela.

Fortunately, longtime Braves scout Rolando Petit was aware of the baseball-rich culture that existed in La Sabana. Acuña was 5'10" and approximately 160 pounds when scouts began evaluating him around the age of 14. The size was a deterrent for some scouts. A long swing led other scouts to pass on the chance to get what became one of the game's best talents.

The Braves and Royals were the only teams who made a strong attempt to sign Acuña. The Braves got the job done with a $100,000 signing bonus, a price that has evolved from a bargain to a ridiculous steal. Nobody knew how special this young outfielder was. He wasn't even ranked among MLB.com's top 30 signings of the 2014 international class.

But it didn't take long for him to grab attention. Bobby Cox saw Acuña playing at the Braves' spring training complex after the 2015 season and knew he was watching a future star. Michael Soroka, who was drafted by the Braves in 2015, also experienced immediate awe.

"The thing I noticed was he was one of the guys whose bat speed I could hear from the dugout on those quiet [Gulf Coast League] fields," Soroka said. "That was kind of my wake up. I was like, 'Wow, that's a professional bat.' I didn't realize it was that special then because I was new to pro ball. But as we got into it, and you could see the kinds of balls he was hitting, you saw him take off. At the time, he was this skinny kid who hadn't been in the weight room."

Acuña was just 20 when he made his celebrated MLB debut approximately a month into the 2018 season. A knee ailment sidelined him for a month that summer. But he still hit 26 homers over 111 games and won the National League Rookie of the Year Award. He showed his incredible potential the following season, when he hit 41 homers and finished three stolen bases shy of the fifth 40-homer, 40-stolen-base season in MLB history.

Acuña impressed again during the COVID-shortened 2020 season and was a top MVP candidate when he suffered the ACL tear while chasing a fly ball on the warning track in Miami. As he completed the long recovery and rehab process, he battled doubts and lingering effects, which hindered him throughout the 2022 season.

"It meant a lot to me to be able to bounce back after I was hurt," Acuña said through an interpreter. "There was some doubt about my ability to do what I accomplished. It meant a lot to me to come back and have that kind of success."

How incredible was Acuña's 40-70 season?

Acuña led the NL in runs (149), hits (217), stolen bases (73), on-base percentage (.416) and OPS (1.012). He ranked second in slugging percentage (.596) and batting average (.337). His 41 home runs and 106 RBIs both ranked among the top six in the league.

Nobody had previously notched more than 46 steals during a 40-homer season. This was also the first time anybody had more than 52 steals during a 30-homer season. So it's safe to say a 40-50 or 40-60 season would have been deemed unrealistic before this year. A 40-70 season? Wow.

Critics said too much value was placed on Acuña's stolen base total, especially with the rule changes implemented in 2023 to benefit base stealers. It's worth noting no other NL player tallied more than 54 steals.

Acuña's numbers stand as historically great even if you remove stolen bases from the evaluation.

The Venezuelan outfielder finished his MVP season with 80 extra-base hits, a 1.012 OPS and 84 strikeouts. He joined Lou Gehrig (1927), Chuck Klein ('30) and Joe DiMaggio ('37) as the only players to hit at least .335 with 40 home runs, 215 hits, 80 extra-base hits, 100 RBIs, 145 runs and a 1.000 OPS with fewer than 90 strikeouts.

Doing something the game hasn't seen since 1937 is pretty incredible, especially when this doesn't even account for a single stolen base.

"I've been playing with Ronald since 2016, and at this point, nothing really surprises me anymore," Max Fried said. "He's that talented, and he's that good."

Acuña's career statistics exiting the 2023 season included a .292 batting average, 161 home runs, 180 stolen bases and a .918 OPS. It's incredible to think where these totals might rest had he not suffered the ACL tear one year after the COVID-shortened season.

Still even with the combination of these long stretches of inactivity, Acuña is the only player in MLB history to hit .290 with 160 homers, 180 stolen bases and a .900-plus OPS through his 25-year-old season.

"He's doing things we have never seen before," Austin Riley said. "You come to the ballpark every day knowing there is a chance he is going to do something special."

Acuña became the second-youngest Braves player to win the MVP Award when he garnered the honor in 2023. He became the franchise's first unanimous winner after serving as the catalyst for what proved to be one of the greatest offenses in baseball history.

The 2023 Braves won an MLB-high 104 games on the strength of an offense that became the first American or National League club to produce a .500 slugging percentage. This lineup also matched the single-season MLB record with 307 homers.

The 2023 Braves might have been one of the best teams in franchise history. But this argument was weakened when the dynamic offense was limited to just four extra-base hits as the Braves were eliminated by the Phillies in the National League Division Series for a second straight year.

Acuña missed the second half of the 2021 season and thus was unable to fully experience the exuberance his Braves teammates felt while winning the World Series that year. But he certainly has the capability to build upon 2023 and help the Braves remain World Series contenders for many years to come.

"I'm not saying what's going to happen next season," Acuña said. "I'm not trying to predict anything. But as long as I'm healthy, I feel like anything is possible."

41

Freeman to Olson

As FREDDIE FREEMAN AND MATT OLSON ESTABLISHED themselves among the top National League MVP candidates in 2023, they added to the zaniness of the story that left a lot of folks in tears in 2022.

Braves president of baseball operations Alex Anthopoulos was the first to publicly shed tears. This occurred on March 14, 2022, as he announced he had just acquired Matt Olson from the Oakland A's. He had made an incredible acquisition. But he had also marked the end of an era.

With Olson in place, there was no longer reason to wonder if Freeman would realize his wish to spend his entire career with the Braves. This, of course, led to an abundance of tears falling in the Freeman household.

The Olson trade closed one of the most successful careers in Atlanta. Among all players who have tallied at least 6,500 plate appearances for the Braves, Freeman ranks fourth in OPS (.893), trailing only Hank Aaron, Chipper Jones and Eddie Mathews. He also ranks among the top 10 in home runs, runs, hits and RBIs.

Freeman's plan was to spend at least another half decade adding to those numbers. But his life changed on the night of March 12, 2022, when he got a phone call as he was at a birthday party. It was his agent Casey Close.

The exact words exchanged weren't revealed, but Freeman remembers walking back into the party and telling his family, "I don't know what just happened, but I don't think I'm still with the Braves."

Close had just completed a conversation with Anthopoulos and made a couple contract requests that Freeman has said far exceeded his wish. The tone of the conversation made Anthopoulos feel like this was an ultimatum.

It was a Saturday night and Anthopoulos would need to get in touch with Braves CEO and chairman Terry McGuirk. So, he asked for an hour. Once the two parties completed their conversing on this evening, Anthopoulos asked whether this was basically the last chance to re-sign Freeman.

Anthopoulos got the feeling that Freeman must have received a similar offer from the Yankees, Dodgers or another club seeking a first baseman.

Close has contended this wasn't an ultimatum. But Freeman and Anthopoulos both interpreted it to be.

So, Anthopoulos spent the next day checking on free agent Anthony Rizzo's availability and wondering if he might get stuck with using Adam Duvall at first base. But there was also always the possibility of acquiring Olson, who was one of the top items available via Oakland's fire sale.

How did this situation get to this point? One thing that has to be remembered is that there was a MLB lockout from

December 2, 2021, to March 10, 2022. So there was no opportunity to negotiate with Freeman or any other free agents during this three-month stretch.

But there was plenty of time before the lockout.

Freeman first publicly voiced the desire to receive a contract extension during spring training in 2019. The Braves said it was too early to discuss this possibility. The following year was damaged by the COVID pandemic. The season was reduced to two months and teams played in empty stadiums.

Along with losing revenue in 2020, the Braves didn't know if the pandemic might have a long-term financial effect. So, there were no negotiations heading into 2021, Freeman's last year on his contract.

Freeman won the 2020 NL MVP, but began the 2021 season slowly. He was stressed by the thought of being away from the two sons he and his wife had brought into their family during the winter. But he was also bothered by the fact the Braves weren't talking to him about his future.

Around the All-Star break, Freeman told Chipper Jones he'd be willing to take something similar to the five-year, $130 million contract extension Paul Goldschmidt received from the St. Louis Cardinals before the 2019 season.

When Jones brought this information to Anthopoulos, the Braves offered a five-year, $135 million deal.

Assuming that was going to be enough, Jones approached Freeman a week or two later and asked whether the deal was getting done. The first baseman said he was now looking for six years. This began to strain what had been a strong friendship.

Jones felt somewhat embarrassed. He told Freeman a five-year deal was essentially the same because if he wanted to stay an extra year, the Braves likely wouldn't say no.

But the next few months elapsed with no further discussions. Once Freeman helped the Braves win the 2021 World Series, the expectation was that a contract would be completed over the next few weeks. Everyone knew there was a possibility of a work stoppage. So, November seemed to be a prime time for discussions.

But the silence continued throughout that month leading up to the lockout. When Freeman met with Close and his other agent, Victor Menocal, at his California home in February, he said all he wanted was to remain with the Braves.

At the same time, the agents walked away thinking the sixth year was also still a requirement.

Close and Menocal had secured Freeman an eight-year, $135 million deal in 2014, after he had played just three full seasons. He was completely confident they would come through again. But if he had it to do all over again, he would have become more involved in the negotiations.

His missteps led Dansby Swanson, who is also represented by Close and Menocal, to approach his free agency much differently the next year. Swanson called Anthopoulos multiple times and even talked to McGuirk, just hoping the Braves might eventually increase their six-year, $100 million deal. He didn't get his wish to stay in Atlanta, but he still seemed to win via the seven-year, $177 million deal he got from the Cubs.

Swanson established himself as one of the game's best shortstops. But nobody in 2021 could have predicted he would end up with more guaranteed dollars than Freeman via free agency.

Freeman ended up signing a six-year, $162 million deal with the Dodgers. He fired his agents a few months later.

When Freeman returned to play the Braves in Atlanta in June 2022, it was obvious how painful this separation still was. As he entered the interview room before the series opener, he began crying uncontrollably and had to leave the room. The tears were still flowing when he returned and seated himself in front of the media.

"I thought I loved this city and this organization a lot," Freeman said as he dabbed his eyes and bloodshot cheeks with a towel. "But you can tell how much I truly do love this organization and this city. I don't even know how I'm going to get through this weekend."

Freeman got through that initial season in Los Angeles just fine. He finished fourth in National League Most Valuable Player balloting, his fifth straight top-10 finish.

Coincidentally, this trade brought the two first basemen back home. Freeman was raised south of Los Angeles in Orange County and Olson was raised about 30 minutes northeast of Truist Park.

Olson's homecoming has also been memorable. He hit 34 homers during his first year with the hometown Braves. But he took his game to another level in 2023, when he hit a franchise-record 53 homers and finished fourth in NL MVP balloting, one spot behind Freeman. His success strengthened the value of the eight-year, $168 million contract the Braves gave him the day after acquiring him from the A's.

Freeman grew happier as he progressed through the early years of his contract with the Dodgers. When he is a free agent after the 2027 season, he'll be preparing for his 38-year-old season. Olson will be prepping for his 34-year-old season with two more guaranteed seasons on his contract.

It's too early to predict whether Freeman and Olson could one day be Braves teammates. But with the designated hitter, it's certainly a possibility.

42

Contract Extensions

REMEMBER THE 1994 MONTREAL EXPOS TEAM THAT THREATENED the Braves' division titles streak? Well, you could say it's also responsible for the Braves' current bid to produce another double-digit streak of consecutive division crowns.

The Expos sat atop the National League East standings, leading the Braves by six games through August 11, 1994, when a work stoppage ended the season. So, no division titles were awarded.

When play resumed in 1995, financial restraints had forced the Expos to part ways with some of their stars. Larry Walker was with the Colorado Rockies and Marquis Grissom back in his hometown playing for the Braves. Moises Alou and Pedro Martínez were among the other players later moved.

This frustrated many Montreal fans, including a young Alex Anthopoulos, whose interest in baseball grew during what had the makings to be a great 1994 season.

"I saw a lot of players leave," Anthopoulos said. "I know what it was like that our good young players were being traded away or that they couldn't keep them. So I think there's a small part of me that feels from a fan base, you can buy this guy's jersey because he's going to be here a while."

Anthopoulos provided this story while explaining some of the reasoning he was willing to assume any risk with locking up so many of the Braves' young stars over the past few years.

Ronald Acuña Jr. and Ozzie Albies signed what still appear to be very club-friendly extensions in 2019. Matt Olson was acquired from the A's in March 2022 and received an eight-year deal a day later. Sean Murphy was acquired from Oakland on December 12, 2022, and inked a six-year deal a couple weeks later.

In between the Olson and Murphy deals, the Braves gave long-term extensions to Austin Riley, Michael Harris II and Spencer Strider. Riley gained his deal just a little more than a year after having to battle Johan Camargo for the starting third base job. Harris and Strider got their deals just a few months into their big-league careers.

There is risk involved. Had the Braves done the same with Michael Soroka after or during his great 2019 rookie season, they would currently be lamenting the decision. Nobody envisioned Soroka tearing his right Achilles tendon twice. But potential injuries or unexpected decline are certainly risks of any contract given to a player.

"We do like the fact that guys can just worry about going out and playing," Anthopoulos said. "They don't have to worry about making a certain salary or getting certain statistics and so on, and that they know they're going to be here."

Murphy (catcher), Olson (first base), Albies (second base), Austin Riley (third base), Michael Harris II (center field) and Acuña (right field) are all under control by the Braves through the 2027 season. So, too, is Spencer Strider, who is the only recent pitcher to gain an extension from Atlanta.

The Braves entered the 2023 season with the ability to project what 66 percent of their lineup might look like four seasons down the road. This provides a great benefit when it comes to payroll planning.

Players under club control through 2027: Murphy, Harris, Strider, Olson, Acuña, Albies ($7 million option in 2026 and '27) and Riley

Through 2028: Murphy, Harris, Strider, Olson, Acuña ($17 million club option) and Riley

Through 2029: Murphy ($15 million club option), Harris, Strider ($22 million club option), Olson and Riley

Through 2030: Olson ($20 million club option), Riley (guaranteed through 2032 with a $20 million club option for '33)

When the Braves signed Acuña and Albies during the early portion of the 2019 season, the overwhelming reaction was that both players had left a significant amount of money on the table. But because both were young enough, they were willing to gain immediate financial security, knowing there would still be a chance for them to sign a big deal at the end of their current contracts.

Acuña signed an eight-year, $100 million deal that includes two club options. If both option years are exercised, the Braves would control the superstar outfielder at an average annual value of $12.4 million over 10 seasons. Acuña will be 30 during what would be the last possible season covered within this deal. Thus, there's a chance he will receive another big payday at the end of it.

"Hopefully, this isn't the last deal we do with him," Anthopoulos said when the current contract was completed. "Hopefully, he ends his career as a Brave and he goes in the Hall of Fame one day as a Brave. But this is a starting point."

As for Albies, he received a seven-year, $35 million deal that also includes two options. If both options are exercised, the Braves would control Albies at a cost of $45 million over nine seasons.

The second baseman fractured his elbow taking a swing while in the minor leagues and he fractured his foot taking a swing during the 2022 season. These are examples of why he was seeking financial security. But he's recovered from both injuries and is again looking capable of hitting 30 homers on an annual basis.

Guys who hit 30 homers a year don't make $5 million per year. But Albies has never shown any hint he regrets signing the deal when he was just one full season into his big-league career.

"I don't look at it just from money because I'm not playing for money," Albies said. "I'm playing for my career. I took it because I want my family to be safe."

The 2022 extension spree began with Olson, who responded by battling Acuña and his predecessor, Freddie Freeman, for the 2023 National League MVP Award. Freeman ended up getting $27 million per year (not accounting for California taxes) when the Braves' acquisition of Olson led him to sign with the Dodgers.

Olson will make an average of $21 million per season through 2029, his final guaranteed season. The Braves recognized Freeman as an annual MVP candidate. But, being four years younger, Olson has less chance of fading over the latter years of the long-term contract that was required to sign either of these first basemen.

The Braves haven't had any remorse since making long-term commitments with Olson or Riley, who exited 2023 with three straight 30-homer seasons. If he continues to show this kind of power, the $21.2 million he will receive annually for 10 years will look like a bargain.

Harris and Strider received their extensions while teaming to be one of the most influential rookie duos the Braves have ever seen. Harris further established himself as an elite outfielder in 2023 and Strider continued to set strikeout records during his second season.

As for Murphy, he joined Acuña, Albies, Riley and Strider on the National League's 2023 All-Star roster. This just added to the significant amount of time these guys will be spending together during much of this decade.

Acknowledgments

MAYBE I SHOULD HAVE KNOWN SO MUCH OF MY LIFE WOULD be spent around the Atlanta Braves. My best friend, Stevie Myers, and I were seven during that summer of 1982, when we realized TBS was bringing this other team to our television sets on a nightly basis. He chose Dale Murphy and the Braves as his favorites. So he got to at least see his team get to the playoffs that year.

I stuck with the Pirates and Tony Peña. My team stayed silent in October the next seven seasons and then made the playoffs each of the following three years. Stevie's team eliminated mine from the playoffs during the last two of those three years. So, as he celebrated, I allegedly threw something on the fourth floor of Stuart Hall at the University of Dayton and got fined $35.

Then there was my Grandma Reilly, who fell in love with the Braves and began watching them on a nightly basis after I left Wheeling, West Virginia, to come to Atlanta in 1996. She loved Andruw Jones, but I knew she was also my biggest fan.

Quite honestly, I'm quite fortunate to have a number of people who would qualify as my biggest fan. This certainly includes my wife, Tammy Bowman, who has shown nothing but patience and support while being roped into this crazy baseball life. She finally got used to all the late nights and long trips. Then I decided to cut into more of our personal time by writing this book.

But I couldn't have asked for more love and support during this endeavor. She knew how much I enjoyed it, and that's all that mattered to her. She has always made me a better me.

My longest-standing fans have been my parents, Ed and Sara Bowman, who never stood in the way of me pursuing my dreams. It has been an absolute joy to share the many experiences you helped create. None of this would have been possible without your love and support.

I too want to thank my sister, Amy Bowman, who spent many years telling me to write a book. She might have skipped the chapter about 1992 National League Championship Series Game 7. Had the Pirates won that night, she had tickets for one of the World Series games in Pittsburgh. Thank you for always being there.

The ride I've experienced since joining MLB.com in 2001 has been incredible. Thank you to Gregg Klayman, Matt Meyers and Jenifer Langosch for allowing me to write this book. Your leadership has been invaluable. Thank you, too, to Dinn Mann and Paul Bodi, two guys who provided incredible support during my earliest years with the company.

This experience has also been enriched by the support I've received from my kids, Tot, Souvana and Taylor. Souvana loves the Braves and Taylor loves everything but sports. But they both provided incredible support. I hope my grandkids, Piper and Baker, come to love this great game of baseball as much as I do.

This has been an enriching experience aided by the wonderful folks at Triumph Books. I hope you enjoying reading this book as much as I enjoyed writing it.